CORPORAL KNOWLEDGE

Corporal Knowledge

Early Christian Bodies

JENNIFER A. GLANCY

OXFORD
UNIVERSITY PRESS

2010

OXFORD
UNIVERSITY PRESS

Oxford University Press, Inc., publishes works that further
Oxford University's objective of excellence
in research, scholarship, and education.

Oxford   New York
Auckland   Cape Town   Dar es Salaam   Hong Kong   Karachi
Kuala Lumpur   Madrid   Melbourne   Mexico City   Nairobi
New Delhi   Shanghai   Taipei   Toronto

With offices in
Argentina   Austria   Brazil   Chile   Czech Republic   France   Greece
Guatemala   Hungary   Italy   Japan   Poland   Portugal   Singapore
South Korea   Switzerland   Thailand   Turkey   Ukraine   Vietnam

Published by Oxford University Press, Inc.
198 Madison Avenue, New York, New York 10016

www.oup.com

Oxford is a registered trademark of Oxford University Press

Library of Congress Cataloging-in-Publication Data

Glancy, Jennifer A.
Corporal knowledge : early Christian bodies / Jennifer A. Glancy.
p. cm.
Includes bibliographical references and index.
ISBN 978-0-19-532815-8
1. Human body—Religious aspects—Christianity. I. Title.
BT741.3.G53 2010
233'.5—dc22   2009019401

9 8 7 6 5 4 3 2 1

Printed in the United States of America
on acid-free paper

To Amy, Bridget, Erin, Jim, and Meghan

Oh bless the continuous stutter

Of the word being made into flesh.

—Leonard Cohen

Acknowledgments

A decade ago Alice Bach encouraged me to read Pierre Bourdieu. I followed her advice and began asking the questions that inform this volume. Alice was there at the end of the process as well, offering exquisite editorial advice on the final manuscript. During the years that I worked on this project, Karmen MacKendrick and I cotaught an interdisciplinary seminar on the Ancient and Medieval World at Le Moyne College. Reading texts together taught me to think differently about ways that bodies know. Elizabeth Salzer read multiple drafts of each chapter. Elizabeth is a physician assistant; her spouse Joanna Shulman is an obstetrician-gynecologist. Their wisdom was invaluable as I worked on chapter 4, "Mary in Childbirth." Any errors that remain are due solely to the author's noncompliance with medical advice. I thank Alice, Karmen, and Elizabeth, who are midwives to this book.

I am grateful to Cynthia Read and the editorial staff at Oxford University Press for their care and attention to this project. Virginia Burrus and Stephen Moore reviewed the proposal, and their perceptive comments helped me sort out what I wanted to accomplish. I gratefully acknowledge the support of grants and sabbatical leave awarded by the Le Moyne College Faculty Senate Committee on Research and Development.

Halvor Moxnes and Marianne Kartzow—who are the best of hosts—invited me to the University of Oslo to participate in a seminar called Jesus in Cultural Complexity, where I presented sections of chapter 1, "What She Knew in Her Body: An Introduction." I thank Halvor, Marianne, and Denise Buell for their comments on my presentation. Closer to home—in fact, across town—Frances Taylor Gench graciously offered me the opportunity to refine my arguments at the Union-PSCE New Testament colloquy.

Those with ears to hear may detect the influence of my teacher J. Louis Martyn on chapter 2, "Boasting of Beatings (2 Corinthians 11:23–25)." I am grateful to Lou both for his encouragement and the example of his own scholarship. Chapter 2 is a revised version of an article that first appeared in the *Journal of Biblical Literature* 123 (2004).

Chapter 3, "Embodying Slavery from Paul to Augustine," was conceived and gestated in the context of the Feminist Sexual Ethics Project (FSEP) that Bernadette Brooten directed at Brandeis University with funding from the Ford Foundation. I presented a version of this material at the FSEP 2006 public conference, "Beyond Slavery: Overcoming Its Religious and Sexual Legacy," and a very different version of the material is to appear in a forthcoming edited volume. I am grateful to all my FSEP colleagues, especially Sheila Briggs, Kecia Ali, and Gail Labovitz; to Emma Wasserman, who helped me clarify my reliance on Bourdieu; and most especially to Bernadette, for her scholarly acumen, her warm encouragement, and her steadfastness. I am grateful to the Feminist Theology Group at St. Paul's, the Episcopal cathedral of the Central New York diocese, for discussing this work with me; special thanks to Laurie Sanderson, theologian. I have benefited from the questions and comments of audiences who attended my lectures at a conference on christianity and slavery at Baylor University organized by John Nordling; at an interdisciplinary symposium on slavery at the University of Rostock organized by Gesa Mackenthun; at Rice University; at Washington University at St. Louis; and at Notre Dame, where I am particularly grateful to Keith Bradley for his hospitality and encouragement.

For a number of years I met twice a semester with a group that calls itself LARCNY: Late Ancient Religion in Central New York. My colleagues in LARCNY read a draft of chapter 4, "Mary in Childbirth." Georgia Frank, Kim Haines-Eitzen, and Patricia Cox Miller offered especially helpful comments. I would also like to acknowledge more broadly the collegiality of that group. While I worked on chapter 4 I had the benefit of the manuscript of Virginia Burrus's *Saving Shame: Martyrs, Saints, and Other Abject Subjects*, which she generously volunteered to share with me. Catherine Anne Playoust agreed to entrust this stranger with the manuscript of her Harvard dissertation, *Lifted up from the Earth: The Ascension of Jesus and the Heavenly Ascents of Early Christians*. To Virginia and Catherine, thanks. Jennifer Knust invited me to present a version of "Mary in Childbirth" as the Brown Lecture at Boston University, and I was glad for the invitation and for the lively conversation. I am also appreciative to Claudia Setzer for an invitation to present a version of the work at the Columbia University New Testament Seminar and to my friends and colleagues who participated in that conversation. Thanks as well to Cal Roetzel, who afforded me the chance to present an early and rough version of "Mary in Childbirth" at the University of Minnesota. I presented a still more premature version in the Le Moyne College Faculty Research Seminar, where I was pushed to refine my thinking. Chapter 4 incorporates material from an article on Tertullian first published in *Henoch* 30.2 (2008), a special issue, "Blood and the

Boundaries of Jewish and Christian Identities in Late Antiquity" that was edited by Ra'anan Boustan and Annette Yoshiko Reed.

Versions of chapters 2, 3, and 4 were also presented at annual meetings of the Society of Biblical Literature. I thank Cornelia Horn and Shelly Matthews for comments on my papers at the 2007 meeting.

The most propitious place for me to write is a cabin on a bluff overlooking Seneca Lake. For use of that cabin and for much else, I thank Ginger and Bill Andrews. I rely on Bridget Short, Jim Glancy, Amy Glancy, Erin Johnson, and Meghan Glancy for essential things (e.g., recipes, music tips, and family photos). Sisters and brother, this book is dedicated to you.

That David Andrews climbs holy mountains should be acknowledged. But how to acknowledge his contributions to my scholarship? Our nightly dinners are seminars that inspire me to think and teach and write. David, thank you.

Contents

Abbreviations

Ascen. Isa.	*Ascension of Isaiah*
Augustine	
Ep.	*Epistles*
Basil of Caesarea	
Ep.	*Epistles*
Cicero	
Verr.	*Against Verres*
Dig.	*Digest of Justinian*
Josephus	
Ant.	*Jewish Antiquities*
J.W.	*Jewish War*
Odes Sol.	*Odes of Solomon*
Origen	
Hom. Lev.	*Homily on Leviticus*
Hom. Luc.	*Homily on Luke*
Pliny	
Nat.	*Natural History*
Plutarch	
Mor.	*Moralia*
Prot. Jas.	*Protevangelium of James (= Infancy Gospel of James)*
Tertullian	
Apol.	*Apology*
Carn. Chr.	*On the Flesh of Christ*
Marc.	*Against Marcion*
Mart.	*To the Martyrs*
Nat.	*To the Nations*
Res.	*On the Resurrection of the Flesh*

CORPORAL KNOWLEDGE

I   ———————————————————————————

What She Knew in Her Body: An Introduction

These then were two very genuine experiences of my own. These were two of the adventures of my professional life. The first—killing the Angel in the House— I think I solved. She died. But the second, telling the truth about my own experiences as a body, I do not think I solved. I doubt that any woman has solved it yet.

             —Virginia Woolf, *Professions for Women*

A woman's blood flowed uncontrollably for over a decade. Her money flowed to doctors but she found no relief. Hearing of Jesus, she made her way to him. Not for the first time, perhaps, she had a hunch that if she even touched the healer's clothes she would be made well. This time she hit the jackpot. Touching Jesus' outer garment, she siphoned his power. Immediately, Mark tells us, the bleeding stopped, "and she knew in the body that she was cured of the scourge" (5:29b). Jesus, likewise, "knew in himself that power had gone out from him" (5:30a).[1] Among the story's vivid details, including the abrupt cessation of the woman's chronic suffering and her theft of power in a corporal exchange Jesus did not will, I am especially intrigued by one Markan turn of phrase: "She knew in the body."

Mark's phrasing is sometimes standardized in translation. The New Revised Standard Version, for example, tells the reader that the woman "felt in her body that she was healed of her disease." The translator's shift from knowing to feeling conforms to commonplace usage. Bodies feel. Minds know. Mark, however, implies that bodies know, that we are capable of corporal knowledge. What do we know in the body? Mark's vignette of the bleeding woman suggests one simple answer. We know when we are sick and when we are well. We also know when the air is sticky and the very moment when a breeze cools the late afternoon. But, I argue, corporal knowing is not limited to matters of health or sense perception. What else do we know in the body? I have written this study as a cultural historian intrigued to flesh out the skeletal remains of early Christian bodies. I have also

3

written this book in an effort to think through the diverse phenomena of corporal knowing, to think through what it might mean to say, "she knew in the body."

In this book I trace the centrality of bodies to early Christian social dynamics and therefore to early Christian discourse. What's new here, the reader may wonder. This territory has been previously, and brilliantly, explored. Peter Brown's seminal *The Body and Society: Men, Women, and Sexual Renunciation in Early Christianity*, first published in 1988, set the agenda for subsequent scholarship. Brown, in turn, helped many scholars of religion in antiquity understand how the projects of Mary Douglas and especially Michel Foucault were relevant to Mediterranean antiquity. Without their bodies of work, my work would have no body. But there is still more to say about bodies, if only because bodies are stubbornly flesh; bodies know the world in ways that exceed our disciplinary ways of knowing; bodies tell stories that press beyond the closures of scholarly telling. Douglas's essential work on the social body intersects only obliquely with the arguments of this volume. Foucault's influence, on the other hand, is pervasive but diffuse. This is not a book about Foucault. After we have said everything about early Christian bodies that Foucault helps us say, those bodies will still have more stories to tell.

I define early Christianity broadly, from the days of Paul to the days of Augustine. My examples are chosen illustratively rather than exhaustively. Later in this chapter, I consider the arguments of philosopher Mark Johnson, who argues that bodily metaphors inevitably structure human knowing.[2] Parallel to Johnson's insistence that bodies structure thought, I work from the assumption that bodies structure social exchange and create worlds of meaning. In that formulation, "bodies" may seem to exist outside of social dynamics, but of course they do not. The Gospel of John includes a story relating an encounter between Jesus and a blind beggar, a story I discuss in the next section. By the time Jesus encounters the blind beggar, the unsighted man's lifetime of making his way in a world that reads sinfulness in his visual impairment would have shaped his corporal being in the world.

I do not dwell on the ways that nascent Christianity and coeval discourses altered practices of self-fashioning and thus wrote new chapters in the cultural history of bodies. Those are important questions about which other scholars have taught us much. I ask instead how the inevitable cultural habituation of bodies inclined Christians of the first centuries toward certain social arrangements rather than others. I ask, moreover, how the inevitable cultural habituation of bodies facilitated certain patterns of theological reflection rather than others. I argue that social location is known in the body and I attempt to demonstrate the significance of that insight for a cultural history of Christian origins. What we know in the body, however, exceeds our social locations. I emphasize the excessive quality of corporal knowing in chapter 4, where I engage a variety of early Christian writers as they examine the body of Mary at the moment she gives birth. I argue that in writing about Mary's parturient body, Christian authors depend on fundamental understandings about selfhood and identity. Those fundamental understandings in turn engage intuitions about a kind of knowing that comes into being as flesh gives birth to flesh.

The Man Born Blind: A Cautionary Tale

My primary concern in this book is not with illness, disability, or healing. At the outset, though, in order to illustrate both the familiarity and strangeness of the notion that bodies tell stories, I pause to consider one common way that bodies were understood to be vessels of truth, in the association of physical debility with moral failure, character flaws, and dishonor. I also introduce this topic in order to illustrate the moral hazards implicit in common readings of storytelling bodies. The Gospel of John includes a story where bodies appear in ways both disturbing and familiar to twenty-first-century sensibilities (9:1–12). Sauntering down a road accompanied by his disciples, Jesus encounters a blind man, a beggar. Because the man had been blind his entire life, the disciples ask, "Who sinned, this man or his parents?" Rejecting the formulation of their question, Jesus says, "Neither this man nor his parents sinned; he was born blind so that God's work might be revealed in him." Jesus then spits on the ground so that he can spread the mud, dirt moistened with spittle, on the man's eyes. Following Jesus' instructions, the man washes in a pool named Siloam. The beggar sees.

Both the disciples and Jesus assume the man's body tells a story. They differ in their readings of that corporal story. For the disciples, blindness convicts someone of sin. When an infant enters the world without sight, the disciples are unsure who the guilty party is. Although in the case of the blind man Jesus demurs from the view that the man's body tells a sinful story, elsewhere in the fourth Gospel Jesus implies a comparable corporal narrative. An immobilized man who has been ill for thirty-eight years is empowered by Jesus to pick up his mat and walk. Jesus later charges the man, "See, you have been made well! Do not sin any more, so that nothing worse happens to you" (John 5:1–14). About the blind man, Jesus infers that the man's body tells what seems to me an equally problematic story: the man has lived his entire life in darkness so that Jesus could manifest himself as light of the world.

With rare exceptions, commentators on the Gospel of John accept Jesus' apparent willingness to link sinfulness and disability in the case of the formerly paralyzed man, just as they nod approvingly at Jesus' interpretation of the beggar's lifelong blindness as a mere foil for magnifying Jesus' glory.[3] On this view, what a paralyzed man knows in his body is not only physical limitation or pain but also moral transgression. This narrative structure persists. A kind coworker of mine became convinced that she developed breast cancer because she had strayed from the Lord. A loving Jesus, she believed, catalyzed cells to metastasize so that she might return to his embrace, an embrace that would shelter her from an eternity of hellfire.

Counternarratives

Susan Sontag's *Illness as Metaphor* and its later companion piece *AIDS and Its Metaphors* take on insidious variants of this narrative. "Everyone who is born holds dual citizenship, in the kingdom of the well and in the kingdom of the sick," Sontag writes. "Although we all prefer to use only the good passport, sooner or later each of us is obliged, at least for a spell, to identify ourselves as citizens of that other place."[4] Sontag's project is to examine, in her words, "not what it is really like to emigrate to the kingdom of the ill and live there, but the punitive or sentimental fantasies concocted about that situation."[5]

In *Illness as Metaphor*, her particular targets are the sentimental fantasies that circulated around tuberculosis and the punitive fantasies that circulate around cancer. First published in 1978, *Illness and Its Metaphors* exposes the shame that in those days attached itself to metastatic disease. Sontag writes, "[C]ancer is notorious for attacking parts of the body (colon, bladder, rectum, breast, cervix, prostate, testicles) that are embarrassing to acknowledge. Having a tumor generally arouses some feelings of shame, but in the hierarchy of the body's organs, lung cancer is felt to be less shameful than rectal cancer."[6] *She has cancer*, it used to be whispered, the location of the tumor unspecified if the malignancy originated in penis or ovary. But the shame of diseased pudenda is only part of Sontag's critique. Her primary concerns are with the punitive narrative that treats cancer as an outgrowth—or perhaps offscouring—of repressed emotion and the equally punitive narrative that treats the sad fact that a person may die from metastatic disease as a failure of will, the obverse of the urgent *You can beat it!*

Illness as Metaphor was a comfort to me during my graduate school days. My mother was diagnosed with ovarian cancer, the disease that eventually brought a premature close to her life. In those years I found it painful to hear common refrains about cancer, especially the cruel refrain that suggested that cancer was the consequence of bottling up emotions, of choking on rage and grief. And yet, in middle age—the age when my mother was diagnosed with ovarian cancer, I note with a melodrama my mother would have despised—I remain confused about how what we call mind interfuses with what we call body. We live in a culture where therapy for emotional distress is likely to be pharmaceutical and where persons with high blood pressure are taught to meditate. What is mental and what is physical? Our culture insists that mental health is somehow fundamental to physical health. Can we affirm that commonplace notion, I wonder, without a purchase on pernicious stories that stigmatize persons with chronic or fatal diseases as emotional and implicitly moral failures?

Even in circles that eschew the concept of sin, we offer secular riffs on the words Jesus spoke to the man who picked up his mat and walked: "See, you have been made well! Do not sin any more, so that nothing worse happens to you." In his memoir of the death of his mother, Susan Sontag, David Rieff writes,

> It is hard enough for any cancer patient to really resist the idea that some failure on his or her own part brought the illness on. After all, Reichian explanations of psychological repression causing cancer have in our own time tended to give way to explanations based on one's having eaten the wrong foods, the basis of such self-blame, and the assumption that the cancer patient is in a deep sense the author of his or her own disease is still very much in the air.[7]

In her writings Sontag rejects the metaphor of a war on cancer and the militarization of discourse about AIDS, which in the 1980s was treated as an invasion of the body of the state. "We are not being invaded," she concludes *AIDS and Its Metaphors*. "The body is not a battlefield. The ill are neither unavoidable casualties nor the enemy. . . . About that metaphor, the military one, I would say, if I may paraphrase Lucretius: Give it back to the war-makers."[8] With guilt rather than irony, Rieff admits that in his mother's final months he colluded in her interpretation of her third and final cancer diagnosis as a winnable battle. Until the final week of her life Sontag believed that she would defeat the cancer.

The stories we read in ailing bodies are not the focus of this book. I introduce them at the outset of the volume to make a simple point. While we are likely to be alienated from at least some of the corporal narratives of Christian antiquity, we know the world as mediated through our own corporal narratives. Contemporary narratives converge in multiple and complex ways with the stories early Christians read in bodies. The puzzle that confronted Jesus' followers in John 9:1–12, how to account morally for the birth of individuals with illness or atypical physical limitations ("Who sinned?"), enters into the speculations of the third-century theologian Origen as he argues that souls exist previous to their birth in bodies. "For if this were not so," Origen muses, "and souls had no pre-existence, why do we find some new-born babes to be blind, when they have committed no sin, while others are born with no defect at all?" (*First Principles*, 1.8.1). Alarmed or appalled as we may be by the assumptions informing Origen's treatment of physical debility as punitive pedagogy, Sontag and her son Rieff remind us that we read our own punitive tales in bodies. As Rieff notes, the assumption that the sufferer "is in a deep sense the author of his or her own disease is still very much in the air."

This book considers the ways that the storytelling bodies of Christian antiquity might inform a cultural history of Christian origins. What did Christians living in the Roman Empire know in their bodies? What stories did their bodies tell, and, a different question, what stories were read in their bodies? Can bodies lie? In raising these questions I also invite the reader to contemplate ways that storytelling bodies of the third millennium mediate our experiences of the world. What do we know in our bodies? What stories do our bodies tell? How do the stories we tell about our bodies complicate the stories we read in ancient bodies?

Scholarly Stories

As I have noted, philosopher Mark Johnson argues that bodily metaphors are foundational to thought. In *The Body in the Mind: The Bodily Basis of Meaning, Imagination, and Reason*, Johnson writes, "The centrality of human embodiment directly influences what and how things can be meaningful for us, the ways in which these meanings can be developed and articulated, the ways we are able to comprehend and reason about our experiences, and the actions we take."[9] In ways conventionally opaque to us, Johnson demonstrates, our perceptions and judgments are corporally located and informed. While "the body" serves as an endlessly plastic metaphor, Johnson's concern is not so much "the body as metaphor" as the often unrecognized corporal inflection of other metaphors, such as metaphors of up and down, of center and periphery, of in and out, all of which arise out of bodily experiences of orientation in space.

Given Johnson's exposition of the centrality of the body to the structure of thought, we should not be surprised that the body as a category of analysis has been a near-ubiquitous category in the scholarship of recent decades. In their widely quoted 1987 article "The Mindful Body: A Prolegomenon to Future Work in Medical Anthropology," a work that has been influential far beyond its home discipline, Nancy Scheper-Hughes and Margaret M. Lock propose a taxonomy of paradigms for analysis of the body: "(1) as a phenomenally experienced *individual body-self*; (2) as a *social body*, a natural symbol for thinking about relationships among nature, society, and culture [e.g., along lines pursued by Mary Douglas]; and (3) as a *body politic*, an artifact of social and political control."[10] Developing their analysis of the body politic, Scheper-Hughes and Lock note that "societies regularly reproduce and socialize the kind of bodies that they need."[11] On this categorization, my analysis of storytelling bodies in chapters 2 and 3 works from the notion of the body as a body politic, with a particular interest in the corporal inscription of implicit rather than explicit social codes. I emphasize habituation rather than studied self-fashioning. I ask how the interactions of habituated or skilled bodies incline communities, in this case early Christian communities, to pursue certain kinds of organization and discourse. My choice of the verb *incline* is intended to imply a resistance to determinism.[12]

To the extent that Foucault is relevant to the analysis of the body politic, we may refer to the Foucault who wrote *Discipline and Punish* rather than the Foucault who wrote *The Care of the Self*. In framing my analysis, however, I have primarily relied on other theorists. The practice-oriented social theory of Pierre Bourdieu, with its notion of habitus, embodied knowledge, is a backbone of my exploration.[13] I have also drawn on works of feminist philosophers, most importantly Linda Martín Alcoff. Bourdieu and Alcoff are both readers of the phenomenologist Maurice Merleau-Ponty—as was Foucault, though Foucault's relationship to Merleau-Ponty's phenomenological philosophy was fraught with the ambivalence of dependency and differentiation. As I develop my argument throughout the book, the contributions of these theorists will be evident. In the final chapter I fold in the arguments of other feminist philosophers, including Elizabeth Grosz and Luce Irigiray, who take Merleau-Ponty's arguments about corporal knowledge in a different—and perhaps more basic—direction.

Knowing Your Place

Earlier in this chapter I discussed one kind of storytelling body, a body whose disease or disability is interpreted as the denouement of sin. As I noted, I chose this example because it is both alien (or alienating; we want to repudiate the view that disease results from sin) and familiar (in Rieff's words, "the assumption that the cancer patient is in a deep sense the author of his or her own disease is still very much in the air"). Classicist Maud Gleason argues that in the Roman world the body was conceived as a "vessel of truth and organ of meaning."[14] Gleason does not have in mind the diseased body so much as the cultural body, the body as shaped and experienced and interpreted as cultural artifact, a notion that may also seem at once alien and familiar. Alien because we do not like to admit that we make assumptions about other persons based on corporal presentation: whether a stranger is lithe or squat, pockmarked or ruddy-faced; whether a new acquaintance returns our gaze. Familiar because we make such assumptions daily: we assume that the deep voice we hear on the phone is male and we do not know how to respond when the speaker identifies herself as Mary.[15]

If the self is a body, what kind of a body is the self? Although Alcoff stresses myriad ways that cultures habituate bodies, and particularly the myriad ways that gender and race are learned and embodied in the United States, she rejects the idea that bodies are blank pages inscribed by society. Rather, following Johnson, Merleau-Ponty, and others, Alcoff understands the body as mindful. She writes that "it makes more sense to think of the body as, oddly enough, a kind of mind, but one with a physical appearance, location, and specific instantiation. . . . We perceive and process and incorporate and reason and are intellectually trained in the body itself."[16] Developing Merleau-Ponty's notion of the habitual body, Alcoff notes that we typically become conscious of what our body knows at moments when such knowledge is disrupted. The example she supplies is driving on the left—or unaccustomed—side of the road. Such disruptions of normalcy, she contends, "bring us face-to-face with the wealth of knowledge we take entirely for granted, knowledge lodged in our bodies and manifest in its smooth mannerisms and easy movements."[17]

Examples of knowledge carried in the body could be endlessly multiplied, including such basic knowledge as how to use a Western-style toilet, a kind of knowing so deeply habituated that our bodies may find it difficult to adjust on camping trips or regions that favor in-ground toilets, however elegantly tiled. An example of bodily knowing that particularly interests me is typing. As I type, I neither look at the keyboard nor think about where my fingers should land. In fact, I cannot even tell you where the key for *o* or *m* is located on the board, but my fingers fly there without hesitation. When asked to spell a word, I often "remember" by typing, either by actually typing or by imagining my fingers on a keyboard. The corporal knowledge implicit in typing interests me because, unlike my crude example of toilet training, typing implicates verbal cognition. No clean line divides the body as mind from the mind that reasons.

What we know in the body is so basic to human communication that we may fail to acknowledge it, but we live out the implications on a daily basis. After televised presidential debates, for example, pollsters regularly survey the American public to decide the winner of the debate. In debate after debate, many viewers explicitly state that they judge the winner based on candidates' body language. A transcript does not convey what actually transpired. A brilliant remark followed by what is perceived as a smirk or dismissive hand gesture blunts the effectiveness of the remark. A relaxed, calm stance conveys comfort with authority; fidgeting suggests that the candidate may not be up to the challenges of serving as commander in chief. Of course none of this is deterministic. One viewer may interpret a candidate's crossed arms as pensive while another viewer may interpret those same crossed arms as belligerent.

Part of what I mean when I say that social location is known in the body is that a person's social location informs the kinds of postures and gestures that, seemingly instinctively, she understands she is permitted in a given situation.[18] With respect to the United States, Alcoff writes:

[R]ace operates preconsciously on spoken and unspoken interaction, gesture, affect, and stance to reveal the wealth of tacit knowledge carried in the body of subjects in a racialized society. Greetings, handshakes, choices made about spatial proximity, tone, and decibel level of voice, all reveal the effects of racial awareness, the assumptions of solidarity or hostility, the presumption of superiority, or the protective defenses one makes when one routinely encounters a misinterpretation or misunderstanding of one's intentions.[19]

Depending on the social location of the audience, an Irish American man who stands with chest thrust forward as he speaks in a deep voice may convey reassuring command of a situation, while an African American man who adopts the same stance and intonation may be taken as threatening. Self-presentation depends on one's company. We hold our bodies differently with friends and with strangers, with men and with women, with people we perceive to share key elements of our social location and with people we perceive as culturally distant. In short, bodily knowledge of social location is profoundly relational.

Finally, bodily knowledge of social location is learned from childhood, but once learned seems natural. What we learn is not only our own social location but how to read the social location of others with whom we interact. In any given exchange, we are unlikely to entertain consciously whether to project our voices or to whisper, to hunch our shoulders and lower our gazes or to lift our heads high and stare boldly. Our bodies decide. Nonetheless, for all the seeming naturalness of what Bourdieu calls habitus, an individual may deliberately cultivate and manipulate posture, mannerisms, and gestures.

Modern categories of race and social class are ultimately of only comparative relevance in helping us perceive ancient categories that were crucial to social identity. More immediately relevant dimensions of social location would include categories of race and ethnicity as understood in antiquity, rank, status, wealth, citizenship (the meaning of which shifts from the early to the later Empire), and liberty.[20] I argue in chapters 2 and 3 that various dimensions of social identity in the Roman world, including gender identity and identity as freeborn, free, or slave, worked similarly to inform interpersonal interactions, which were, inevitably, embodied interactions. Corporal inflection of identity informed the kinds of social arrangements Christians constructed and ultimately informed moral imagining in Christian circles. Alcoff argues that because social identities "are correlated to certain kinds of perceptual practices and bodily knowledges," they are likely to "fall below the cracks of the sort of explicit beliefs and assumptions that can be assessed in rational debate."[21] As a result, she concludes, behavior based on gender and race is corporally intransigent, complicating rational attempts at reform.

Influenced by Alcoff, I argue that in the Roman Empire social identity was a kind of bodily knowledge, a knowledge that affected an individual's experience of being in the world and shaped his or her interactions with other people. In shaping their communities, Christians did not subject this knowledge to critique. I have argued that no clean line divides the body as mind from the mind that reasons. I would argue, moreover, that everyday moral knowing and moral distinctions are also mired in the body as mind. The result is that, despite lessons that were occasionally taken from the body of Jesus or the body of Paul, Christian communities were far more likely to reproduce than challenge social distinctions, distinctions that often carried moral connotations.

Old Stories

How can we read the stories told by early Christian bodies? We are outside the cultural codes and we lack the bodies—the flesh, if not, as it were, the bones. The problem arises as soon as word is separated from voice. In his 1966 essay "Paul's Boasting in Relation to Contemporary Professional Practice," E. A. Judge brings this point home. Acknowledging that Paul incorporates irony into his self-presentation in 2 Corinthians, Judge asks, What kind of irony?

> Though how one should distinguish, in a letter, between *sarkasmos*, or "flesh-tearing" irony done with bared teeth, *mykterismos*, a "snort" done with visible dilations of the nostrils, and *epikertomesis*, the "jeer" accompanied by *chleuasmos*, or curling of the lip, is an awkward problem if one hopes to do full justice to Paul's candour. The unhappy elders who had to read his letters to their churches must already have been tempted to intone them poker-faced, as we do in ours, if it had indeed been possible for anyone in antiquity to have contemplated so barbaric an impoverishment of speech.[22]

The modern reader lacks both Paul's corporal presence, his bared teeth or dilated nostrils, and the shades of meaning those facial movements carried in what I will call a corporal vernacular.

The challenge presented by our distance from cultural codes is not entirely insurmountable. In his 1963 monograph *Gesture and Rank in Roman Art: The Use of Gestures to Denote Status in Roman Sculpture and Coinage*, Richard Brilliant argues, "The symbolic gesture was used in works of art as a principal instrument of status identification because gestures were familiar social acts and their significance was accessible to all."[23] Brilliant's work exploits the centrality of rhetorical training to elite Roman self-cultivation and the centrality of gesture to rhetoric. He thus helps us both to understand the significance of corporal self-presentation in Roman social dynamics and to interpret specific gestures and postures. His work helps us see that a cultural code exists and it helps us crack that code.

Inasmuch as bodies, culturally conditioned and culturally experienced, informed social dynamics, our lack of access to those bodies frustrates our analysis of those social dynamics and our appreciation of the textual legacies left us by ancient Christian hands. Both Brilliant and Judge help us understand that rhetoric was a corporal practice, a point that Maud Gleason and Erik Gunderson have more recently developed in important treatments of Roman rhetoric as a corporal technology.[24] Because gestures and postures were taught formally by rhetoricians, we have various sources, both visual and textual, to help us decode them.

Rhetorical training was the provenance of elite men, a work of studied self-fashioning. In fact if we have the patience to sort through the evidence, we can begin to interpret the corporal codes of elites in the Roman Empire. Techniques of the body were presented as natural insignia of character that should be cultivated from youth. The stories read into bodies were moral tales predicated on the subject's social status, wealth, and gender. For example, in his treatise *On Duties* Cicero addresses his son. He presents proper bodily comportment as a moral duty. He writes, "But as for us, let us follow Nature and shun everything that is offensive to our eyes or our ears. So, in standing or walking, in sitting or reclining, in our expression, our eyes, or the movements of our hands, let us preserve what we have called 'propriety' [*decorum*]" (1.35.128). Cicero reinforces gender and status training by emphasizing that decorum forbids both effeminate (or soft, *mollioribus*) dawdling and crude vigor (1.35.128). Note that, for Cicero, proper gait is simultaneously natural and a matter to which a young man should give deliberate attention. He admits no contradiction between nature and cultivation.

A text such as this presents particular challenges for the modern reader, who is likely to have difficulty recognizing Cicero's paternal advice as advice about morality. A modern reader is more likely to interpret Cicero's parental instructions on gesture as quaint training in manners, not entirely unlike my mother's irritated instructions to her five daughters to "be ladylike," by which she meant that we should sit with knees together and, in her words, cultivate dulcet tones. Maintaining a moderate gait is unlikely to strike us as quintessentially moral behavior. But Cicero's parental instructions fall within the boundaries of intentionally moral discourse. To dismiss the significance of bodily deportment in a treatise on morality is to misunderstand the boundaries of Roman conceptions of morality. At issue is the virtue of *modestia*. Alongside Cicero's insistence on the civility of restrained gait, he also insists that emotions should be restrained, neither buoyant nor depressed, and that assorted appetites should be subjected to rational control.[25]

Roman concern with the skilled body as the instantiation of social location has emerged as a significant area of research among classicists, a number of whom acknowledge Bourdieu's influence.[26] In his monograph *Dining Posture in Ancient Rome: Bodies, Values, and Status*, for example, Matthew B. Roller seeks to contribute to "the history of the body, and specifically if the ways in which a Roman's social position and subjectivity were expressed in and constructed through bodily dispositions and movements."[27] Expressing a mild lament that Roman diners did not formally theorize their practices in the same way that rhetoricians elaborated their corporal practices, Roller sets out to establish that through their bodily dispositions Roman diners "claimed for themselves (and ascribed to others) particular locations within the hierarchies of gender and status."[28] In *Nature Embodied: Gesture in Ancient Rome*, Anthony Corbeill analyzes a wide spectrum of Roman body language, ranging from the gestures of priests and doctors to women's mourning practices to the gaits of politicians—particularly as those gaits were mocked by Cicero. Corbeill is interested in quotidian movements and gestures precisely because they ordinarily escape the interest of writers. "When our sources mention a gesture being performed," he argues, "and its intention being understood by a viewer, we gain access to a shared area of knowledge, one based not on the expression of individual will but on cultural circumstances."[29] Corbeill ultimately argues that bodily postures and movements, albeit scripted, were read as natural markers of morality and character. Everyday interactions of bodies helped to establish and control social and political boundaries.

Early Christian Bodies

How do studies of Roman bodies, studies like those by Brilliant, Gleason, Corbeill, and Roller, help us understand the impact of bodily habitus on Christian thought and practice? Paul may well have benefited from rhetorical training, but I am at least as interested in other bodies, bodies outside the narrow confines of properly disciplined bodies, bodies outside the confines of those privileged to discipline their own bodies: the bodies of slaves, male and female; the bodies of elite women; parturient bodies whose oozing effluvia defy categorization as interior or exterior; the body of a crucified, low-status provincial. What stories do these bodies tell? What secrets do they know? How do they give birth to theological discourse—or act as midwife to our birthing of theological discourse?

We cannot get our hands on early Christian flesh. We can nonetheless study early Christian sources for traces left by bodies, that is, for clues about corporal postures, dispositions, and interactions. We will thus be in a position to question whether early Christian sources represent bodies as replicating or resisting imperial habitus. One limitation of all work on ancient sources is the predominance of elite-authored texts, and, in the realm of material culture, elite-sponsored artifacts. We will thus learn more about how elite men expected subordinates to comport themselves than we will learn about how habituation to a subordinate bodily posture affected the moral imaginings of subjects occupying those social locations.

Although our sources frequently reflect the situation among low-status provincials at the margins of the Empire, we have reasonable expectation that those sources significantly share a corporal vocabulary with other representations of Roman bodies. Or so Corbeill argues. He writes that he assumes *"a continuity of gesture across the time and space of the ancient Roman world unless there exists clear evidence to the contrary"* (italics original). This assumption of "gestural continuity" is crucial, Corbeill explains, "since the limitations of our sources for bodily movement often force me to employ evidence not only from different media but from different centuries."[30]

Although we cannot specify the precise contours of the psychic impact of corporal training—as free or slave, for example—such impact seems inevitable, both on individuals and on communities. One lesson that we may glean from studies of Roman bodies is that in the ancient world corporal communication was taken for granted. If we neglect our sources' clues about bodily dispositions and corporal interactions, we are likely to misunderstand those sources. A mere transcript of a verbal exchange misses facial and postural clues to what actually transpired. Even if we do not fully understand the dynamics at work in representation of a corporal exchange, we do well to note textual clues about such dynamics.

Body Language in the Gospel of Mark

At this point in my discussion, early Christian bodies may seem remote, more ghost than matter. To flesh out those bodies, I consider the corporal vernacular at work in the Gospel of Mark. As Corbeill observes, "When our sources mention a gesture being performed and its intention being understood by a viewer, we gain access to a shared area of knowledge, one based not on the expression of individual will but on cultural circumstances."[31] I thus pay particular attention to Mark's representation of gesture and movement. In order to keep the discussion focused I pay special attention to the woman, described as a Greek who is Syrophoenician by ethnicity, who falls at Jesus' feet as she petitions him to intervene with her daughter. My goal in this analysis is to help the reader become aware of ways that one first-century Christian text relies on notations regarding bodily deportment, posture, gesture, and movement to express negotiations of power and status.

On Mark's telling, our heroine seeks out Jesus in the house where he has taken refuge. Throwing herself at his feet, she begs for his assistance. Her physical gesture enacts her petition.[32] In physically falling before Jesus as she seeks help, the woman is hardly alone. Mark describes a sequence of other individuals in related postures, postures variously described as stooping, kneeling, and falling on the ground or at Jesus' feet.[33] Although the varying postural descriptions may evoke somewhat different images, each is an act of self-lowering that participates in a corporal vernacular expressing emotion, social location, and perception of power.[34] Not surprisingly, in the iconography of the Roman Empire—and indeed of adjacent territories—the image of one person sunk on the ground in the presence of another person was the most common visual marker for submission to superior power and authority.[35] The same gesture enacted by different bodies elicits varying responses, as we will see.

Mark especially favors the image of a person lowered before another person to enact deference. Mark's John the Baptist, for example, expresses his secondary status by saying, "The one who is more powerful than I is coming after me; I am not worthy to *stoop down* and untie the thong of his sandals" (1:7). Neither Matthew nor Luke retains Mark's explicit reference to John's self-lowering.[36] In Mark, the rich man who seeks instruction on how to inherit eternal life expresses his deference to Jesus when he runs toward him and then kneels before him (10:17).[37] In Matthew's and Luke's versions of the story the privileged questioner does not lower himself before Jesus (Matt. 19:16; Luke 18:18). Finally, Mark pictures Roman soldiers parodying the familiar gesture of deference. After the soldiers clothe Jesus in a purple cloak, crown him with thorns, salute him, and spit on him, they drop to their knees in mocking obeisance (15:19).[38]

In a number of instances, Mark represents people on the ground before Jesus in the midst of healings and exorcisms.[39] In scenes of healing and exorcism the person who falls to the ground may be the person who suffers or a third party interceding for a sufferer. The motion of falling to the ground may have multiple meanings in contexts of healings and exorcisms. When a leper kneels before Jesus, his kneeling posture expresses his plea to be healed (1:40).[40] Mark characterizes the Gerasene demoniac's gesture by the verb *proskuneō*, thus presenting the man's drop to the ground as a gesture expressing obeisance consistent with the demoniac's address to Jesus as "Son of the Most High God." In another scene, however, a man in a crowd brings his son to Jesus. The man confides that his son is possessed by a spirit so violent that the boy is regularly thrown to the ground. When the boy is in Jesus' presence, the spirit propels the boy to the ground as if on cue. In this story the afflicted person's falling to the ground is characterized as evidence of spirit possession rather than of deference to Jesus (9:14–29).

The woman who hemorrhaged for over a decade also falls to the ground before Jesus.[41] Both F. Scott Spencer and Joel Marcus detect a close parallel between the gestures of the hemorrhaging woman and the Syrophoenician women.[42] Spencer writes of the Syrophoenician, "[S]he approaches Jesus with deferential body language rather than with brazen impudence, bowing at his feet as she begs for mercy on behalf of her tormented daughter (7:25–26). This position recalls that of the hemorrhaging woman, except for the notable distinction that the Syrophoenician *starts* with bowing before Jesus instead of first grasping him from behind."[43] I believe that Spencer and Marcus overemphasize the parallel between the movements of the two women. In fact, I argue, Mark presents their corporal movements differently. The Syrophoenician falls to the ground as a suppliant. When the bleeding woman falls before Jesus, she has already reached out and siphoned healing power from him. Not a petition, her fall expresses her fear. Moreover, Jesus asks who touched him. Mark says that the long-suffering woman "fell down before him and told him the whole truth." Falling to the ground is an act of self-identification and thus of truth telling.

I argue that we can find a more illuminating comparison between the embodied petitions of two parents, Jairus and the woman from Tyre. In both these stories the petitioner asks for intervention for a daughter. Mark's phrasing is close in the two accounts: both petitioners fall at Jesus' feet.[44] More significantly, in both cases the gesture of falling at Jesus feet is constitutive of the act of supplication. What differs is not the petitioner's physical gesture but Jesus' response to that gesture. Meaning is embodied and interactive; physical comportment appropriate for a person of one social status may be perceived as inappropriate for a person of a differing social status. Jesus responds positively to one petitioner. He recoils from the other.

Perhaps hinting that Jesus is initially resistant to Jairus, Mark states that the synagogue leader begs Jesus repeatedly. Nonetheless, the shape of the story emphasizes Jesus' positive response. Unlike the Syrophoenician, who accosts Jesus when he seeks privacy in an alien region, the synagogue leader accosts Jesus when he is in the midst of a crowd by the Sea of Galilee, one of his preferred venues. In that context Jairus, a Galilean who is both a male parent and a synagogue leader, physically enacts his petition. Jesus, in turn, a male Galilean who is neither a parent nor a pillar of the synagogue, physically enacts his positive response. He accompanies Jairus to heal his daughter.

Joanna Dewey argues that in petitioning Jesus, Jairus acts in a countercultural way. She writes, "One would not expect a synagogue leader . . . to fall at Jesus' feet indicating his social inferiority to Jesus."[45] While Jairus is deferential and acknowledges Jesus' power in the area of healing, I do not think his deference can be generalized as an acknowledgment of social inferiority. Roller argues that in literary depictions of Roman dining scenes, bodily elevation is not the sole important marker of social location. "A different hierarchical principle is at work here: the body that must move or take action in response to another body or bodies is inferior."[46] Such logic is evident in the story that appears in Matthew and Luke of the centurion who seeks help from Jesus the healer.[47]

In Luke's version, the centurion sends emissaries to Jesus to beg him to heal a valued or honored slave. Jesus begins to follow the emissaries to the centurion's home, but again the centurion sends emissaries with a message. The centurion says that he is unworthy to receive Jesus under his roof and encourages Jesus to heal by verbal command. "For I also am a man under authority," the centurion is reported to say, "with soldiers under me; and I say to one, 'Go,' and he goes, and to another, 'Come,' and he comes."[48] The centurion's message to Jesus acknowledges that Jesus' word can heal at a distance. At the same time, the centurion defers to Jesus' authority by making clear that he is not beckoning Jesus like a subordinate who comes and goes at the pleasure of one who outranks him.

In the Gospel of Mark, both the synagogue leader and the Syrophoenician woman fall at Jesus' feet, a gesture of self-abasement. With Jairus, however, Jesus responds by following him to his home, movement that implicitly acknowledges Jairus's status. Of all Jesus' healings in the Gospel of Mark, this is the only instance where he is specifically said to travel in order to perform the healing. In other instances Jesus encounters the sufferer, the sufferer is brought to him, or, as in the case of the Syrophoenician woman, Jesus heals at a distance. Falling to the ground, Jairus defers to Jesus' authority. Accompanying Jairus home, Jesus affirms Jairus's status.

With the woman from the region of Tyre, Jesus' reaction is quite different. Why? Sharon Ringe writes, "The fact that the woman's approach to Jesus—falling at his feet—parallels the deferential request of Jairus on behalf of his daughter (5:22), to which Jesus responds positively, suggests that either her ethnicity or her gender might be at the root of the response."[49] Perhaps, Ringe suggests, Jesus may turn away from the woman because she is a resident of a region that exploited the Jews of Galilee, and, as a Greek, an elite resident of that exploitative region. Is the woman doglike because of her gender? Her religion? The region in which she lives? Her Greek identity? Her Syrophoenician heritage? Her possible wealth and privilege?[50] The complexity of the woman's cultural identity is in play when, like Jairus, she falls at Jesus' feet.[51] Her body is precisely the location that makes present this complex cultural identity, just as Jairus's body is precisely the location that makes present his complex cultural identity.

Those who write about the scene often stress the submissiveness and even abjection of the woman's physical posture. While those same scholars sometimes note in passing the submissiveness of Jairus's gesture, the woman's physical self-lowering invites more extended comment. In their commentary on Mark, John Donahue and Daniel Harrington wonder whether the reader is "intended to visualize her still at the feet of Jesus" while she engages in conversation with him.[52] I think the answer is yes. On the other hand, I think the reader is intended to visualize Jairus at the feet of Jesus when he begs him repeatedly, entreating, "My little daughter is at the point of death. Come and lay your hands on her, so that she may be made well, and live" (5:22). However, Jairus's abject posture does not evoke an equal sense of abjection. Why? As I have noted, a crowd witnesses Jairus lowering himself to beg assistance from Jesus. The same crowd follows Jesus as he accompanies Jairus to his daughter's bedside and thus also witnesses an action that reaffirms Jairus's ranking place in the community.

David Rhoads writes, "The posture of the woman in begging for a healing is integral to Jesus' description of her as a scavenger dog."[53] (*Pace* Rhoads, it is the woman rather than Jesus who turns the dog into a scavenger.) Rhoads's point is that the dialogue between Jesus and the woman presupposes the abasing associations of a physical location near the ground. Moreover, the scene plays with the tension between woman's deceptively abject acceptance of Jesus' tagging of her as a dog and her bald-faced assault on Jesus' authority. Donahue and Harrington pick up on the tension, commenting, "Despite her seeming posture of humble suppliant, . . . she responds with equal alacrity to Jesus' insults."[54] Jesus, who responded with hostility to the woman's embodied plea, demurs to her verbal challenge.[55]

In these Markan scenes, deference and authority are negotiated through posture and gesture as well as through words. Such negotiations of the hierarchies of power and social status would have been familiar to Mark's readers and indeed throughout the Roman Empire. Pliny, for example, notes that all peoples adopt similar postures of supplication, lowering themselves and reaching toward the knee of the person being petitioned. Pliny supposes that the commonality of the gesture derives from a life force peculiarly resident in the knee.[56] Social status as known in the body is not immutable but functions as part of a wider system of hierarchies. The person accustomed to having others kneel before him may himself fall to the ground in supplication. Thus when we reach the scene in Mark where Jesus falls to the ground in Gethsemane, we should be prepared to interpret the motion as expressing Jesus' desperate petition to be kept from harm, a petition addressed to the one Jesus calls Father (14:35).[57]

My Body, My Self?

Even as I have explored the social dynamics of early Christian bodies, I have mused about a more fundamental question. What is the relationship of one's identity to one's body? In many ways this is the question that informs chapter 4 of the present volume, my analysis of early Christian writings on Mary in childbirth. In the midst of Alcoff's argument that social location is known in the body, she offers a critique of the view that "allows one to say, 'I am not really my body,' as if one were actually housed elsewhere and only there as a tenant."[58] Who might hold such a view? A Cartesian, for example; or the early Christians who composed *The Apocalypse of James, The Letter of Peter to Philip*, the Nag Hammadi *Apocalypse of Peter* (all dated to the second or third century), and other Christian works that, in Karen King's words, repudiate the identification of body with self. (In chapter 4

I consider at length the representation of bodies in *Ascension of Isaiah*, a little-known text that in complex ways distances selfhood from corporeality.) In *The Apocalypse of Peter*, the Savior reveals to Peter an alternate vision of the crucifixion. In the vision, a figure suffers on the cross while another figure is "glad and laughing on the tree." The Savior explains, "He whom you saw on the tree, glad and laughing, this is the living Jesus. But this one into whose hands and feet they drive the nails is his fleshy part, which is the substitute, being put to shame, he who came into being in his likeness" (81.16–24).

In contrast, in the *Letter of Peter to Philip*, Peter teaches that Jesus was crowned with thorns, crucified, and buried, but he goes on to say that Jesus was "a stranger to this suffering" (139.21–25). For some early Christians, the incarnation, crucifixion, and resurrection demonstrate the freedom of incorruptible spirit from the corruptible body. About these works, King writes,

> At issue is more than the affirmation that the Savior truly had a body, suffered, and died. Not only Christology but anthropology—the fundamental issue of what it means to be a human being—was at stake. Is the true self located in the body or in the soul/spirit? Tertullian argued vociferously that the soul and the body came into being as a unity and would continue as a unity for all eternity in the resurrection. *ApJames* [*Apocalypse of James*] and *LetPetPhil* [*Letter of Peter to Philip*] disagree: the location of the soul in the body is a temporary arrangement; only the spiritual soul will rise to life with God.[59]

The Nag Hammadi sources are witnesses to a theological movement commonly called Gnosticism. Gnosticism is routinely said to be anti-body. King helps us see the limits of that truism.

In her monograph on the *Secret Revelation of John*, King elaborates on the understanding of the relationship between body and identity as represented in a single major treatise from Nag Hammadi. King argues that the *Secret Revelation of John* presupposes that true identity, the true self, resides in the divine spirit rather than in the body. Bodies in themselves are not evil. Bodies are perfectible. Freed from wickedness, they can become luminous.[60] Within this textual world, King claims, "the body is an important—if not the most important—site of revelation and the purveyor of true knowledge."[61] King asks, "What is the truth which the body teaches?"[62] On King's convincing exposition, the *Secret Revelation of John* conforms to the ancient view of the body as a microcosmic map of reality. The *Secret Revelation of John* subjects the rulers of socially oppressive reality to critique. As microcosm and map of that oppressive reality, the body is not exempt from critique. King concludes, "To say that the *Secret Revelation of John* considers the body to be evil by nature misses the complexity of the text's presentation of the human body as both map and territory, as both revelation and background, as the soul's ally and the demiurgic weapon against which it must struggle."[63]

In the Johannine scene of the man born blind we encounter the common ancient view that read physical debility as a signature of moral failure. In face of such a view, it is easy to understand why someone would say—in the view Alcoff attempts to rebut—"I am not really my body." In chapters 2 and 3 I continue to develop the view that the body is conditioned to be a skilled interpreter of social relations. Again, in view of the oppressive nature of social relations in the Roman Empire, it is easy to understand why someone would distance selfhood from the habituated body, to say, "I am not really my body." My intention here is not to become a partisan in early Christian debates about the relationship of self to body, debates that return in the argument of chapter 4. My intention is to point out that Alcoff's insistence that the self is a body has important consequences for the views we hold—and the views we reject—about human identity. King helps us see a thoughtful adjunct and alternative to the view of the body-self that Alcoff advances, an alternative expounded in documents from Nag Hammadi and scattered in other ancient Christian sources.

Being a Body

Bodies exceed the stories they tell. I have a long-standing frustration with analyses of bodies that tell us nothing about what it means to be a body—even, dare I say, Peter Brown's field-altering *The Body and Society*. Not that I think those analyses are wrongheaded. As will be obvious, my own work is deeply indebted to them. My frustration is simply that those analyses do not help me tell the truth about the experience of being a body, to echo Virginia Woolf's words in this chapter's epigraph.[64] In focusing on the stories told by the body of John's vision-impaired beggar, for example, we overlook the question of whether the world was blear or crisp when the beggar first glimpsed it; what visual sense he made of a world he had previously known through hearing and touch; whether the mud Jesus rubbed into the blind man's eyes was gritty or slimy on the thin flesh of his eyelids. If we think such questions at all, we bracket them as homiletic.

"The Case of the Missing Body" is hardly confined to studies of religion in antiquity. Thomas Csordas notes, "At the 1990 meeting of the American Ethnological Society dedicated to the theme of 'the body in society and culture,' it was evident that many participants were using the term 'body' without much sense of 'bodiliness' in their analyses, as if body were little more than a synonym for self or person."[65] An exclusive focus on what Scheper-Hughes and Lock term the body politic eclipses attention to the tactile quiddity of bodies, to the experience of being a body, to what Scheper-Hughes and Lock term "the phenomenally experienced *individual body-self*." Chapter 2, "Boasting of Beatings (2 Corinthians 11:23–25)," asks how Paul's scarred body would have been read in Corinth and considers the theological discourse generated by that body. Paul's body becomes on this telling a semiotic or representational body, a body to be read. In chapter 3, "Embodying Slavery," I focus on ways that corporal habituation shapes identity and thus confines social arrangements and informs—or deforms—the moral universes of early Christian communities. In asking how corporal habituation shapes identity I circle around the experience of being a body. Still concerned with semiotic or representational bodies, I also want the reader to think about what it means to be a particular body-self, to be, for example, a female slave or a female slaveholder. As I move in chapter 4 to an extended treatment of Mary's body in childbirth, my approach shifts from a semiotic or representational approach to bodies to a stronger emphasis on a phenomenological approach to bodies, to pick up on a distinction articulated by Csordas.[66] This shift is not an attempt to displace a semiotic approach to bodies but to expand it, and in so doing to invite reflection on the body as "the existential condition of possibility for culture and self."[67]

The strange bodies we glimpse in a variety of early Christian writings offer curious angles on this insight, which Csordas derives from Merleau-Ponty, who writes of the body as "our general medium for having a world."[68] So, for example, Ignatius writes to Roman Christians in the early second century, begging them not to interfere with his martyrdom. He imagines himself condemned to the beasts, an image known from mosaics and other artifacts scattered throughout the Mediterranean. In these visual representations, the naked body of the condemned man is bound to a post, the lions goaded by an attendant lest they prove themselves picky eaters.[69] Let me be ground by their teeth, Ignatius pleads, and when my body is no more, then I will be found in Christ. This is not a variant on the Stoicism current in Ignatius's day. Ignatius is not indifferent to the fate of his body. Rather, Ignatius positively identifies his cosmological metamorphosis, his desired unity with Christ, as a literal incorporation. Through the general medium of his body he anticipates that his world will be transformed. Christian writers who image Mary in childbirth likewise picture a strange body that can help us think in different ways about the body and selfhood.

At stake in discourses of childbirth, ancient and modern, are questions related to corporeality, epistemology, and selfhood. What I offer in chapter 4 is not a systematic treatment of childbearing bodies but an invitation to engage selected writings on the nativity as meditations on being a body. I have found the early Christians who evoke, narrate, or analyze the nativity to be thinkers contending with the whatness of bodies. By *whatness* I do not mean *thingness*. Following Merleau-Ponty, I do not see bodies as things or objects; rather, I understand my own body to mediate my relations with the world—with things, with other persons, even with ideas. So many scholars have written so very well about the ways that early Christians made sense of bodies bloodied in martyrdom. I have deliberately chosen to offer instead a sustained treatment of some ways that early Christians attempted to make sense of a body bloodied—or not—in childbearing. I ask: What do images and narratives of Mary in childbirth suggest about Christian attempts to grapple with what it means to be a body? Whether she is heavy with child or pressing her newborn to her breast, what does Mary know in her body?

As I have said, bodies exceed the stories they tell. I do not expect to tell such consummate stories of early Christian bodies that there will be nothing left to say about them. I do expect to help the reader understand how bodies figure into a cultural history of early Christianity. Moreover, and more ambitiously, I propose a nonreductive corporal epistemology. Through my readings of early Christian sources, then, I invite the reader to reflect on what is known in the body.

Boasting of Beatings (2 Corinthians 11:23–25)

> *Is it then the case that it is the whole woman I want, that my pleasure in her is spoiled until these marks on her are erased and she is restored to herself; or is it the case (I am not stupid, let me say these things) that it is the marks on her which drew me to her but which, to my disappointment, I find, do not go deep enough? Too much or too little: is it she I want or the traces of a history her body bears?*
>
> —J. M. Coetzee, *Waiting for the Barbarians*, 64

Paul writes that in his body he bears the marks of Jesus, *ta stigmata tou Iēsou* (Gal. 6:17). J. Louis Martyn comments, "Considering his physique to be a major form of communication, alongside the words of his letter, Paul points literally to his own body. He can do this because his body tells the story of the forward march of the gospel, just as do his words."[1] Martyn shares the widely held view that Paul's *stigmata* are literal scars "from Gentile stones and from Jewish whips" (2 Cor. 11:24–25).[2] These Jesus scars, Martyn continues, "reflect the wounds of a soldier sent into the front trenches of God's redemptive and liberating war."[3] Tracings of whips and magistrates' rods, however, are not prima facie the wounds of a soldier, cicatrices ennobling a warrior's breast. They are, typically, markings of a servile body, insignia of humiliation and submission. Who, then, reads Paul's somatic markings as badges of martial valor: The Christians of Galatia? The Christians of Corinth? Scholars? Paul himself?

Paul may understand his storytelling body to narrate "the forward march of the gospel," as Martyn suggests, but those who catch a glimpse of what Stephen D. Moore calls "the map of his [Paul's] missionary journeys that has been cut into his back" may well read other stories, some shameful, scored there.[4] This chapter is distinctive in that I focus narrowly on a single passage of a single early Christian document. In reading the body language of 2 Corinthians 11:23–25, where Paul, boasting, elaborates on the character of the beatings he has endured, I ask how

24

Paul's boasting of beatings contributes to the complex argument of 2 Corinthians 10–13. What does Paul know in his lacerated and bruised body? How does he situate this dubious knowledge as a source of improbable power?

Paul talks smack—boasts of beatings—in the context of a letter to the Corinthian Christian community. Founded by Paul, the community has subsequently come under the sway of rival teachers whom Paul accuses of self-vaunting. Paul parries, "But whatever anyone dares to boast of—I am speaking as a fool—I also dare to boast of that" (11:21b). He boasts that, like his rivals, he is a Hebrew, an Israelite, a descendant of Abraham, and minister of Christ. Indeed, he claims, he is a better minister than they: "Are they ministers of Christ? I am talking like a madman—I am a better one: with far greater labors, far more imprisonments, with countless floggings, and often near death. Five times I have received from the Jews the forty lashes minus one. Three times I was beaten with rods. Once I received a stoning" (11:23–25a). Paul continues with a litany of other hardships on land and sea before he boasts obliquely of another kind of journey, an astral journey. He writes, "I know a person in Christ who fourteen years ago was caught up to the third heaven—whether in the body or out of the body I do not know; God knows" (12:2). "Caught up into Paradise," Paul claims, he "heard things that are not to be told, that no mortal is permitted to repeat" (12:4). Paul thus claims astral travel as a source of ineffable knowledge. I argue that Paul also claims the humiliating violations he endured as an improbable but incontrovertible source of knowledge and thus of power.

In his influential study of hardship (*peristaseis*) catalogues in the Corinthian correspondence, John T. Fitzgerald argues that, in Greco-Roman literature, "[t]he scars that the good man sometimes bears on his body are visible tokens of his virtue, 'so that not by hearsay but by evidence of their own eyes men can judge what manner of man he is' [Xenophon *Agesilaus* 6.2]. The endurance of hardship is thus the *proof of virtue*, the seal of integrity."[5] Fitzgerald implies that, in the corporal idiom of Mediterranean antiquity, a man's scarred body tells a virtuous, virile story. By extension, Paul's scars attest to a praiseworthy endurance of hardship. However, Fitzgerald's quotation from Xenophon is selective. Xenophon addresses Agesilaus's manly courage (*andreia*), established in battle.[6] Xenophon writes that, as a consequence of valor in combat, Agesilaus bears "in his own body visible tokens [*sēmeia*] *of the fury of his fighting* [emphasis added], so that not by hearsay but by the evidence of their own eyes men could judge what manner of man he was." By effacing the explicitly martial context in which scars are legible as signs of virtue, Fitzgerald leaves the impression that the endurance of any physical ordeal is equally exemplary. On a first-century view, however, hardships might ennoble or degrade a man; scars might testify to heroism or contemptibility. Impressed by lash and rod, the scars that some men bore in their bodies testified not to virtue but to a lack of integrity. Recognition of the semiotic distinction between a breast pierced by a sword and a back welted by a whip is crucial to reading Paul's body language in 2 Corinthians 11:23–25. In boasting of beatings, Paul boasts not of his manly courage but of his humiliating corporal vulnerability.

Pierre Bourdieu argues that we make sense of human bodies—and human bodies make sense—through a "system of structured, structuring dispositions, the *habitus*."[7] Habitus, which Bourdieu describes as "embodied history, internalized as a second nature and forgotten as history," translates itself into knowledge borne in the body:[8]

> Adapting a phrase of Proust's, one might say that arms and legs are full of numb imperatives. One could endlessly enumerate the values given body, *made* body, by the hidden persuasion of an implicit pedagogy which can instil a whole cosmology, through injunctions as insignificant as "sit up straight" or "don't hold your knife in your left hand," and inscribe the most fundamental principles of the arbitrary content of a culture in seemingly innocuous details of bearing or physical and verbal manners, so putting them beyond the reach of consciousness and explicit statement.[9]

Reading Paul's body language is difficult because, with the passage of time, the discourse of the familiar fades. Downcast eyes, a blush spreading across a face, the deliberate exposure of dermal markings: facial expression, demeanor, and posture cease to bear shared meanings.[10] We do, however, have clues for interpreting what Bourdieu calls "bodily hexis," that is, "political mythology realized, *em-bodied*, turned into a permanent disposition, a durable way of standing, speaking, walking, and thereby of feeling and thinking."[11] The scars of a first-century body instantiate relationships of power, of legal status (freeborn, freed, or enslaved), of domination and submission, of honor and shame, and of gender. In drawing attention to his *stigmata* and enumerating his beatings, Paul relies on a vocabulary of corporeality shared by his readers.

Interpreting the story Paul expects to be read in his body is further complicated by the social location of 2 Corinthians 10–13, written to urban Christians shaped by intersecting Greek, Roman, and Jewish thought worlds.[12] These thought worlds were not mutually exclusive, nor were they isomorphic, nor were they stable. What it meant to be Greek, Roman, or Jewish was in flux in the first century.[13] Where, then, shall we look for clues on how the Corinthians might have responded to a glimpse of Paul's back? In Acts of the Apostles, Luke relates an incident that takes place in Philippi: magistrates, responding to public pressure, order the flogging of Paul and Silas. Luke emphasizes the Roman identity of the city, of the accusers, and of the beaten missionaries (Acts 16:19–39).[14] That Paul and Silas are Jewish, Greek-speaking Roman citizens, strangers in a Macedonian city whose inhabitants appeal to Roman officials on the basis of shared political allegiance, illuminates the complexity of (self-)identity under the empire. Nonetheless, Luke's recurring emphasis on explicitly Roman elements of the scene focuses the reader's attention on the meaning of flogging and flogged bodies in a mien wherein signal aspects of Roman "political mythology" are embodied. In untangling strands of meaning woven into the fabric of Paul's reference to his repeated beatings in 2 Corinthians 11:22–25, I follow Luke's lead and emphasize dimensions of Roman hexis that imbue with significance a man's public exposure of his own wounds. Like Philippi, Corinth is, of course, a Roman colony.[15]

As now the corpus of Paul's writings conjures for us images of Paul's physical corpus when still alive, so in his own day his words prompted those who knew him to recall his absent body. Paul bids the reader to remember his wounds. Did Paul, when present in a community, use his body to persuade, to exhort, or to inspire? If Paul expects the Galatians to understand his *stigmata* to be marks on his back, they are likely to have seen those marks, and, with or without his guidance, to have read the story of his punishments inscribed there.[16] Perhaps when Paul stood in the midst of a congregation, he bared his back and offered an interpretation of the history of its markings, reminding his dubious audience that whips had similarly lacerated Jesus' flesh. In this scenario his painfully acquired corporal knowledge might imbue him with a peculiar authority, but we may imagine other scenarios as well. For example, we might easily imagine that, shamefaced and tongue-tied, Paul was cornered into explaining his stripes during chance encounters in the baths.[17]

In this chapter I argue that through the repeated violation of his body Paul claims a corporal knowledge that unites him with Jesus. Paul does not try to represent this corporal knowledge as glorious. The whip teaches abasement and humiliation. Nonetheless, because his experiences of physical abuse unite him with Jesus, Paul presents his abject body as evidence of his authority. In order to make sense of Paul's somatic rhetoric, we must learn to read the storytelling bodies of the Roman world.

Battle Scars

In his *War against Jugurtha*, Sallust supplies a speech for Gaius Marius as he garners support for war. He contrasts two kinds of self-boasting. His aristocratic rivals, he claims, boast of family and lineage. He, on the other hand, boasts only of what is his own: his accomplishments, his difficulties, and, ultimately, the marks on his own body.[18] Consideration of his rhetorical strategy helps situate Paul's self-boasting in 2 Corinthians 11:23b–33 and introduces the rhetorical functions of war wounds in Roman discourse.

Marius mentions his triumphs in passing while emphasizing obstacles overcome and privations endured. He asserts, "From my childhood to my present time of life I have so lived that I am familiar with every kind of toil and danger" (85.7). His rivals, noble in heritage but not in manly valor, "begrudge me my office; then let them begrudge my toil, my honesty, even my dangers, since it was through those that I won the office" (85.17). Marius calls attention to his hardships for a variety of purposes, although not, as a Cynic or Stoic might, to highlight his serenity amid turmoil. Through his struggles, Marius says, he has established himself as a man. In response to those who rest their claims to authority in ancestry, Marius replies that he is more like the valiant ancestors than the soft descendants. He insists that he has not lived through a lifetime of tribulations in order to glorify himself, but rather to promote the good of those before whom he now stands. His opponents display portraits of their noble ancestors. Marius offers to set before them evidence of his own nobility: "I cannot, to justify your confidence, display family portraits or the triumphs and consulships of my forefather; but if occasion requires, I can show spears, a banner, trappings and other military prizes, as well as scars on my own breast. These are my portraits, these my patent of nobility, not left me by inheritance as theirs were, but won by my own innumerable toils and perils" (85.29–30).

Some in Sallust's audience would have been more impressed by the display of family portraits than of wounds. Many, however, would have fallen in formation behind the soldier who, though lacking a pedigree, referred proudly to the marks carved into his own chest. As ancestral portraits could be read as evidence of familial nobility, so Marius's scars could be read as evidence of personal nobility. Both like and unlike Paul, Marius presents his scarred body in competition over authority. The act of exhibiting a wounded and scarred body was a standard move in Greco-Roman self-presentation. I outline the rhetorical function of war wounds— and the display of such wounds—before turning specifically to the question of whether the recipients of 2 Corinthians 10–13 would have read the latticework of lacerations on Paul's flesh as honorable manly emblems of a soldier's courage.[19]

Throughout Greek and Roman literature, scars incurred in combat serve, in Plutarch's words, as "inscribed images of excellence and manly virtue" (*Mor.* 331C).[20] Matthew Leigh argues that the display of war wounds as the climax of argumentation is a distinctively though not uniquely Roman practice.[21] Orators referred verbally to their battle scars. They opened their tunics in order to exhibit those scars. A Roman crowd milling about an orator required no instruction to decode his gesture when he bared his chest. Without speaking another word, his scar tissue testified to a brave confrontation with an adversary's sword. Quintilian conceded that a person's display of his or her body as a spectacle could be more credible than declamation. He offered an example familiar to his readers: "Thus when Antonius in the course of his defense of Manius Aquilius tore open his client's robe and revealed the honorable scars which he had acquired while facing his country's foes, he relied no longer on the power of his eloquence, but appealed directly to the eyes of the Roman people" (*Institutio oratoria* 2.15.7). Manius Aquilius could not be dishonorable, his honorable scars implied, a claim that apparently negated the evidence presented by the prosecution. Before Roman eyes, a man's cicatrized breast was the incarnation of a martial narrative.

Quintilian, following Cicero, referred to the orator's *sermo corporis*, his body language.[22] The orator's *sermo corporis* exemplified a bodily hexis, an embodiment of political mythology and values. Specifically, the semiotic significance of invoking or displaying dermal insignia of valor was widely appreciated. Josephus supplied the example of Antipater the Elder, who appeared before Julius Caesar to defend himself against charges of disloyalty. His defense relied not on spoken but on somatic language. In fact, he claimed to have no use for words: "his body, while he was silent, shouted it [his loyalty] aloud" (*J.W.* 1.197). Maud Gleason comments, "This shouting, silent body did indeed affect a successful cross-cultural communication, probably because the display of one's scars as testimony in self-defense was a Roman gestural convention."[23]

Within the Roman *sermo corporis*, the vocabulary of battle scars was finely calibrated. An unfriendly audience could read a tale of cowardice in unbroken flesh on a man's chest.[24] The forensic gesture of a defendant baring his war-battered chest was sufficiently familiar to be the subject of parody. Cicero, having informed his audience that Verres made a practice of satisfying his lust by forcibly bedding the wives and daughters of respectable households, demanded to know whether Verres's defense would entail the customary display of wounds.[25] Would Verres, Cicero asked, "bare his breast, show the people of Rome his scars—scars made by women's teeth, the imprinted records of lechery and foulness?" (*Verr.* 2.5.33).

Not all battle wounds are honorable. Scar tissue marking chest, throat, or face tells a story of courage in combat. Scar tissue marking a man's back tells a story of cowardice.[26] Allusions to war wounds typically specify their location. So Livy's Servilius proclaims, "I possess a body adorned with honourable scars, every one of them received in front" (45.39.16). Aelian preserves the tradition that, when a Spartan mother received word that her son had died in battle, she personally sought his body on the battlefield. If the wounds on her son's corpse were in the front, she arranged for burial in the family plot. If the wounds were in the back, she slunk away; the corpse was left for anonymous burial (12.21). Like Spartan mothers, ancient audiences were critical readers of the stories told by corporal inscriptions.

In a footnote to his observation that Paul's *stigmata* reflect his military role in advancing the gospel, Martyn alludes to the battle scars on Antipater's body limning his loyalty to Caesar: "As Antipater was said to bear on almost every part of his person the marks of wounds showing his loyalty to Caesar . . . so Paul points to his body as it testifies to his belonging to the crucified Jesus."[27] But who would designate Paul's *stigmata* "signs of excellence," as Josephus refers to Antipater's scars (*J.W.* 1.193)? Is Antipater's exposure of his scars parallel to Paul's insistence in various passages that the reader acknowledge his wounds and the incidents in which he was wounded? Ancient audiences distinguished between the mark of a sword slashing a courageous breast and the mark of a sword slashing a cowardly back. They distinguished even more sharply between the martial tracing left by a sword and the servile tracing left by a whip or a rod. The Corinthian Christians would have appreciated the nuances implicit in the markings of a man's corpus: not every scarred body told an honorable story.

The Whippable Body

In Roman *habitus*, whipping was the archetypal mark of dishonor.[28] In his litany of hardships endured in the course of training and military campaigns, Sallust's Marius includes some details that Paul also registers. He speaks of being hungry, cold, and forced to sleep in conditions that deprive him of slumber. Such conditions were at times associated with poverty and misfortune, and thus the potential dishonor of poverty and misfortune, but they were at the same time the kinds of experiences that hardened a man, made him virile. Being subject to beating, being vulnerable to the power of another man (or woman) to order a whipping, was not a rite de passage associated with maturing to manhood, but a state which diminished any claim to manliness. Whipping played a pedagogic and ultimately epistemological function, imparting knowledge of degradation and dishonorable submissiveness. (I discuss later an exceptional case, the ritual flagellation of elite Spartan youths at the altar of Artemis Orthia.) Stoic and Cynic moralists regularly contended that beatings, however brutal, were not a source of veritable injury. Richard Saller notes that this philosophical contention had no impact on a conventional wisdom that persisted in seeing beating and other corporal punishment as inherently degrading.[29]

The scars of a man's body tell a story, but not every man's body tells a war story. We have considered the function of the display of war wounds in first-century somatic rhetoric. Josephus describes an incident that illustrates the function of the display of a different kind of wound. In Tarichaeae, Josephus claims, a crowd massed in opposition to him. Feigning capitulation, he agreed to meet with representatives of the crowd. Then he dragged the delegates into the building "and whipped them until their innards were laid bare" (*J.W.* 2.612). Throwing open the doors, he exhibited the delegates' flesh, drenched in blood. Intimidated and terrified, the mob dispersed. Commenting on the incident, Maud Gleason writes, "This is the body language of dominance."[30] Josephus's action endowed him, Gleason notes, "with an air of decisive manliness on the Roman aristocratic model."[31] Relationships of power, of domination and submission, and of honor and shame were enacted somatically.

Not all instances of the exhibition or uncovering of marks inflicted by whips were so dramatic. Flogging was the most common form of corporal punishment. The ability to order a whipping signaled a person's dominance over another; the inability to resist a whipping, the dishonor of the person whipped. Within an idiom that was distinctively though not uniquely Roman, corporal punishment was routinely associated with slaves, and thus vulnerability to corporal punishment signaled servility. Over the course of the history of the Roman Republic, the de jure right of all citizens to immunity from corporal punishment in the public sphere, notably from the lictors' rods, was established; the citizen's expectation of corporal inviolability extended into the empire.[32] Richard Saller has argued that this privilege was translated into domestic bodily hexis. As a result, although Roman fathers had the legal right to beat their sons, the association of being beaten with dishonor, servility, and submissiveness usually protected the backs of legitimate sons from the scars that characterized the backs of slaves.[33] Dishonorable bodies were whippable; honorable bodies were not.[34]

Because vulnerability to beating was a servile liability, any free person who was whipped or struck suffered an injury to honor far in excess of whatever temporary pain or permanent mark was inflicted.[35] A whipping was a lesson in servility. Philo's account of Flaccus's campaign against the Jews of Alexandria relies on a corporal idiom associating honor and status with immunity from beating and gradations of dishonor and low status with various kinds of beatings. Philo reports that Flaccus ordered the members of the Alexandrian gerousia to be rounded up and taken to a theater, where they became a spectacle. "Then as they stood with their enemies seated in front to signal their disgrace he ordered them all to be stripped and lacerated with scourges which are commonly used for the degradation of the violent malefactors" (*Against Flaccus* 10.75).

While beating itself dishonored the victims, that dishonor was intensified by Flaccus's choice of implements: "There are differences between the scourges used in the city, and these differences are regulated by the social standing of the persons to be beaten" (10.78). Members of the gerousia were whipped with the scourge used against the Egyptians, an implement that struck forcibly against the dignity of the Jewish leaders. Philo stresses that Flaccus exhibited his contempt through this choice:

> For it is surely possible when inflicting degradation on others to find some little thing to sustain their dignity. . . . Surely then it was the height of harshness that when

commoners among the Alexandrian Jews, if they appeared to have done things
worthy of stripes, were beaten with whips more suggestive of freemen and citizens,
the magistrates, the gerousia, whose very name implies age and honour, in this
respect fared worse than their inferiors and were treated like Egyptians of the meanest
rank and guilty of the greatest inequities. (10.78, 80)

Philo plays on the reader's comprehension of the semantics of corporal control as
enacted within the corporal vernacular of Alexandria. The goal of the exercise was
not only to humiliate the gerousia before the general population. Rather, the punitive exercise was also pedagogical. Members of the gerousia were supposed to
limp away from their exposure as spectacles knowing shame deeply within their
bodies.

Roman history records a number of instances where honorable persons whose
bodies should have been inviolate were nonetheless subject to whippings by public
authorities. Such treatment brought dishonor and ignominy to the one who endured
it. Both Cicero and Philo sought to discredit the perpetrators of what they saw as
illegitimate violence. They did not set out to intensify or reinforce the shame of the
victims, but they could not erase it. As the climax of his charges against Verres,
Cicero recounted the story of the flogging and crucifixion of a Roman citizen,
Gavius of Consa. For an audience that would not balk at the sight of a slave being
brutalized, Cicero detailed Verres's treatment of Gavius. Verres ordered that Gavius
should be "flung down, stripped naked and tied up in the open marketplace" (*Verr.*
2.62.161). Gavius attempted to avert the beating by announcing his citizenship, but
Verres ignored his plea: "He then ordered the man to be flogged severely all over
his body. There in the open market-place of Messana a Roman citizen, gentlemen,
was beaten with rods; and all the while, amid the crack of the falling blows, no
groan was heard from the unhappy man, no words came from his lips in his agony
except 'I am a Roman citizen'" (*Verr.* 2.66.162). Cicero did not argue that Gavius
was impervious to Verres's insult. On Cicero's view, Verres was wicked, but he
also effectively degraded Gavius, into whose skin an emblem of submissiveness
was beaten.

Whether Gavius, Paul, or any other victim of the magistrates' rods was able to
resist internalizing such stigmatization is another question. Acts of the Apostles
reports that after Peter and other apostles were beaten, they rejoiced that they had
been deemed worthy to be dishonored for the sake of Jesus' name (5:40–41), a
formulation that encapsulates the nexus of flogging and dishonor while expressing
the idiopathic Christian elevation of abasement. Kathleen McCarthy has argued
that, in Plautus, the clever slave "may not relish the actual pain involved in whipping but refuses to see this physical act as depriving him of honor."[36] Nonetheless,
in ordering a slave to be whipped, a slaveholder acted out a script through which
he or she demonstrated mastery over a submissive body. Those witnessing the act

appreciated these semiotics; those who later viewed the cutaneous evidence, raw or cicatrized, had no doubt about the story etched by strokes of the whip.

This point is difficult for modern audiences to appreciate. For us, the slave-holder occupies a morally untenable position. The practice of corporal punishment is an onerous symbol of the immorality and dishonor of slaveholding. Quite the opposite was the case in antiquity. Matthew Roller argues, "Physical and legal degradation corresponded in Roman society to moral degradation."[37] That one's body was whipped and therefore whippable constituted evidence of suspect char-acter.[38] Moreover, with every stroke of the lash a slave or other low-status person was expected to learn the lesson of his or her own contemptibility. Degradation was corporally known. Paul's whippability—for his announcement that he had been repeatedly lashed and beaten with rods defined him as eminently beatable—marked him as dishonorable, even contemptible.

From a distance of two millennia, we may find it difficult to read Paul's body: are those badges of valor or marks of dishonor? In the first century, however, scar tissue on a breast pierced in battle was readily distinguished from a crosshatching of weals on a back. One variety of anecdote found in Roman histories turns on the semiotics of this dermal distinction.[39] During the Sabine wars, Livy tells us, in the days before Roman citizens were guaranteed the immunities later promised them by custom and law, men who should have been recognized as heroes were instead reduced to the indignities of debt bondage. Those whose military service had helped guarantee Roman liberty were virtually enslaved. One old man's body viv-idly testified to this outrage. Making himself an example, the old man stood in the forum and "displayed the scars on his breast which bore testimony to his honour-able service in battle" (2.23.4).

The veteran then told the story of what his life had been like since he had returned from duty. He arrived home to discover his property damaged by the en-emy: crops stolen, house torched. Falling into the hands of usurers, his financial situation worsened, until finally his creditors carried him off, "to the chain-gang and the torture-chamber. He then showed them his back, disfigured with the wales of recent whipping" (2.23.6–7). The sight of the old man's wounds, front and back, incited the crowd. To Roman eyes, a man whose breast was nobly cicatrized should not know the ignominy of the lash. The point of the story is not that the veteran who demonstrated his manliness in battle continued to demonstrate his manliness in other harsh circumstances. Rather, the point is that the veteran whose semeio-phoric breast verified his claim to honorable manhood should not be degraded by being treated as less than a man, that is, by treatment only appropriate for those whose contemptibly low status rendered them beatable. Livy does not confuse bat-tle wounds and disciplinary stripes. In fact, his anecdote is predicated on the sym-bolic distinction between these two kinds of corporal markings.

Earning His Stripes

Scored in the skin of Livy's ill-used veteran, front and back, are stories of martial valor and of degradation. Livy is not alone in exploiting the simultaneous sameness and differences of scars. For example, the (mis)identification of humiliating insignia—stripes welted into a back by a whip—as martial crests is familiar from comedy. In a different vein, ancient writers marveled at the Spartan contest in which the blood of flagellated ephebes soaked the altar of Artemis Orthia. Generally touted as a ritual enactment of manly courage, the Spartan contest nonetheless elicited scoffing from some who refused to perceive any instance of subjection to the whip as the mark of a man. A question in reading 2 Corinthians 10–13 is whether Paul's contemporaries might read his body as battle scarred, a question that turns on whether Paul's contemporaries would treat his endurance of repeated bouts of whipping as noble, admirable, or even respectable. Before we consider the place of 11:23–25 in the argument of chapters 10–13, we therefore consider texts where the marks of whipping or other (typically) humiliating physical assaults are (mis)taken for honorable signs of masculinity.

The comedies of Plautus are prominent in discussions of the literary representation of slavery and physical abuse. As William Fitzgerald observes in *Slavery and the Roman Literary Imagination*, Plautus "continually finds new ways of figuring the immutable fact that the slave is the being who is beaten."[40] Preferring corporal pain to moral or emotional submission, Plautus's slaves laugh off the incessant stream of abuse directed at them. Why would the audience find these exchanges funny? Fitzgerald argues that in the complex hierarchy of Roman society, where each audience member had to submit daily to the authority of some dominant figure, the intransigence of comic slaves evoked appreciative laughter. He writes:

> [P]hysical pain is only part of the effect of whipping intended by the master; what whipping is supposed to accomplish is branding the slave with marks of shame and dishonor that go far deeper than the scars on the skin. . . . But when we think of the clever slave's attitude towards whipping, it is exactly this degradation that is missing. . . . In fact, the most consistent attitude expressed by clever slaves is to talk about their scars as a mark of honor.[41]

In short, the whip is supposed to teach a slave that he or she is contemptible; humor arises when a clever slave constructs forbidden knowledge from that abuse.

The Plautine slave's identification of bruises and welts as marks of honor relies on martial imagery. In *Asinaria*, for example, the slaves Libanus and Leonida produce lists of each other's acts of valor. Leonida notes that Libanus was repeatedly suspended and beaten by eight strong men. Libanus, in turn, notes that, by his indifference to beating, Leonida wore out eight lictors. Combat duty, Libanus suggests: "All these regiments, battalions, and armies of theirs have been put to flight, after fierce fighting. . . . Who's a more valiant man than I am at absorbing blows?" (555–557). McCarthy argues that the audience derives pleasure from such verbal bandying because they identify—temporarily—with the slaves who resist customary submissiveness. Through this limited identification, the audience member imagines acting out of a subjectivity that is not inscribed by the dominating will of another.

While McCarthy offers a compelling reading of the social function of humor in the comedies of Plautus, the success of individual jokes is nonetheless contingent on the audience's instinctive acknowledgment of the difference between dishonorable and honorable corporal marks. A scene from *Curculio* offers an example of another servile character jesting that his dishonorable markings should be construed as badges of valor. Curculio is not a slave but a parasite. According to literary stereotype, parasites, in service to their bellies, are willing to dishonor themselves by absorbing both verbal insults and the physical humiliations of vicious practical jokes.[42] A banker named Lyco encounters Curculio on the street and mocks him by calling attention to the fact that one of his eyes is bandaged. Curculio insists that he lost his eye to a catapult shot. Lyco replies, "Oh well, little I care whether it was shot out, or knocked out when a pot of cinders was cracked on your head" (396–397). In an aside, Curculio acknowledges Lyco's prescience, but he still parries, "I won the honorable wound beneath this bandage in defense of my country and, I beg you, do not outrage me in public" (399–400). Curculio, Lyco, and the audience know that Curculio has not fought for anything other than the satiety of his guts. The humor of the scene is contingent on the incongruity of calling a brand of dishonor a badge of honor.

Paul never labels his own marks battle scars, nor does he use the language of military engagement to describe his subjection to whip and rod. Perhaps one reason that he avoids such an explicit comparison is the realization that the analogy would open him to mockery, a mockery that, at least in Corinth under the influence of the rival superapostles, would further erode recognition of his authority as an apostle. At the same time, Paul's habit of listing his beatings alongside his other tribulations raises the possibility that, like a slave in a comedy, he refuses to be defined by the whip's degrading inscription of his skin, that he has derived alternative knowledge from his lessons. I return to this question in my analysis of the place of Paul's boasting of beatings (2 Cor. 11:23–25) in the argument of 2 Corinthians 10–13. First, however, I consider a ritual in which strokes of the whip spelled honor rather than dishonor, the marks of a whipping signs of manhood rather than imprints of servility.

In the Spartan flagellation contest, elite young men vied at the altar of Artemis Orthia to determine who would be last to withdraw from the savage whipping: blood

saturating the shredded flesh of his back, the winner's indifference to pain proclaimed his virile courage and self-control.[43] Tertullian cited the contest as the
pinnacle of pagan fortitude (*Apol.* 50.9; *Mart.* 4.8; *Nat.* 1.18). The bloody competition was a popular spectacle in the Roman era. Some contestants apparently died
as a result of the severe whipping. Plutarch, a spectator, claimed to have witnessed
contestants at the point of death (*Lycurgus* 18.1).[44] Cicero, who also alluded to
visiting Sparta for the ritual, typifies the assessment of most who refer to the ritual:
the flagellation contest was exemplary training in masculinity (*Tusculan Disputa-
tions* 2.14.34, 2.18.43). After you have witnessed the fortitude of Spartan youths,
Cicero demanded, would you, "if some pain happen to give you a twitch, cry out
like a woman and not endure resolutely and calmly?" (2.19.46). The spectacle of
the city's elite bloodied by the lash thus represented one highly circumscribed
instance in the script of ancient masculinity where the degrading connotations
of being whipped were overwritten by the hegemonic masculine virtue of self-
control.[45] At the altar of Artemis Orthia the identification of stripes from a whip
with insignia of valor was not a laughing matter.

Still, some laughed. So strong was the association between flogging and dishonor that even the stylized whipping of Sparta's finest elicited expressions of
contempt. Both Lucian and Philostratus record such voices. In Lucian's dialogue
Anacharsis, or Athletics, two legendary figures—the Athenian Solon and the
Scythian Anacharsis—debate the merits of the quintessentially Greek practice of
athletics. The dialogue culminates in a discussion of the Spartan competition.
Anacharsis diagnoses the Greek belief that this ritual whipping of young men
inculcates manliness in them as a risible sign of madness. He asks Solon why, if the
practice is so meritorious, the Athenians have not adopted it. When Solon responds
that the Athenians are content with their own exercises, Anacharsis guffaws:
"No: you understand, I think, what it is like to be flogged naked, holding up one's
arms. . . . Oh, if ever I am at Sparta at the time when they are doing this I expect I
shall be very soon stoned to death by them publicly for laughing at them every time
I see them getting beaten like robbers or sneak-thieves or similar malefactors"
(39). So indelible is the imprint of humiliation on one who is whipped that Anacharsis insultingly refuses to allow the possibility that the whip might inscribe honor
on a man's body.[46]

In Philostratus's *Life of Apollonius of Tyana*, the association of whipping with
servility prevents the Egyptian sage Thespesion from perceiving any wisdom in the
Spartan contest. Thespesion asks Apollonius to confirm what he has heard, that
Spartans are beaten publicly. Apollonius assures him that the most noble and distinguished are so beaten. "'Then what do they do to household slaves,'" Thespesion asks, "'when they do wrong?'" Learning that the Spartans employ the same
whip at the altar of Artemis Orthia and in the punishment of servile wrongdoers,

Thespesion presses further: "'Then these excellent Hellenes are not ashamed . . . to reflect that they are governed by men who are whipped before the eyes of all?'" Rebutting the argument that ritual submission to the whip teaches virile self-control and fortitude, Thespesion asks: why teach a patient endurance suited only for a slave? (6.20).

For Thespesion, a whipping is a form of pedagogy that teaches not nobility but degradation. A whippable body knows humiliation. Regardless of circumstances, Thespesion implies, a man who is whipped loses his claim to honor: so what kind of people would acknowledge the authority of leaders who had been publicly whipped? Neither the dialogue between Solon and Anacharsis nor the dialogue between Thespesion and Apollonius has a victor. The genre of dialogue allows multiple voices to be heard and to remain in play. However, discussion of the flagellation contest effectively brings each dialogue to a close. Both Solon and Apollonius claim that there are further arguments to be made in defense of the ritual. Each demurs from making such arguments.

Spectators gazing at the naked bodies of adolescents lashed until bloody assure us they are soberly witnessing a ritual of initiation into manhood. Mocking laughter from Anacharsis and Thespesion challenges the contention that a back may honorably earn its stripes. Although most writers who refer to the ritualized lashings emphasize the virile self-control of the contestants, the laughter we hear from Anacharsis and Thespesion is predicated on the servile and degrading associations of any subjection to the whip. A male slave's endurance of countless floggings was not validation of masculine fortitude but confirmation of his exclusion from a socially recognized manhood.[47] Who might have interpreted the stripes on Paul's back as honorable emblems of battles fought, contests won? In Corinth, a chance glimpse of Paul's *stigmata*—or a recital of his humiliations by whip and rod—would have been more likely to elicit contempt than admiration. In 2 Corinthians 10–13, Paul must reassert his apostolic authority while countering Corinthian reaction to his evident whippability.

Paul Talks Smack

As known in the Corinthian churches, Paul's story is an embodied story. He writes that his rivals contend, "His letters are weighty and strong, but his bodily presence is weak, and his speech contemptible" (2 Cor. 10:10). The Corinthian Christians are familiar with his history of abuse. In 1 Corinthians, for example, he writes (referring to himself), "To the present hour we are hungry and thirsty, we are poorly clothed and beaten and homeless" (4:11; see also 2 Cor. 6:5). We may easily imagine that Paul spoke about incidents of abuse when he was in Corinth, and even speculate that he had—intentionally or not—exposed fleshy souvenirs of those episodes.[48] In 2 Corinthians 11:23–25, Paul provides greater detail about the blows to which he has previously alluded. Moreover, he boasts about those beatings. An emerging consensus holds that Paul's boasting in the fool's speech (11:21b–12:10) exhibits familiarity with protocols of self-praise in rhetorical theory and practice.[49] No such consensus holds regarding the content of Paul's boasting. While some scholars treat Paul's listing of hardships in 11:23b–33 as an ironic inversion of first-century values, others—seemingly a majority—argue that this same listing is consistent with the Greco-Roman rhetorical practice of acknowledging hardships, often as demonstrations of virile fortitude. Few scholars distinguish among the hardships listed in 11:23–33. Survival of a shipwreck thus appears to be as dishonorable—or honorable—as endurance of lash and rod.[50] Acknowledgment of the specific meanings of flogged bodies in a first-century habitus is essential for appreciation of Paul's rhetorical strategy in the fool's speech.

Ancient Scars, Modern Eyes

Writing of Paul's tribulations, scholars sometimes imply that the very fact of adversity carried a social stigma in the first century. For example, Timothy B. Savage writes that 2 Corinthians 11:23–29 is "a list of personal afflictions so horrific that it would have elicited feelings of extreme contempt among his readers. By boasting of such humiliations the apostle would seem to be reveling in his disgrace."[51] Such a broad assertion that the Corinthians would find the tribulations of 2 Corinthians 11:23–33 to be contemptible is untenable.[52]

We considered at length the speech Sallust composes for Marius. In a number of respects, his iteration of hardships is parallel to Paul's. Marius boasts repeatedly of toil and dangers, including exposure to the elements, rough sleeping conditions, fatigue, and privation of necessities, just as Paul's speech itemizes his "toil and hardship, through many a sleepless night, hungry and thirsty, often without food, cold and naked" (2 Cor. 11:27).[53] Both Marius and Paul follow standard canons of self-praise by including such elements.

In his treatise on the acceptable parameters of self-praise, Plutarch outlines the reasons one might, in the context of self-praise, speak of what is not transparently praiseworthy. He writes, "when faults not altogether degrading or ignoble are set down beside the praise they do away with envy. Many blunt the edge of envy by occasionally inserting into their own praise a confession of poverty and indigence or actually of low birth" (Mor. 544B). Along with such extrinsic "antidotes [pharmaka] to self-boasting," one may boast even more effectively of hardships and perils "inherent in the very content of the praise," that is, challenges confronted for the sake of the audience one addresses. Plutarch supplies the example of Cato, who went without sleep for his country's good (544D). To characterize the entirety of 11:23–33 as a catalog of humiliations thus ignores the theory and practice of self-praise in antiquity.[54]

While even poverty and low birth could surface in boasting of oneself, Plutarch tells us that what is *aischros*—degrading, infamous—plays no role in a litany of self-praise (*Mor.* 544B), a point overlooked by many scholars who argue that, in boasting of hardships, Paul adheres to first-century canons of self-praise. For example, Hans Dieter Betz notes that "Plutarch argues that men fighting Tyche are admired for propping up courage and for overcoming self-pity, lamenting, and self-abasement"; thus, Betz infers, Paul's boasting of weaknesses (2 Cor. 11:30) was "by no means alien to the culture."[55]

As he details his labors and hardships, Paul exhibits familiarity with conventions for self-praise. However, his enumeration of repeated instances in which he was publicly flogged violates expectations for such boasting. As we have seen, subjection to whip and rod was disgraceful, even infamous. Beatings were pedagogical; those who were beaten carried knowledge of their humiliation and unmanly submissiveness in their bodies. In their emphasis on the manliness of confronting manifold physical challenges, contemporary scholars assimilate the stripes scored in Paul's flesh to cicatrized emblems of martial valor while ignoring the power relations—of legal status, domination and submission, honor and shame—incarnated in flogged bodies by Roman habitus.[56]

Several influential works on Paul's use of hardship (*peristaseis*) catalogs lay the groundwork for the position held, that Paul's endurance of tribulations testifies to his fortitude.[57] J. Fitzgerald argues that Paul's opponents boasted "of their hardships as *diakonoi* of Christ and that their letters of recommendation contained *peristaseis* catalogs."[58] While Fitzgerald suggests that the content of Paul's boasting would resemble that of the superapostles, he does not offer a systematic analysis of 2 Corinthians 11:23–33.[59] In his treatment of 6:3–10, he classifies Paul's "blows, imprisonments, and riots" under the putative category of "catalog of punishments" (noting that riots, while not themselves a punishment, frequently provoke punishment). However, the examples that Fitzgerald cites in his treatment of "catalog of punishments" do not establish that boasting of corporal punishment was an established practice.[60] Moreover, while he adumbrates examples from Greco-Roman literature in which heroic men boast of scars, he fails to note that these men are war heroes who earned their scars in combat.[61]

Both Robert Hodgson and Martin Ebner cite traditions of Alexander and Heracles as a context for understanding Paul's self-boasting in 11:23–29.[62] They quote at length from passages in Plutarch and Arrian where Alexander itemizes dangers he has confronted. Hodgson comments that the Alexandrine tribulation lists are "reminiscent of the buffetings, famines, storms, rivers, and treachery of

2 Cor 11:23–29."[63] Alexander announces, "My body bears many a token [*symbolon*] of an opposing Fortune" (Plutarch *Mor.* 327A). He then details the dangers of a sustained military campaign, including not only famine but also "storms, droughts, deep rivers" (327C). Since Paul writes of shipwrecks, drifting at sea, and dangerous rivers, the parallelism is, to a certain extent, clear. Alexander's "buffetings," however, have nothing to do with subjection to whip and rod, but with combat injuries. According to Arrian, Alexander challenges his troops: "Let anyone who carries wounds strip himself and show them; I too will show mine. For I have no part of my body, in front at least, that is unwounded; there is no weapon, used at close quarters, or hurled from afar, of which I do not carry the trace" (Arrian *Anabasis* 7.9.1–2). Without explicitly describing the markings of Paul's body as battle scars, Hodgson reads Paul's body as telling a soldierly tale: he mistakes the humiliating insignia carved on Paul's flesh by whip and rod for virile emblems of martial valor.[64]

Fitzgerald and Ebner draw extensively on Stoic and Cynic *peristaseis* catalogs, particularly those of Seneca and Epictetus.[65] For Seneca and Epictetus, physical pain and public humiliation are matters of indifference. They argue that, while a man should not deliberately seek such experiences, endurance of wrongful corporal punishment is nonetheless virtuous. To advocate indifference to the pain and ignominy of being whipped, however, does not establish beatings as a legitimate subject for boasting. Moreover, as we think about Paul's storytelling body in a Corinthian context, we should recall Saller's insistence that the philosophical contention that being whipped did not degrade a man had no impact on the perceptions of a public shaped by a habitus in which servility and dishonor were incarnated by whippability.[66]

This is due, in part, to the conservatism of habitus, which, Bourdieu argues, "tends to ensure its own constancy and its defense against change through the selection it makes within new information by rejecting information capable of calling into question its accumulated information."[67] An argument for the moral indifference of a whipped body would not expunge the ingrained habit of reacting to a whipped body with contempt. Moreover, a beaten or whipped man whose corporal experiences were informed by Roman habitus would be likely to internalize the intended meaning of the violence; he would walk away with discomfiting somatic knowledge of his own contemptibility.

The question of attitudes toward endurance of pain and humiliation crystallizes a difficulty inherent in relying on Seneca and Epictetus to reconstruct an intellectual background for Paul. Seneca is a contemporary of Paul's, Epictetus a generation younger. If Seneca and Epictetus transmit changeless Stoic doctrines, then we may be justified in relying on them as we flesh out an intellectual milieu that also shaped Paul. However, Seneca's writing represents a break with earlier Stoic traditions on a number of counts, particularly with respect to the body in pain. Catharine Edwards notes a tension between Seneca's concern with the body and older Stoic indifference to bodily status.[68] Brent D. Shaw similarly notes that Seneca treats the "nexus of pain, torture and endurance/patience" with a novel intensity.[69] Seneca plays a pivotal role in the story of Roman letters during the first century, a century in which traditional values were being transformed.[70] As a result, although the relationship between Senecan and Pauline attitudes toward corporal pain and public degradation merits consideration, we cannot rely on Seneca (or Epictetus) to reconstruct the habitus that shaped Corinthian response to Paul's whippable body.

The paradoxical nature of Paul's boasting of beating eludes many commentators. Regarding Paul's declaration that on three occasions he had been beaten with rods, commentators are chiefly concerned to establish that, although Roman law prohibited magistrates from ordering the flogging of a citizen, social reality did not always conform to legal mandate.[71] De facto, citizens were, occasionally, beaten. But by focusing on the juristic implications of the scene—whether Paul's vulnerability to the magistrate's rod belies Luke's ascription of citizenship to him—commentators overlook the meaning of such treatment for those shaped by Roman habitus. Citizen or not, free or slave, a beaten body was a dishonored body. As a result, any free person who was publicly stripped and battered with rods suffered an effective reduction in social status.[72] Even a single occasion of flogging dishonored a man. Multiple occasions of flogging would raise questions about the character of a man unable or unwilling to guard his body against violation, who might even be perceived to invite such treatment.[73]

On five occasions, Jewish leaders whipped Paul. According to Deuteronomy, official whippings were restricted to forty lashes because more stripes would degrade the recipient of the blows (25:3).[74] Gentiles in the Corinthian churches were unlikely to be familiar with this scriptural scruple: thirty-nine lashes would constitute thirty-nine strikes against the recipient's integrity.[75] Perhaps more important, other references to the thirty-nine lashes dating from the Roman era insist on the degrading character of the punishment. Josephus represents the thirty-nine lashes as an explicitly disgraceful penalty, inflicted on free persons only because they first outrage their own honor through enslavement to wealth (*Ant.* 4.8.21). The story Josephus reads in the imposition of the thirty-nine lashes is informed by a Roman habitus: whipping, which brings dishonor to the one who is whipped, is suitable only for slaves, so one who is whipped, even if legally free, warrants description as servile.

The Mishnaic elaboration of administration of the thirty-nine lashes dwells on abasing dimensions of the practice, with no recognition of the scriptural hesitancy to avoid inscribing degradation along with the stripes (*Makkot* 3.12–14): the offender may not stand upright during the whipping, but must bend low. Synagogue officials bind the offender's hands to pillars and grab the offender's garments, ripping them so that the upper torso is naked. With all his strength, the synagogue leader wields the leather whip, delivering one-third of the strokes to the front of the torso and two-thirds to the back. (Marks of a whip slashing across a man's chest would not, however, be mistaken for pectoral war wounds.)

The rabbis consider possible denouements for the beating. It may be so severe, for example, that the one who is whipped dies. Or the humiliation of the beating may have a scatological outcome, in which case the punishment is halted, presumably because the end of abjection has been achieved: "If he [that was scourged] befouled himself whether with excrement or urine, he is exempt [from the rest of the stripes]. R. Judah says: A man [is exempt only if he befouled himself] with excrement, and a woman [if she befouled herself] with urine" (3.14).

Given both the later dating of the Mishnah and the complex relationship of legal texts to lived reality, we should not take the Mishnaic scene as an accurate description of the delivery of the thirty-nine lashes in the first century. Moreover, few (if any) Corinthian Christians would have witnessed a synagogue whipping. They had, however, observed many other whippings, mostly of slaves. They could envisage more easily than we can the public humiliation, the instantiation of relationships of dominance and subjection, honor and dishonor, carved into Paul's lowered, stripped, flinching body, a body that may well have soiled itself in the midst of a whipping.

Paul says that, if he must boast, he will boast of things that exhibit his weakness (2 Cor. 11:30). When he boasts of beatings, he boasts of what is *aischros*: dishonorable, degrading, and ultimately, morally suspect. To us, Paul's endurance of brutal whippings may be more likely to betoken heroism than contemptible weakness and abasement. In our postures and demeanors, we embody a different sociopolitical mythology.[76] Shaw argues that Paul's writings played a key role in modification of the classical corporal hexis. He writes:

> The connection between bodily position and moral evaluation, and the revolution in values connected with valuing the inferior, the humble, the womanly, that which merely accepts and endures (from a prone position) is clearly indicated by the history of the words that were used to describe being low to the ground or prone—*tapeinos*—and allied terms (meaning low, prone, close to the ground, and consistently associated with being poor, weak, insignificant, and womanly). . . . The almost palpable association of moral status and bodily position was so strong and so inalterable that the classical conceptions that pervaded the thought-world of the Greek *polis* and all its successor ideologies surrendered no ground on this matter. To be *tapeinos* . . . had an indelible connection with shame, humiliation, degradation and, inexorably, with that which was morally bad. . . . It is the Christian writings . . . that revolutionize these values wholly by their total inversion. Paul boasts of his self-abasement and humility. . . . Indeed, he actually creates a new virtue—*tapeinosophrune* (ταπεινοσοφρύνη) [*sic*]— the voluntary abasement of the self and one's body.[77]

The Story of a Body

As Paul confronts a challenge to his apostolic authority in Corinth, he commits what may seem like a tactical error. He boasts of his beatings. Why does he highlight his corporal abasement during a crisis of Corinthian confidence in his apostolic authority? On a strategic level, Paul's whippability is already an issue in Corinth. Thus, he cannot avoid the topic. Paul has previously written—and likely spoken about—his beatings. As we have seen, the charges brought by the superapostles implicate his somatic vulnerability. One gambit for confronting such charges is to disarm the opponent by admitting the accuracy of the charges. Beyond such practical considerations, Paul perceives that in his marked body the story of Jesus' passion is legible. In his body he knows the power of Jesus' sufferings. He thus has both tactical and theological reasons for boasting of his publicly humiliating beatings.

We learn from 2 Corinthians 10:1–11 that the Corinthians already have Paul's body on their minds. As I have noted, 1 Corinthians 4:9–13 informs us of one way Paul presented his beaten body at a time when his authority was not under attack from the superapostles, a self-presentation relevant to later Corinthian reaction to Paul's corpus. Describing himself as weak and dishonored (4:10), Paul writes, "To the present hour we are hungry and thirsty, we are poorly clothed and beaten and homeless, and we grow weary from the work of our own hands" (1 Cor. 4:11–12a).

Two vivid images bracket this list of hardships. Introducing the list, Paul pictures himself as a prisoner condemned to death in an amphitheater in a cosmic spectacle orchestrated by God (4:9). Concluding the list, Paul describes himself as filthy waste (4:13). The latter metaphor suggests that Paul perceives his travails as a missionary, including the public abuse of his body in beatings, to leave him in a state of abject contemptibility.[78] How does the inaugural metaphor of spectacle inform a reading of Paul's body, limp from beatings? Carlin A. Barton writes of the "extreme ambiguity" associated with gladiators and also with those, not themselves gladiators, condemned to die in the arena: "Gladiators were the defeated and humiliated outcasts from society and the most highly charged and sacred warriors within the community. They inspired both worship and disgust, emulation and loathing, sympathy and revulsion."[79] Within the frame of the spectacle, one who scorned pain and death might elicit admiration. As the spectator stepped back from the frame, the courage of the gladiator—still less the condemned man—could not erase the degradation that forced him into the arena. A man whose life was so expendable that he could be killed to amuse others qualified as rubbish or dregs, terms Paul applies to himself (v. 13). Of the various sufferings Paul lists in vv. 11–12, battering is the only one in which he would be publicly exhibited, stripped of his clothes, physically vulnerable to those intent on subjecting him to violence— like a condemned man in an arena. Paul does not suggest that his endurance of beatings is virile or heroic. Rather, the vocabulary of 1 Corinthians 4:9–13 evokes the abject habitus of a beaten body.

During Paul's absence from Corinth, the superapostles have challenged his apostolic authority. They have maligned him on a number of counts, including, for example, his rejection of financial support from the Corinthian churches (2 Cor. 11:7–11). They have also ridiculed Paul's body. Face to face, they claim, his appearance is base (*tapeinos*, 2 Cor. 10:1), his speech contemptible, and "the presence of his body is weak" (10:10). What do the superapostles mean by the accusation, "the presence of his body is weak?" Scholarly opinion varies, from the position that Paul is sickly to the contention that "it is unlikely that one who was so inured to incessant hardship and journeying could be described as a weakling."[80] In general, though, even scholars who acknowledge that the superapostles may allude to some physical weakness of Paul's argue that the adjective *weak* refers ultimately to low social status, a lack of honor, or simply a weak claim to apostolic authority.[81]

Because New Testament scholars have not acknowledged that relationships of power were embodied, they have not appreciated the centrality of Paul's body to the superapostles' campaign against him.[82] An important exception is J. Albert Harrill, who argues that Paul's opponents targeted his body in their invective. Harrill contends that, through the superapostles' allegation that Paul's bodily appearance was weak, they "tried to question Paul's manhood and right to dominate others."[83] The superapostles' jab at Paul's physical fitness impugns him as servile. Harrill's survey of ancient sources, especially his treatment of physiognomic handbooks, documents the widespread understanding that social status was somatically expressed.[84]

The allegations that Paul was base, weak, and contemptible were parallel (10:1, 10), calling into question both his social status and his apostolic authority. These allegations were also, not incidentally, somatic. As moral degradation was understood in the first century to be expressed in physical degradation, so corporal degradation was construed as a marker of a fundamental contemptibility.[85] For the superapostles and some members of the Corinthian churches, the debility of Paul's somatic presentation undermined his claim to authority in the community. Remembering Paul's storytelling body from clues in his epistolary corpus, we also know that he had been repeatedly flogged and that, most likely, his body still bore souvenirs of those beatings. The weakness of Paul's corporal self-presentation thus seems inseparable from his evident whippability. Like Thespesion mocking the Spartans for submitting to governance by men who have been publicly whipped, perhaps the superapostles asked: What is it like to follow an eminently beatable leader?

The question of Paul's authority to discipline the community underlies 10:1–11. Paul presents his abasement as parallel to Jesus' meekness (10:1) but discourages the Corinthians from interpreting this self-abnegation as an inability or unwillingness to exercise authority (10:1–2, 11). In this context Paul refers to the charge that the presence of his body is weak, and indeed context and charge may be linked. Paul was perceived as a nail, not a hammer; as the sort who was subject to the rod, not the sort likely to wield a rod.[86]

The superapostles, on the other hand, seem game to pick up the rod. Immediately before he commences his foolish boasting in 2 Corinthians 11:21b, Paul refers to the humiliation of the Corinthian churches by the superapostles: "For you put up with it when someone enslaves you, or preys upon you, or seizes you, or takes advantage of you, or slaps you in the face" (11:20).[87] Paul's association of the acceptance of physical and verbal blows with servility confirms his fluency in a first-century corporal vernacular.[88] With the crack of an open palm across a cheek, the superapostles have asserted their dominance. The Corinthians have submitted. For Paul, the problem is not that the Corinthians have humbly absorbed the stinging blows. The problem is that, in their submission to the authority of the superapostles, they have subjugated themselves and the gospel Paul preaches. To characterize the effect the superapostles have had on the Corinthians, Paul relies on the analogy of enslavement.[89]

If the superapostles have enslaved the Corinthians by disciplining them, have synagogue officials and magistrates enslaved Paul by flogging him? Paul moves from his mockery of the Corinthians for permitting the superapostles to abuse them to his foolish boasting, self-praise that prominently features a catalog of tribulations, most of which do not qualify as ignominious (11:23–33).[90] He lists his beatings near the outset of the catalogue (vv. 23b–25a). He does not deny or minimize his somatic history, with which the Corinthians are already familiar, a history that has already been targeted by the superapostles in their attack on his authority. As Martyn observes, "On the whole, Paul drew no distinction between malevolent persecution at the hands of various authorities and such disasters as shipwrecks and floods."[91] Indeed, in his lists of tribulations faced, Paul treats his subjection to floggings in the same fashion that he treats his travel escapades and privations of such necessities as food, drink, and shelter (1 Cor. 4:9–13; 2 Cor. 5:4–5, 11:23–27). Paul does not represent insignia of humiliation as emblems of valor, but neither does he acknowledge that those who have flogged him have mastered him. His resistance to definition by those who have whipped him is an implicit criticism of the Corinthians, who have, Paul alleges, been mastered by the superapostles.

If Paul does not concede that the wales of his back tell a story of his enslavement by those who have lifted whip and rod against him, what story does his body tell? We return to Paul's allusion to the *stigmata* of Jesus, widely taken to be a reference to the scars he has acquired in the course of his missionary activity, particularly the tracings made by lashes, rods, and stones (Gal. 6:17; 2 Cor. 11:24–25).[92] *Stigma* has servile connotations. Delinquent slaves were often tattooed or branded.[93] On one reading, through the stigmatic metaphor, Paul implies that the marks inscribed in his flesh by whips and rods brand him as Jesus' slave. That reading, however, is vexed. A slaveholder brands a slave; Paul did not receive his scars at the hands or directive of Jesus, but at the hands of those who opposed the gospel. Moreover, Paul's reference to *stigmata* grounds his demand at the close of Galatians that those who have opposed him should cease to trouble him.[94] Under Roman law, when a slaveholder tattooed a slave, he or she not only marked the slave as his or her property but also increased the slave's vulnerability to physical or verbal assaults by others.[95] If Paul's *stigmata* identify him as a slave of Christ, his expectation that his *stigmata* would protect him may seem fundamentally misplaced.

These inconsistencies prompt consideration of other readings of the metaphor. Martyn argues that Paul's scars make manifest the tracings of Roman whips on Jesus' own body, tracings that are inherently servile.[96] Paul not only claims that he bears in his body the *stigmata* of Jesus. He also claims that in his body he always carries "the putting to death of Jesus" (2 Cor. 4:10).[97] For Paul the stigmata of Jesus offer evidence that he knows in his own body the putting to death of Jesus.[98] Paul's welted skin is parchment on which is legible the agonizing story of Jesus' humiliations preceding his life-giving death (cf. 2 Cor. 4:11); the flagellation of Jesus figures prominently among those humiliations.[99] Because Paul believed that in the stripes of his own flesh the story of Jesus' passion could be read, he ascribed phylactic properties to his stigmata. He warned: "From now on, let no one make trouble for me; for I carry the stigmata of Jesus in my body" (Gal. 6:17). Nonetheless, to those informed by Roman habitus, his whipped body inevitably announced that he was whippable.

Paul writes to the Corinthians that he boasts of things that show his weakness (11:30, 12:9–10). In boasting of beatings, he has done precisely that. He has already mentioned the charge of the superapostles that the presence of his body is weak (10:10). He does not deny this charge. To those habituated to a first-century somatic idiom, Paul's physical weakness, which I have argued is expressed in his whippability, would raise suspicions about his claims to authority. He nonetheless boasts of his beatings, and not only because the Corinthians are already cognizant of his history of floggings. His debility unites him to Christ: "For he was crucified out of weakness, but lives by the power of God. For we are weak in him [or: with him], but in dealing with you we will live with him by the power of God" (13:4). In writing that Jesus was crucified "out of weakness," Paul acknowledges the socially conditioned meaning of a condemned, flagellated, and ultimately crucified body. Jesus' vulnerability to corporal abuse and violation—being whipped, spat upon, and crucified—incarnates his degradation and dishonor. Paul is weak in—or, with—Jesus (13:4), bearing in his own body the marks of the events leading to Jesus' death (4:10).

The superapostles have convinced many Corinthian Christians that Paul's abused body testifies to the weakness of his claim to apostolic authority. Paul does not try to revamp the prevailing habitus; he does not call dishonor honor. Rather, he represents his abject mien as cruciform. He knows Christ in his body. His scars are visible evidence of that knowledge. In his somatic weakness, both consequence and condition of his beatings—for, on a first-century view, only a whippable body is whipped, and whipped repeatedly—the Corinthians should read the degrading and powerful story of the passion of Jesus.

Conclusion

Martyn suggests that Paul treats his physique as a medium of communication. But what story does his body tell? Many scholars identify Paul's scars as tokens of virtue. I have argued that, within a Roman habitus, scars that established a man's virtue or virility were typically incurred in battle. Display of war wounds was a common feature of Roman somatic rhetoric. Those habituated to a first-century corporal idiom distinguished between a breast pierced in battle and a back welted by a whip: not every scarred body told a war story. Whippability was not a token of honor, excellence, or virility. As I argue in the next chapter, slaves knew dishonor, abasement, and servility in their bodies. In analyzing Paul's boasting of beatings, scholars often cite examples of heroism attested by wounded bodies, although they do not always acknowledge the martial context of those wounds. Scholars have, moreover, passed over the semiotic distinction between a battle-scarred body and a flogged body. In a straightforward way, when Paul boasts of beatings, he does what he says he does. He boasts of things that show his weakness.

Whips and rods had inscribed Paul's flesh. Habituated to a first-century corporal idiom, the Corinthians could not read a straightforward tale of manly valor in Paul's storytelling body. Paul does not suggest they should. Rather, he makes clear to the Corinthians that in his own body he knew the sufferings of Christ. I have argued that Paul boasts of beatings for strategic reasons: his abused body is already the subject of discussion and even derision in Corinth. He also boasts of beatings for theological reasons: he believes that the story of Jesus' death is legible in the scar tissue that has formed over welts and lacerations inflicted by rod and whip. Paul's share in the sufferings of Jesus is a source of corporal knowledge and ultimately of personal power. As he elsewhere writes, "I want to know him [Christ] and the power of his resurrection and the sharing of his sufferings by becoming like him in his death, if somehow I may attain the resurrection from the dead" (Phil. 3:10–11).

3

Embodying Slavery from Paul to Augustine

My subject for this evening is Slavery as it is, and its influence upon the morals and the character of the American people.

I may try to represent to you Slavery as it is; another may follow me and try to represent the condition of the Slave; we may all represent it as we think it is; and yet we shall all fail to represent the real condition of the slave. . . .

Slavery has never been represented; Slavery never can be represented.
—William A. Brown, Fugitive Slave, 1847, "A Lecture Delivered before the Female Anti-Slavery Society," 82

I have argued that, in Paul's whippable body, the Corinthian community could read the degrading but theologically charged story of the execution of Jesus. Finding positive meaning in the crucified flesh of Jesus or the striped flesh of Paul stands as a challenge to the bodily habitus of the Roman Empire. In light of that corporal nonconformity, one might expect that the Christian community would have developed its own modes of corporal deportment and interaction, modes of corporeality that would embody a distinctively Christian set of values. In some ways, of course, over the following centuries the Christian community did just that, especially in the various forms of ascetic practice that emerged. At the same time, however, ordinary Christians perpetuated modes of relating to one another that did not differ perceptibly from the relations of those outside the community.

I am especially interested in the perpetuation through late antiquity of a particular system of corporeality, the system defined by slaveholding. Christians consciously modeled themselves on Christ. Why didn't they perceive the gospel to be incompatible with the habitus of slaveholding? I have argued that social location is known in the body. Such deeply held bodily knowledge is rarely subjected to conscious moral scrutiny. In this chapter I argue that the tenacious grip of a slaveholding habitus deformed Christian moral imaginations. I focus, though not exclusively, on habituated distinctions between the bodies of slave women and the bodies of free women. To paraphrase the words of slavery resister William Brown that open this chapter, my subject is the corporal practice of slavery and its influence upon the morals and the character of early churches.

Foot Washing

I have noted that the crucified body of Jesus stands in tension with the later Christian embodiment of standard Roman slaveholding values. Moreover, according to early Christian memory, Jesus actively taught his followers to embrace the posture of slave rather than slaveholder. In the synoptic tradition, Jesus taught, "Whoever wishes to be first among you must be slave of all" (Mark 10:44; cf. Matt. 20:26–27, 23:11; Mark 9:35; Luke 22:26). According to Matthew and Mark, Jesus grounded this teaching in the example of his own service and death: "For the Son of Man came not to be served but to serve, and to give his life a ransom for many" (Mark 10:45; cf. Matt. 20:27). According to Luke, Jesus evoked more narrowly the image of a slave waiting at table to ground this teaching: "For who is greater, the one who is at the table or the one who serves? Is it not the one at the table? But I am among you as one who serves" (22:27). John does not include this saying, but an episode he narrates enacts its message. According to John, Jesus, in the hours before his betrayal, washed his disciples' feet and instructed them that they must likewise serve one another. "So if I, your Lord and Teacher, have washed your feet, you also ought to wash one another's feet. For I have set you an example, that you also should do as I have done to you" (13:14–15). Foot washing was a chore assigned to one of the least regarded slaves in the household. By washing his friends' feet at the meal where he predicted his betrayal by one of those friends, Jesus embodied the part of the slave of all, a slave who desired "not to be served but to serve, and to give his life as a ransom for many."

Although readers in the twenty-first century can appreciate the message of the foot-washing scene, the story told by Jesus' body as he stooped to wash another man's foot would have been understood more acutely by residents of the ancient world who were themselves implicated in the corporal dynamics of Roman dining practices. Matthew Roller analyzes a series of anecdotes from Roman authors in which dinner guests were humiliated by being required to stand rather than recline throughout the meal. For example, Suetonius offers a glimpse of Caligula's humiliation of elite men. Suetonius writes that Caligula required his disfavored guests "to stand as he dined, now at the back of the couch and now at his feet, wearing a linen garment girded at the waist." Thus, Roller assesses, "the specific humiliation experienced by these lofty senators is that they observe the function, posture, and appearance of slaves in convivia."[1] Of course, to stoop to wash feet—as Jesus does—would be even more degrading.

To set the scene for the foot washing, John supplies details related to clothing and gesture: Jesus left his place at the meal, stripped himself of his garments, and girded himself with a towel, a towel he used to dry feet. When he finished serving his followers, he again dressed himself in his familiar garments and resumed his familiar place at the table. In Latin, *habitus* refers broadly to manifold dimensions of self-presentation, of physical condition or character: demeanor, bearing, expression, posture, as well as manner of dress, especially mode of dress appropriate for a particular occasion or social status.[2] To strip garments of respectability that shield private body parts from view, to kneel before another and cradle his foot in hand, to wear a towel as an apron and thus to use one's own body for so base an action as the drying of another's foot: to an ancient audience shaped by the habitus of slavery, such actions conveyed more powerfully than words Jesus' exhortation to his followers to imitate him by abasing themselves.

Although in keeping with the spirit of Jesus' instruction Christians were encouraged to cultivate humility, their cultivated humility seems to have had little impact on the behavior of Christian slaveholders. The first Christians were not in a position to challenge the system of slaveholding in the Roman world. Nonetheless, they made no documented attempt to bar slaveholders from church membership, as some nineteenth-century American churches did, nor to eliminate slaveholding in their communities, as Philo and Josephus claimed the Essenes did.[3] (An interesting thought experiment: ponder how differently Christianity might have developed if churches had required manumission of slaves as a precondition for the baptism of slaveholders.) While early Christians typically insisted that God did not judge according to status, individual Christians were nonetheless shaped by, and thus embodied, a slaveholding habitus. Some early Christians were slaveholders, freeborn or freed; others were freeborn or freed persons not wealthy enough to own even a single slave; others were enslaved. For each of these persons, the practices of slavery constituted a habitus that trained his or her body and conditioned perceptions of other bodies. Conditioning to slavery was habitual, a dimension of a corporal vernacular rather than an area of conscious moral decision making.

Habitus

I have already introduced sociologist Pierre Bourdieu's notion of habitus. I briefly review that discussion here and I also bring Bourdieu into conversation with Alcoff and other feminist theorists. Bourdieu's practice-oriented social theory analyzes the logic of practice, the operations of the ordinary, by which a society perpetuates itself and advances its values. He argues that we make sense of human bodies, and human bodies make sense, through a "system of structured, structuring dispositions, the habitus."[4] Habitus, "embodied history, internalized as a second nature and forgotten as history," translates itself into knowledge borne in the body.[5] Through habitus takes place the process of socialization that marks a person, Bourdieu writes, "as an eldest son, an heir, a successor, a Christian, or simply as a man (as opposed to a woman)."[6] I rely on Bourdieu's treatment of habitus to illuminate the ways that a slaveholding culture informed the development of Christian sexual ethics and, more broadly, Christian attitudes toward bodies inevitably inscribed by gender, sexuality, and status. His formulation allows us to see that social processes construct, though not deterministically, distinctions between the bodies of free persons and slaves.

What kinds of bodily distinctions do I have in mind? In the first chapter I focused, though not exclusively, on gesture and posture; in chapter 2 I concentrated on the dermal inscription of a single body; in this chapter, I broaden the scope of my consideration. We can find apt comparisons by considering bodily distinctions produced by wealth and poverty in contemporary society. (In thinking through the effects of slavery on ancient bodies, I find it helpful to consider a range of comparative material. In the next section, for example, I rely on analyses by American freedpersons of the bodily habitus they experienced under a modern system of slavery.) Here are the words of a welfare recipient quoted in an article by Vivyan Adair, a literary critic concerned with American representations of poverty:

> My kids and I been chopped up and spit out just like when I was a kid. My rotten teeth, my kids' twisted feet. My son's dull skin and blank stare. My oldest girl's stooped posture and the way she can't look no one in the eye no more. This all says that we got nothing and we deserve what we got. On the street good families look at us and see right away what they'd be if they don't follow the rules. They're scared too, real scared.[7]

Adair identifies the speaker of these words as a white, single mother of three from Olympia, Washington. In thinking about the bodily effects of poverty, the speaker does not distinguish effects that would easily be characterized as purely physical, such as dull skin or stooped posture, both associated with poor nutrition, with effects that might be characterized as psychological, such as a blank stare or inability to return a gaze. Moreover, the speaker understands that the corporal traces of poverty are interpreted in moralizing terms by the wider public. Adair's analysis insists that injury to the body is injury to the self. Identifying herself as a child of poverty, Adair writes, "At an early age my body bore witness to and emitted signs of the painful devaluation carved into my flesh; that same devaluation became integral to my being in the world."[8] My discussion of habituated distinctions between free bodies and enslaved bodies thus raises the question of whether and in what ways slavery and freedom were integral to the selfhood of enslaved persons and free persons, especially enslaved women and free women, in ancient churches. What did it mean to know slavery in the body? To know freedom?

A consistent critique of Bourdieu is his failure to account for individual subjectivity.[9] I do not think an emphasis on "techniques of the body," to use Marcel Mauss's oft-quoted phrase, necessarily implies determinism or denial of individual subjectivity.[10] As Alcoff argues—without using the language of habitus—to think of the body as a kind of mind does not impute to the body "*transparently* meaningful or *stable and fixed* meanings." Rather, she writes, "We perceive and process and incorporate and reason and are intellectually trained in the body itself."[11] In relying theoretically on Bourdieu and Alcoff, I attempt both to acknowledge that enslaved persons and slaveholders were moral actors who were more than the sum of damages done to them and to argue that slavery was damaging at a corporal level and ultimately deforming of moral imagination. Partly to highlight individual subjectivity within the corporal system of slavery, I close the chapter by examining evidence from late antiquity that suggests that several isolated groups of Christians, Christians stigmatized and suppressed by more powerful Christians, seem to have embodied resistance to slavery and its corporal habituation. At the same time I do not want to denigrate the forced "choices" made by the vast majority of slaves who lived and loved within the violent parameters of the Roman slave system.[12]

Another consistent critique of Bourdieu's notion of habitus is its inability to account for social change.[13] Bourdieu's theory of practice better accounts for perpetuation of the status quo than for shifts in the status quo.[14] On the one hand, this limitation of Bourdieu's notion of habitus is an asset for me in my analysis of slavery during the first five centuries of Christianity. What I find problematic and thus seek to account for is the perdurance of slaveholding practices in the face of Christian anthropology that frequently—though not consistently—proclaimed the equality of human persons in the eyes of God. On the other hand, I do need to account for change on an individual level. If slavery and freedom are known in the body, as I argue they are, how could a person negotiate movement from free to slave, or, more frequently, from slave to free?

To know one's place in a system is to have (located) knowledge of that system. To know one's place in a system is also to have some implicit understanding of other people's places in that system. Bodies interact; a body that moves deferentially responds to the movements of a body that moves with authority. Moreover, in the course of a single day the same body might move both deferentially and with authority. In the Matthean parable of the unforgiving slave, for example, the well-positioned slave who owes his master a vast sum of money falls on his knees before his master. That same slave shortly thereafter is represented as responding to a less well-placed slave falling on his own knees in petition (Matt. 18:23–35). Maturity also affects bodily comportment. A girl learns to walk like a woman who eventually learns to move differently—and not only because of the travails of aging—as she assumes the role of a matriarch. Individual bodily comportment is thus not fixed or absolute. Rather, bodily comportment, posture, movement, and gesture are inevitably interactive. At the same time, I would argue, the effects of habitus are durable. In moving to a new status in society, a person may be conscious, sometimes fleetingly, of readjusting gait or posture or tone of voice, but the body does not forget its early training. The Christian community's memory that Jesus attempted to teach them to behave as slaves to one another highlights the ability to become conscious and critical, on an individual level, of the corporal dynamics of social hierarchy. The failure of the community to reform its practices highlights the tenacity of habitus.

Abolitionist Bodies

Joan Martin draws on Bourdieu's analysis of the "logic of practice," including his concept of habitus, in her analysis of the ways that the experience of slavery affected American slave women. Summarizing Bourdieu, Martin writes that practices, such as the practice of slavery, "arise from deep levels of structuring the nature of reality, a structuring which first takes place in the human body. In this sense, the body metaphorically acts as the organizing location of learning."[15] Although forms of unfree labor in colonial America bound persons of European and Native American origin as well as persons of African origin, as time passed chattel slavery was increasingly restricted to trade in persons of African descent. Distinctions between slave bodies and free bodies thus came to include racial distinctions. As Martin argues, however, the practice of slaveholding also inculcated a deeply seated corporal knowledge of slavery.

American slaves and freedpersons left us a written legacy describing their experiences of slavery. We lack a parallel trove of ancient writings by slaves or freedpersons. I thus find it useful to consider the observations of those in the nineteenth century who were caught up in the habitus of the American slave system.[16] In drawing on this material I hope to flesh out my description of the effects of slaveholding habitus. The comparative material has its limits. First, there were significant differences between Roman and American slave systems, including, for example, different patterns and frequencies of manumission. Second, although slaves were sexual property under both systems, American writers who commented on sexual exploitation had already been shaped by an established tradition of Christian moralizing. Finally, the American material still does not give us anything resembling unmediated access to bodies. Writers like Frederick Douglass and Harriet Jacobs were skilled prose stylists attempting to persuade audiences. When we read American sources, then, we encounter stylized representations of bodies, representations that will nonetheless help us think about the durable effects of habitus.[17] As Walter Johnson writes of the corporal pedagogy of American slavery, "For enslaved people the most basic features of their lives—feeling hungry, cold, tired, needing to go to the bathroom—revealed the extent to which even the bare life sensations of their physical bodies were sedimented with their enslavement. . . . And yet those things were never reducible to simple features of slavery."[18]

Of a kind mistress, the great American abolitionist Frederick Douglass wrote that in her company his early instruction in how to embody slavery was out of place. "The crouching servility of a slave, usually so acceptable a quality to the haughty slaveholder, was not understood or desired by this gentle woman. So far from deeming it impudent in a slave to look her straight in the face, as some slave-holding ladies do, she seemed ever to say, 'look up, child; don't be afraid.'"[19] According to Douglas, his early instruction led him to express his status as a slave somatically, in cringing posture and averted eyes.[20] Downcast eyes were a standard trope in the stereotyped language of advertisements for tracking down fugitive slaves. A particular slave might be said to have "a 'down look' when any ways examined," or simply "'looks down when spoke to.'"[21] Douglass's comment coupled with the evidence of fugitive slave ads document strong expectations from slaveholders regarding the postures of the persons they held in bondage. Slaveholders relied on violence to teach slaves how to behave as slaves, behavior then interpreted as evidence of innate servility.

In the nineteenth century, a number of former slaves recorded observations of the visible imprint of slaveholding relations on human bodies, observations that can help us picture the corporal traces of slavery on enslaved women and freeborn women in antiquity. I draw on the writing of Harriet Jacobs, an American who was enslaved from birth until her escape as an adult, in my analysis of the impact of sexualized slaveholding practices on female slaves, especially those born and raised as slaves. Let us imagine the differential impact of freedom and slavery on two young bodies in a hypothetical—but not improbable—ancient household that included two half sisters, one a freeborn and legitimate daughter of the house-holder's wife, the other an illegitimate daughter of a household slave. I argue that each half sister would learn to embody her legal status. How?

Jacobs describes the violence and sexual coercions of slavery in pedagogical terms: "The slave girl is reared in an atmosphere of licentiousness and fear. The lash and the foul talk of her master and his sons are her teachers."[22] In our hypo-thetical household, repeated brutal beatings would educate the enslaved half sister, scarring, shaping, and disfiguring her body. Such marking of the slave body was often noted by observers of American slavery. Douglass, for example, remembered feeling the festering sores on the head of a slave named Mary who was the frequent butt of lashings by a cruel mistress. According to Douglass, "So much was the poor girl pinched, kicked, cut and pecked to pieces, that the boys in the street knew her only by the name of 'pecked,' a name derived from the scars and blotches on her neck, head, and shoulders."[23] Fearing the whip, the enslaved sister would learn to move so as not to attract the attention of a volatile master or mistress.

Dwelling in a household where the erotic appeal of young slaves was unaccompanied by cultural norms of basic respect would affect the ways the enslaved half sister projected her sexuality. Of course the impact of her sexual schooling would vary from girl to girl and woman to woman. Jacobs described the knowledge a typical slave girl carried in her body as she came of age: "Soon she will become prematurely knowing in evil things. Soon she will learn to tremble when she hears her master's footfall."[24] Jacobs's resistance to the sexual demands of her owner was overtly shaped by her Christian beliefs.[25] A slave living in the early first century would not share that heritage; a slave living in the fifth century might. Seeking to avert unwanted sexual attention, a slave might minimize or conceal physical charms. Alternatively, a slave might cultivate the ability to magnify and enhance desirable attributes when sexual attention was likely to save her from other forms of physical abuse, relieve her of other labor, gain her additional nourishment or other goods, or allow her to protect her loved ones. By the time she became an adult, the deportment, posture, and affect of the slave sister in our hypothetical household would express servility somatically.[26]

Relations of slavery also marked the bodies of free persons. Douglass described a slaveholder named Captain Auld. After a childhood in poverty, Auld became a slaveholder as an adult. By focusing on the fact that Auld was not habituated as a slaveholder, Douglass drew indirect attention to the subtle ways that growing up as a slaveholder marked a person's body, deportment, and affect. According to Douglass, slaves "readily distinguish between the birthright bearing of the original slaveholder and the assumed attitudes of the accidental slaveholder." In Auld's case, Douglass's verdict is this: "There was in him all the love of domination, the pride of mastery, and the swagger of authority but his rule lacked the vital element of consistency."[27] Douglass's description encodes his own class prejudices. His words reflect a perception that relations of slaveholding are known and expressed in the body of the slaveholder. As Alcoff and Bourdieu suggest in different contexts, we become aware of an action qua performance when that performance is, in some way, off. On Douglass's telling, Auld rehabituated himself to enact the role of a slaveholder. Those who interacted with Auld nonetheless perceived him to be clumsy in his embodiment of a role he learned as an adult rather than a child.

Further exploration of the writings of nineteenth-century African American authors complicates my analysis of the knowledge that slaves and slaveholders carried in their bodies. Bodies tell stories. Some corporal stories are ambiguous, some deceptive. In the nineteenth century, many persons of African descent relied on habitus, specifically on cultural expectations of how African and European

Americans should present themselves, to pass as white. Moreover, African Americans relied on their bodies to resist the system of slavery. Some instances of resistance were dramatic. Slave rebellions, for example, were violently suppressed.[28] Other instances of resistance were more mundane. In *Scenes of Subjection: Terror, Slavery, and Self-Making in Nineteenth Century America*, feminist theorist Saidiya Hartman puzzles, "how does one determine the difference between 'puttin' on ole massa'—the simulation of compliance for covert aims—and the grins and gesticulations of Sambo indicating the repressive construction of contented subjection?" The answer, she continues, is not evident based solely on observation of performance. "One performance aimed to reproduce and secure the relations of domination and the other to manipulate appearances in order to challenge the relations and create a space for action not generally available. However, since acts of resistance exist within the context of relations of domination and are not external to them, they acquire their character from those relations."[29]

These complications ultimately underscore my argument that the practice of slavery was predictably—but not deterministically—embodied. This argument holds for the ancient world as well as the American context. Although slaves and free persons in the Roman Empire could not be visually distinguished by race as they often were in the Americas, the practice of slavery conditioned bodies that were typically legible as either slave or free. Moreover, inhabitants of that world expected to be able to read the bodies they encountered in order to know how to treat each person encountered: with deference, with respect, or with a superior air. However, more than one ancient comedy derived its humor from the fact that slaves and free persons could not be reliably distinguished from one another.[30]

Spectacular Status

To illustrate habituated differences between free bodies and slave bodies in antiquity, I consider narratives of two martyrdoms, the martyrdom of Perpetua and the martyrdom of Blandina. It is a truism that in martyrdom social distinctions were washed away in blood. I argue instead that representations of the deaths of the elite Perpetua and the enslaved Blandina rely on and perpetuate expectations regarding corporal distinctions between slave and free. Evidence suggests that Perpetua knew freedom in her body and Blandina knew slavery. Or at least, in narrating the deaths of the two women, ancient writers represented their bodies as habituated by status.

As I argued in chapter 2, in the Roman Empire vulnerability to corporal violation was perceived as feminine or servile, and vulnerability to corporal abuse was perceived as servile. The shame of being treated like a slave intensified the suffering of a free person subjected to private or public violence; a man who was abused was additionally shamed by the feminine associations of corporal vulnerability. One second-century petition in Roman Egypt complained of gross injustice, which was "to beat and to give a thrashing and to treat the freeborn like slaves."[31] Conditioning by the whip was a significant and stereotypical part of the slave's habitus. Moreover, Roman law generally—although not universally—protected the bodies of freeborn persons from grosser instances of state-sanctioned violence. By the second century C.E., this system was breaking down. Nonetheless, a fundamental distinction persisted between the limited vulnerability of enslaved bodies and the protected status of free citizen bodies. The events leading to the death of Jesus, from the whipping by Roman soldiers to the painful exposure of his stripped body on the cross, were shameful. Contrast, for example, a martial death by sword. Along with the excruciating physical pain associated with martyrdom, exposure in the arena was also supposed to disgrace the martyr, to publicize her or his dishonorable status.[32] While the physical pain of martyrdom was undeniable, the Christian community refused to view the brutalities of martyrdom as diminishing the martyr in any way. Indeed, Christians interpreted the outrageous violation of martyrs' bodies as a source of ennoblement and power. While this rehabilitation of the humiliated body represents a reversal of values and of habitus, this process plays out differently in accounts of the martyrdoms of persons of elite backgrounds and of slaves.[33]

Perpetua

Imprisoned and martyred in early third-century Carthage, Vibia Perpetua was one of the few women in antiquity to leave a literary legacy, her prison diary. The Passion of Perpetua consists of her diary as well as additional material, including an introduction, a briefer text by one of Perpetua's fellow martyrs, and an account of her tribulations and death in the arena, compiled by the editor of the diary. In *The Suffering Self: Pain and Narrative Representation in the Early Christian Era*, Judith Perkins argues persuasively that early Christians participated in a larger cultural trend in which suffering became a source of identity. In that context, Perkins writes that Perpetua's diary records "a growing sense of her empowerment through suffering."[34] While I am convinced more broadly by Perkins's argument, I argue that Perpetua's own words and the editor's comments consistently portray her as a woman whose confidence in her own power was allied to her elite status, a status translated via her privileged habitus into bodily comportment.

We learn the broad parameters of that habitus from the editor. Perpetua is "of high rank, liberally educated, a respectable married woman."[35] Throughout the narrative, those with whom she interacts treat her with deference. Two members of

Perpetua's family, her brother and her father, address her as *domina*. "Lady" is too prissy a translation. A Roman husband, himself a *dominus*, addressed his wife as *domina* as a title of respect. *Domina* was also the title used by slaves to signal deference when they addressed a female slaveholder or mistress of a household.[36] Richard A. Saller argues that the practice of slavery enhanced the ability of elite Roman women to act independently. Although she was limited in her personal conduct of business dealings, a woman who owned slaves could rely on her slaves and freedmen as agents. For Saller, the title *domina* capsulizes the ability of the elite, slaveholding woman to conduct her business independently of her husband or father.[37] Perpetua describes her father's persistent efforts to dissuade her from her Christian beliefs in order to preserve her life. Recalling that in raising her he favored her above her brothers, he finally implores her "no longer as his daughter but as mistress [*domina*]" (5), a rare form of address from a Roman father to his daughter.

The text thus establishes Perpetua's own sense of her social status, a sense of status respected by her father and others with whom she interacts. Because of her social status, she is a leader among the imprisoned Christians. At the outset of her imprisonment she has not yet been baptized, so her leadership role cannot be attributed to seniority in the Christian movement. She dreams of herself as a person of power, stepping on the head of a dragon as she climbs a ladder to heaven and besting an Egyptian in a wrestling match. Privileged in the social arena, Perpetua assumes authority in the spiritual arena. In her dreams that privilege is expressed somatically.

The narrative of her execution extends Perpetua's own presentation of herself as a woman of stature. Perpetua ends her account, "About what happened at the contest himself, let him write of it who will" (10). Responding to what he terms Perpetua's order or commission (*mandatum*), the author rehearses an incident that, he claims, exposes the quality of Perpetua's soul. Perpetua confronted the military tribune in charge of the imprisoned Christians and challenged him to take better care of the prisoners in order that they might make a more impressive showing in the games. Embarrassed, the tribune ordered more humane care for the prisoners. Even in a moment of greatly reduced legal status, Perpetua projected the authority of a *domina*. Perpetua again challenged the authorities when they commanded the Christians to don the garb of devotees of Saturn and Ceres for the spectacle of their death, and again, those who prepared to execute her deferred to her. The imprint of habitus was so strong on Perpetua that she exacted compliance from those who ostensibly wielded power over her.

In narrating the scene of Perpetua in the arena, the author relies on the common Roman vocabulary of gesture. Even when confronted by beasts and armed men, Perpetua's elite demeanor purportedly did not crack. In a trance after being tossed by a mad heifer, Perpetua adjusted her tunic to cover her thighs. Despite her painful delirium, she was conditioned by habitus to protect her reputation for modesty and chastity; as I argue later in the chapter, maintenance of reputation for modesty was a prerogative associated with women of higher status. Perpetua's fellow martyrs included the slave woman Felicitas. When Felicitas was crushed in the arena, Perpetua lifted her up. Perpetua, not Felicitas, had the strength and confidence to address the catechumens as they faced death. Far from dissolving the distinctions between freeborn woman and slave, the martyrdom account reinforces the distinctions of habitus dividing the two brave women.

The narrator tells us that, in the end, Perpetua took the frightened hand of the neophyte gladiator and guided it to her own throat. She died by the sword like the aristocrat she was. Did the historical Perpetua actually have the grace to guide her executioner's hand? Whether she did or not—I have my doubts—the narrator relies on a corporal vernacular in representing Perpetua's final moments, emphasizing those gestures and postures appropriate for a dignified and influential matron.

Perkins characterizes Perpetua as an "unruly woman" who displaces patriarchal power of family and state structures.[38] However, this characterization accords gender disproportionate weight. Perpetua defied gender roles, yet gender determined neither her actions nor the responses of others to her words and deeds. Even as Perpetua, *domina*, rejected the comforts of her social status, embracing instead the dishonorable punishment of death in a theatrical spectacle, a lifetime habituation to a role of authority informed her commanding presence. An elite woman, Perpetua is represented as knowing authority deep in her guts, a kind of knowing utterly consistent with her lifelong habituation to an elite role.

Blandina

A different habitus conditioned the body of the slave martyr Blandina, who died in Gaul in 177 C.E.[39] We learn about Blandina from book 5 of Eusebius's *Ecclesiastical History*. Just as Perpetua's commanding presence was consistent with the authoritative presence of an elite woman habituated as a *domina*, so Blandina's excessive suffering inhabited the quintessential slave body. How different were their tribulations and deaths? Blandina did not bequeath us a diary. We are even more limited in the conclusions we may draw about the facts of Blandina's death than we are regarding the facts of Perpetua's death. However, Eusebius, who introduced Blandina by saying that, through her, "Christ proved that the things that men think cheap, ugly, and contemptuous are deemed worthy of glory before God" (17), explicitly relied on the categories associated with the liabilities of servile status to describe Blandina's suffering. I am necessarily concerned here as much with the writer's habituation to a set of bodily norms as I am with the martyr's flesh.

As Perpetua's fellow martyrs included the slave Felicitas, so Blandina's fellow martyrs included the woman who owned legal title to her. "All of us were in terror; and Blandina's fleshly mistress, who was herself among the martyrs in the conflict, was in agony lest because of bodily weakness she [Blandina] would not be able to make a bold confession of her faith." (18). The mistress was influenced by prevailing cultural habitus to expect that a slave would weakly capitulate under torture: torture was part of the usual procedure in Roman culture for attempting to extract information from slaves.[40] Maureen Tilley has argued that the preparation of ascetic practices permitted the martyrs to endure brutal tortures without destroying them mentally; a lifetime of abuse, however, could also condition a slave to disassociate from what was done to her body. On this view, unsanctified abuse might thus condition a woman to endure abuse that she could at least interpret as sanctifying.[41] Contemporary analysis of the experiences of survivors of childhood abuse suggests that in some cases, conditioning to pain leads not to fearful capitulation but to a capacity to displace oneself emotionally and mentally from such bodily torment.[42] Eusebius indeed claimed that Blandina was able to dissociate from the trauma experienced by her body: "This blessed woman like a noble athlete got renewed strength with her confession of faith: her admission, 'I am a Christian; we do nothing to be ashamed of,' brought her refreshment, rest, and an insensibility to her present pain" (19).

What most captures the reader's imagination about Blandina is the extraordinary scene of her first exposure in the amphitheater, although she would not actually die until a later occasion. In that first ordeal, Eusebius writes, "Blandina was hung on a post and exposed as bait for the wild animals that were let loose on her. She seemed to hang there in the form of a cross, and by her fervent prayer she aroused intense enthusiasm in those who were undergoing their ordeal, for in their torment with their physical eyes they saw in the person of their sister him who was crucified for them" (41). None of the animals touched Blandina.[43] Blandina, in any case, survived only to die on the final day of the games. Blandina's death, however, is not so memorable as her near-death, at the moment when, in Elizabeth Castelli's well-chosen words, "shape-shifting into the body of Christ," Blandina became "a remarkable form of counter-spectacle."[44] Here, indeed, we have a figure who epitomizes, as Judith Perkins argues, "the ability to endure suffering as power."[45]

Blandina figures the Christian rehabilitation of the humble, the elevation of an abased figure: in the intensity of her slavelike suffering she represents Christ. Eusebius is not alone in recognizing the resemblance of battered slave bodies to the battered body of Christ. 1 Peter encourages slaves to accept unjust beatings from their masters by noting that Christ himself had been abused and suffered, a formulation that, while giving meaning to the suffering of slaves, inculcates submissiveness (2:18–25). A parallel corporal vocabulary was exploited by American writers responding to the depravities of slavery. In her classic—and complex—abolitionist novel *Uncle Tom's Cabin*, Harriet Beecher Stowe made the logic explicit. Confronted with the choice between betraying two fugitive slaves and being killed, Tom chooses silence and a painful death. Stowe comments, "But of old, there was One whose suffering changed an instrument of torture, degradation and shame, into a symbol of glory, honor, and immortal life; and where His spirit is, neither degrading stripes, nor blood, nor insults, can make the Christian's last struggle less than glorious."[46] Just as Blandina is said to metamorphose into Christ, so Christ stands with Tom in his suffering. Perhaps any Christian might be said to embody Christ, but both in antiquity and in the Americas writers were especially drawn to the stereotypically abused bodies of slaves to exemplify one somatic mode of Christian faithfulness. In their endurance of whippings, slaves were thought to have privileged knowledge of the passion of Christ.

Blandina's empowerment did not accord her the kind of personal authority exercised by Perpetua. Blandina did not give orders to those who executed her. She did not lead the other martyrs. Even her mistress, who presumably knew her well, did not anticipate her strength. In Eusebius's representation of Blandina, her power derived from her ability to suffer. In effect, she became a pain artist. She was able to embody Christ because, particularly in his passion and death, Christ embodied the corporal vulnerability of a slave (cf. Phil. 2:5–8). By suffering as Christ had suffered, Blandina too became the slave of all. A revision of modes of perception invited the Christian to view the suffering of the enslaved woman as the suffering of Christ himself, yet this rehabilitation of habitus in martyrdom had no effect on the somatic presentations of the elite woman and the enslaved woman: the elite woman commanded, the enslaved woman endured, with a kind of long suffering associated with the pathetic condition of slaves.[47] Eusebius writes that "tiny, weak, and insignificant" as Blandina was, she inspired those who witnessed her Christic metamorphosis, who saw her "put on Christ" (42). He observes that, by the time Blandina was finally put to death, after every variety of torture and atrocity had been perpetrated on her body, even the pagans conceded that she had suffered more than any other woman (56). We have what may seem a transformation of values: the one who is low is lifted up, the one who is despised is praised. This is an ironic elevation, contingent on Blandina's embrace of injury to her body, injury that was, ultimately, an extreme manifestation of conditions endemic in the lives of Roman slaves.

Slaveholding Sexuality as Habitus

The Greek concept of *aretē*, typically translated virtue, connoted excellence: physical, mental, even social excellence. In classical culture, slaves were caricatured as lacking the capacity for such *aretē*, virtue or excellence. Both Stoicism and Christianity challenged this classical precept. A slave was said to have the same capacity for virtue as a free person, a capacity dramatically evident, for example, in Blandina's Christomorphic endurance of suffering. I argue that in daily practice the habitus of slavery effectively undermined this principle, especially for female slaves. The Christian body developed an obsessive concern with female chastity. This preoccupation was, I believe, a corporal expression of a slaveholding habitus that translated a cultural expectation for elite women into a moral qualification that tended to exclude from the highest spiritual ranks women of humbler social statuses, especially slaves. By elevating self-abasement, Christian writers challenged classical conceptions of virtue. However, as a rule those Christians who were actually enslaved did not benefit from this moral revolution.[48] I argue that many Christians simply discounted the possibility that female slaves could know a certain kind of virtue in their bodies.

In order to appreciate the tension between oft-stated Christian egalitarian ideals and slaveholding habitus, it is necessary to come to terms with the impact of slavery on sexual practice and ideology in the Roman Empire. In a survey article on sexuality in the Roman Empire, classicist Amy Richlin writes, in stark terms, "Slavery would have introduced conquered peoples to the Roman sex/gender system at the lowest level."[49] Richlin argues that the impact of slavery on sexual expression and experience in the Roman world was pervasive. In order to answer the kinds of questions posed in the Kinsey report, she reviews writings from the Roman Empire, including Jewish and Christian writings, asking: What is the respondent's attitude toward sex between men and boys? Between adult men? Conjugal sex? Sex between women? After assembling a sampling of quotations from ancient sources, Richlin begins her own observations by noting, "The institution of slavery underlies all responses."[50] In fact, Richlin opines, "Respectable women's self-definition seems to have depended on sexual self-differentiation from slave women."[51] Richlin's verdict applies broadly to the Roman world. I contend that Christianity intensified existing preoccupation with women's sexual purity. Perhaps in theory a slave was understood to have the same capacity for virtue as a free person, but in practice, a female slave habituated to sexual violation was vehemently denied to be as virtuous as a properly married woman or a free woman in (relative) control of her own sexuality who opted to refrain from sexual activity.

An emphasis on the habitus of slavery thus highlights the differential effects of slavery on free women and slave women. The bodies of female slaves were conditioned and perceived as sexually available; the bodies of free women, especially elite women, were conditioned and perceived as sexually sacrosanct. Women and men who joined the church did not shed their postures, manners, and affects when they walked into congregational gatherings; they did not lose their bodily knowledge of social location. The waters of baptism did not wash away or dissolve the durable and visible effects of bodily habitus. Those who shaped the Christian body had themselves been marked by their upbringings as freeborn, freed, or enslaved persons, and their perceptions, expectations, and preoccupations, which in countless ways lay beneath the level of conscious interrogation, structured the possibilities they were able to articulate for new life in Christ. By late antiquity, after the Roman Empire adopted Christianity as a state religion, a handful of Christian writers explicitly raised moral questions about the sexual use of slaves and about the moral status of slaves whose owners required sexual duties of them. Although I will cite these authors, my ultimate concern lies with the vast numbers of Christians in antiquity who never actively considered such questions at all, though their moral valuations of both slaves and free women were implicitly shaped by their reactions to the sexually available bodies of slave women and the inviolate bodies of elite women.

Inhabiting Slavery and Freedom

In Seneca the Younger's *Trojan Women*, written in the mid-first century C.E., Hecuba, Trojan queen, addresses the women of the vanquished city to prepare them for inevitable enslavement. She speaks to her companions in defeat: "Let the crowd expose its arms in readiness; ungird your breasts, letting fall your garments, and let the body be stripped even to the womb. For what marriage do you cover your breasts, O captive modesty [*captive pudor*]?"[52] Royal authority informs Hecuba's speech, at once appropriately and ironically: shaping her elocution is a lifetime of privilege, but that privilege, with Troy itself, is burnt to ash. The women to be distributed as booty include Hecuba, her daughters, and her widowed daughters-in-law.[53]

To figure involuntary reduction of status, Seneca relies on the contrasting habitus of a free woman and of an enslaved woman. Having directed the Trojan women to strip themselves of those aspects of attire most obviously necessary for elite women to insulate themselves from the intrusive gaze and touch of unauthorized men, Hecuba sighs, "There, this manner of dress satisfies me [*placet hic habitus*]." The training and habits of a lifetime nonetheless shape Hecuba's royal mien as she commands her (former) subjects: a deeply cultivated habitus cannot be slipped off as easily as a garment can be slipped off the shoulders and knotted around the hips. Romans expected that they should be able to recognize, by dress, by habitus, a woman's status: according to Roman law, liability for an insult against a respectable young woman was lessened if the woman was dressed in a way more appropriate to a slave (*Dig.*, 47.10.15.15). In Seneca's Rome, wearing the dress known as the *stola* was the exclusive right of matrons who were freeborn or, if freed-women, married to freeborn men; no uniform was officially established for slaves.[54] The shift in habitus dictated by Hecuba does not, however, involve a costume change so much as a modification of self-presentation. The same garments are draped differently, no longer to signify sexual exclusiveness but sexual availability.

Hecuba directs her remarks to the abstraction of *captive pudor*, translated by Elaine Fantham as an address to "captive modesty," a necessarily misleading translation: *pudor* is difficult to capture in a single English term. *Pudor* encompasses modesty, but also connotes a sense of shame, chastity, an awareness of what is proper, and attention to propriety, especially sexual propriety, in conduct, dress, and speech.[55] At the outset of her kaleidoscopic treatment of *pudor*, Carlin A. Barton identifies it as an "inhibiting emotion."[56] *Pudor* belongs to the free woman, not to the slave: the abstraction *captive pudor* to whom Hecuba speaks is thus an impossible creature.[57] Inability to maintain corporal integrity, vividly evoked by Hecuba in her directions to the Trojan women to disrobe, characterizes the condition of a slave.[58] In the liminal moment of enslavement, the prerogatives and liabilities of differing legal statuses are brought into sharp relief, as a freeborn woman, previously assured that her status protects her against sexual violation, confronts the familiar realities of slavery with new eyes, viewing the sexual availability of the enslaved body no longer with contempt but with horror. As slaves, as sexual property, Hecuba, her daughters, and the other Trojan women must retrain their bodies: to open themselves to sexual access by slaveholders, to uncover their heads and bodies to the gaze of men outside their own families.

For women, virtue was inseparable from chastity. Consignment to the category of slavery endangered a woman's claim to *pudor*. Even enslaved women who avoided sexual use by their owners lacked the reputations essential to *pudor*, as the very fact of enslavement and hence sexual availability cast doubt on their sexual histories. So in a declamation by the elder Seneca, a freeborn woman's bid for a priesthood was challenged because she had been kidnapped, enslaved, and forced to display herself in a brothel, even though she claimed to have maintained her virginity, at the end by killing an armed man who tried to compel her to have sexual relations. Her detractors argued that, even if they conceded that she had somehow managed to avoid defloration, her very vulnerability as a slave obviated her claims to sexual purity: "Do you regard yourself as chaste just because you are an unwilling whore?—She stood naked on the shore to meet the buyer's sneers; every part of her body was inspected—and handled."[59]

How widespread was the expectation that female slaves had been used sexually? Seemingly at a far remove from the sensationalist declamation of the elder Seneca, the Mishnah dictates that converts, former captives, and freed slaves cannot be married as virgins. The presumption is that they have been sexually active, even if that sexual activity has been coerced. This is true for any female who has experienced a period of enslavement from the age of three onward. The presumption is not that toddler slaves would be exempt from sexual violation. Rather, the rabbis believed that hymens ruptured before age three could regenerate themselves.[60] While I cannot think of evidence to confirm that such very young slaves were commonly the sexual playthings of their owners—nor can I think of where one might seek either evidence or counterevidence—it is clear that throughout the Roman world female slaves and former slaves were shut out from the kinds of reputations essential to *pudor*.

To paraphrase a question literary critic Toni Irving asks in another context, if, as Merleau-Ponty suggests, the body is our general medium for having a world, how did female slaves in antiquity structure a sexual body in spite of less-than-ideal bodily experiences?[61] The knowledge of slavery borne in the bodies of many girls and women was a sexualized knowledge.

Sarah and Hagar

Elite authors in antiquity cared more about the indignities and sufferings of women raised as aristocrats than about the indignities and sufferings of women raised as slaves. More fundamentally, they were *aware* of the potential indignities an aristocratic woman might suffer, oblivious to the indignities a slave woman might suffer. Christian authors were not exempted from this blind spot. To illustrate this corporally conditioned blind spot, I turn to Christian treatments of Sarah and Hagar, freewoman and slave, from the first century and the fourth.

Paul moves from a conscious declaration that the categories "slave and free" are outmoded in the new creation (Gal. 3:28) to his development of the Sarah-Hagar allegory in Galatians 4, a critique of the Jerusalem church. Assimilating the Jerusalem church to the slave woman Hagar, Paul writes: "But what does scripture say? 'Drive out the slave and her child; for the child of the slave will not share the inheritance with the child of the free woman'" (Gal. 4:30). Paul closes the allegory without telling the whole story. He does not mention that God responds to Hagar's distress by assuring her that her son, like Sarah's son, will be the ancestor of a great nation. He does not mention that at her bleakest moment, the moment where she turns away from her own son because she cannot stand to see him die of thirst in the desert, God meets her in her distress. A spring gushes in the desert. Paul's version of the Sarah-Hagar story turns on deeply embedded prejudices about slaves and free women. He was conditioned to perceive the bodies and offspring of free women as meriting protection. He was conditioned to perceive the bodies and offspring of slave women as vulnerable to sexual exploitation and other dangers. Paul does not temper his midrash with sympathy for the moral position of the slave. Without any recognition of the active role of Sarah in persecuting Hagar, Paul claims that the enslaved child persecuted the freeborn child. The free woman's hostility is displaced onto the slave child.

Ambrose, fourth-century bishop of Milan, was a descendant of an established and well-placed Roman family. At the time he wrote, Christianity had been established as the imperial religion. Old habits die hard. The slaveholding men in Ambrose's churches were still conditioned by ancient Roman habitus to assume as a matter of course that they had the legal, cultural, and moral right to use their slaves sexually. Writing of the patriarch Abraham, Ambrose comments on the story of Sarah and Hagar. The biblical account of Abraham conceiving a son by his wife's slave creates a problem for Ambrose. If Abraham could carry on with a female slave, a Christian man might ask, why can't I? Ambrose offers several justifications for his counsel to men to avoid sexual relations with their slaves. He instructs men that they, like their wives, are obligated to sexual exclusivity. He also points out that some wife might take her husband's sexual liaison with a slave as a pretext for divorce. He urges women to refrain from jealousy.

Most of all, Ambrose sympathizes with Sarah's treatment of Hagar as, to use the vernacular, "uppity." He apparently perceives the same phenomenon in his own world. He complains that a female slave who is her owner's concubine becomes arrogant and insolent toward her mistress (*On Abraham* 1.4.26). Ambrose knew that, regardless of his exhortations, many Christian men would continue to have sex with their slaves. He therefore writes that Christian men who regrettably continue to pursue sexual relations with their slaves should insist that those slaves subordinate themselves to their mistresses. Like Paul, Ambrose develops the implications of Hagar's story in the context of a cultural script unconcerned with the moral and physical costs of enslavement for a slave. Paul blames the enslaved child for the maltreatment of mother and child. Ambrose blames the uppity slave woman for defying her mistress. Neither Paul nor Ambrose hints at the moral harm done to the slave. They treat her as a source of immorality, not a victim of immorality. I return to Ambrose's double standard for elite women and slave women later in this chapter.

Just as Christians in antiquity contended with the story of Sarah and Hagar, so Christians in the Americas have contended with the story. In her treatment of African American appropriations of Hagar's story, Kimberleigh Jordan argues, "The actual *physical* location of the reader can also reflect one's experience of freedom and liberty. Where one's body is and how it is oriented serves as a canvas of learning."[62] She holds that the reader's reactions to Abraham and Hagar depend "on his or her relationship to embodied power."[63] Before the Civil War, European American novelists relied on the figure of Hagar to symbolize resistance to patriarchy. In doing so, however, they often defended slavery and reinforced stereotypes of African American women as wanton sexual creatures.[64] In quite a different vein, the figure of Hagar has been especially important to African American women. Ambrose of Milan was unable to feel the moral and physical harm done to Hagar. African American women have felt that harm in their bones. Jordan writes that African American women "have known unfreedom through their bodies."[65] From the period of slavery to the present, many African American women have even explicitly named themselves daughters of Hagar, as Delores Williams spells out in a classic work of Womanist theology.[66]

African American interpretations of the Sarah-Hagar narrative hint at the suggestive possibility that alternative interpretations might have circulated in early churches, but no such interpretations are preserved. The *Acts of Andrew*, a work dated as early as the second half of the second century, offers a disturbing variant of the story of Sarah and Hagar, a variant that assumes a moral distinction between the bodies of slaves and of free women. The story is all the more disturbing in its tacit approval of the free woman's behavior. Under the influence of the apostle Andrew, who decries all sexual activity as polluting, Maximilla upsets her husband Aegeates, a proconsul, with her refusal to sleep with him. To preserve her own purity, Maximilla grooms her slave Euclia and dresses her in luxurious clothes, then sends Euclia to Aegeates's bed. Maximilla achieves her end, the deception of Aegeates. Euclia boasts of favors she receives from Maximilla and thereby provokes bitterness among other slaves in the household. The embittered slaves inform Aegeates of the deception. Aegeates directs his initial fury at Euclia for her boasting. He brutally kills her and executes other slaves to hush up the affair. The *Acts of Andrew* condemns the hubris of a slave who overestimates the significance of a sexual relationship with her owner but does not condemn the sexual use of slaves, especially since that practice permits an elite Christian woman to remain unsullied by sexual contact. The work exempts Maximilla from blame in the subterfuge, implying that Euclia's actions were completely explicable in the context of her nature, which is depicted as both lascivious and greedy. Maximilla "summoned a shapely, exceedingly wanton servant girl and told her what she delighted and desired. 'You will have me as a benefactor of all your needs, providing you scheme with me and carry out what I advise.'"[67] Euclia's own curvaceous body indicts her.

The branch of Christianity that produced the *Acts of Andrew* was unusual in its wholesale condemnation of sexual activity, even within marriage. The story should not be taken as a historically accurate account of a typical Christian woman (or even a historically accurate account of an atypical Christian woman). The author of the account, however, accepted without protest the sexual exploitation of a slave, an exploitation that occurred precisely to preserve the interests of an elite woman.

Not only was the inviolable body of a freeborn woman distinguished from the violated body of a slave, but the freeborn woman's corporal integrity was directly
dependent on the abuse of that slave. As I have noted, the story of Maximilla and
Euclia echoes, in a disturbing way, the story of Sarah and Hagar. Sarah arranged
for her husband to have sex with her slave in order to reproduce. Maximilla
arranged for her husband to have sex with her slave so that she, Maximilla, could
avoid having sex. In both instances, the Christians who relayed these stories were
more concerned by the slave's purported misbehavior than the gross sexual exploitation of a female slave by a female slaveholder.[68] I argue that this double standard
derives from unquestioned assumptions associated with slaveholding habitus.

Lucretia

The slaveholding habitus of Roman antiquity, I argue, deformed Christian moral
imaginations. I offer the exemplum of Lucretia as a valorized prototype of an elite
woman's exemplary storytelling body, an exemplum that brings brings into focus
the sexual double standard for elite women and enslaved women. Corporal knowledge of sexual violation was routinized for women of lower status while threatening to the identities of women of higher status. From the days of the Republic until
the days of Augustine, the fabled Lucretia reflected and shaped the morals of pagan
and Christian alike. Even Augustine, who offers a dissenting opinion on whether
Lucretia's suicide was praiseworthy, shares wider cultural expectations about the
usual inviolability of freeborn women's bodies and the inevitable sexual vulnerability of slave bodies.

Spinning wool through the long days and nights of her husband's absence,
Lucretia exemplified the chastity of a Roman matron. As the legend goes, Sextus
was the son of the last king of Rome, Tarquinius Superbus. He became enflamed
not only by Lucretia's beauty but also by her chastity. When Lucretia refused Sextus's advances, he threatened to kill her and also to kill one of his own male slaves.
After placing them in bed together, Sextus threatened, he would announce that he
had killed them when he caught them together in bed. *Pudor*, specifically, the horror that others would believe her body had been sexually penetrated by a slave, led
Lucretia to capitulate to Sextus's sexual demands. Afterward, she sent for her father
and husband from their military encampment. After narrating the events, she
begged them to avenge the wrong. Both father and husband tried to reassure her
that she bore no burden of guilt. She replied, according to Livy, "Though I acquit
myself of the sin, I do not absolve myself from punishment; nor in time to come
shall ever unchaste woman live through the example of Lucretia" (*The History of
Rome*, 1.58.10). With that, she plunged a sword into her own breast and died. The
incident supposedly incited such anger against the arrogance of the royal family

that it catalyzed Junius Brutus to lead the revolt that brought the Roman monarchy to a close.

Widespread allusions to Lucretia in pagan and Christian sources suggest the powerful hold of her dilemma on Roman imaginations. Both ancient and modern allusions to the tale focus on the question of whether corporal violation necessarily involves a diminution of chastity and on Lucretia's unwillingness to live with even a suggestion of unchastity. Typically unexamined is Lucretia's horror at the prospect of sex with a slave. The story codifies a primitive horror at the thought of a freeborn woman's body joined carnally to a slave's body, an attitude toward the purity of the freeborn woman that exceeds the bounds of the moral to become a fear of pollution by what is defined as base. According to ancient mores, the conditioning of the freeborn woman should lead her to recoil physically from such pollution. The purity of the matron's body requires complete dissociation from what is ignoble. Even the appearance of sexual union with an enslaved man would taint that purity.

Roman law discouraged unions between free women and slaves or freedmen. According to an edict of Claudius, a free woman who married a slave could be claimed as a slave by the putative husband's owner. Constantine renewed the Claudian prohibition on unions between free women and slaves in 314. Like much of Roman law, this law was probably not consistently enforced. The majority of free women who cohabited with slaves or freedmen were women of low status and little wealth, the conduct of whose personal lives was of little interest to authorities. Writing in the early third century, Tertullian cited the legal prohibition of such unions in his explanation of why the church forbade Christians from wedding non-Christians. According to Tertullian, the Christian was like a free person, the non-Christian, a slave. He claimed that pagan women, "even those of noble birth and blessed with wealth, unite themselves promiscuously with mean and base-born men whom they have found able to gratify their passions or who have been mutilated [castrated] for purposes of lust. Some give themselves to their own freedmen and slaves, disregarding public opinion, as long as they have men from whom they need fear no check on their licentiousness." Tertullian thus implied that a woman's indifference to the scandal of choosing a partner of low status was itself blameworthy, a token of deficient *pudor*.

Tertullian's analysis of the reasons why free women might make such choices points to his formation in a Roman habitus. Such conditioning by Roman habitus should come as no surprise in an author who cited the example of Lucretia on a number of occasions. Arguing against remarriage, for example, Tertullian touted Lucretia: "Because she knew a man who was not her husband, though it was by violence forced on her at night, she cleansed the defilement of her flesh by shedding her own blood, willing to make compensation for the loss of her chastity at the cost of her life" (*Monogamy* 17).[69] *Pudor*, a concern for sexual propriety, was so deeply offended by the thought of a free woman's body defiled by the embrace of a slave that suicide became defensible, even admirable.

Attesting to the degree to which Christian bodies continued to be conditioned by Roman habitus, the exemplum of Lucretia exerted a powerful hold over Christian imaginations into late antiquity. In the fourth century Jerome wrote, "The virtue of a woman is, in a special sense, purity. It was this that made Lucretia the equal of Brutus, if it did not make her his superior, since Brutus learnt from a woman the impossibility of being a slave" (*Adversus Jovinianum* 1.49; see also 1.46). In labeling purity the defining virtue for women, Jerome counterposes the virtue of Lucretia to servile submissiveness. In what ways did Lucretia exemplify the moral opposition between a virtuous person, implicitly defined as free, and a slave? Perhaps in her refusal to even appear to have been erotically paired with a slave, as the free body of the female was defined in part by its sexual distance from the body of the male slave, but more likely in her unwillingness to live with questionable *pudor*.

Jerome's implicit association of virtue and free status ultimately belies the oft-quoted suggestion that Christians believed that in the eyes of God distinctions between slave and free were obliterated. For many years Jerome worked to distance himself from the views of the third-century Alexandrian theologian Origen, views that over time had come to be characterized as heretical. A particular point to which Jerome returned repeatedly was Origen's argument that hierarchies of gender and virtue would be dissolved at the resurrection. Jerome was as upset by Origen's suggestion that virgins would no longer outrank prostitutes as he was by Origen's suggestion that Lucifer would share rank with cherubim and seraphim.[70] On Jerome's view, sins would be pardoned, but the rewards of resurrected life would be greater for virgins than for those who violated sexual norms. Thus, on his view, even among the blessed a woman privileged to preserve her virginity would outrank a household slave who had no effective control over her own body and would certainly outrank any slave who was prostituted by her owner.[71]

Basil of Caesarea

The strictures of purity essential for a proper woman were evoked by visceral reactions, Roman and then Christian, against sexual contact between a free woman and an enslaved man. The necessity of maintaining somatic integrity became, at times, an obsession, an obsession understood by many Christians as a virtue, and indeed as a woman's defining virtue. But this defining virtue was not equally accessible to all women. Only in unusual circumstances did a free woman confront the question of whether forcible sexual violation compromised her virtue. Slave women confronted this dilemma routinely. Lucretia's story points to the tensions in ancient Christian attitudes toward the virtue of slaves who had no choice in their sexual use by their owners. Writing a century ago, Paul Allard detailed instances in which free women chose death over rape. He noted that, if slaves made similar choices, the historical record does not memorialize their choices.[72] The disinterest of Christian sources in the choices of slaves confronted by forcible sexual demands underscores the degree to which a Roman habitus conditioned Christians to accept the sexual vulnerability of servile bodies.

Basil of Caesarea, writing in the fourth century, believed that the fact of slavery or of freedom informed a person's very potential for virtue. He cited as a mystery why a wicked person flourished while a righteous person suffered, "why one man is a slave, another free, one is rich, another is poor—and the difference in sins and virtuous actions is great: she who was sold to a brothelkeeper is in sin by force, and she who immediately obtained a good master grows up with virginity" (*On Psalm 32.5*). Sensitive to the constraints under which women were forced to act, Basil specified that women who were corrupted by force should not be held responsible for that corruption and added: "Thus even a slave, if she has been violated by her own master, is guiltless" (*Ep.* 199.49). Conscious that the regulations laid down for marriage applied only to free women, Basil also laid out the conditions for marriage of female slaves. He wrote that just as a free woman required her father's participation to marry, so a slave should secure her master's permission (*Ep.* 199.40, 42). Basil thus recognized the ways that the demands of slavery informed slave women's conduct and tried to ordain structures whereby slaves could lead lives reckoned as virtuous.

Like the overwhelming majority of ancient Christians, however, Basil did not oppose slavery itself. He insisted, for example, that, unless a slaveholder required that a slave violate God's law, a monastery was bound to return a runaway slave to the owner (Basil, *Longer Rule*, Question 11). Although he acknowledged that some persons were reduced to slavery through the vicissitudes of life, he also suggested that unwise persons benefited from enslavement to sage owners (*Spiritu Sanctu*, 20.51). Moreover, as Bernadette Brooten points out, although Basil made allowances for enslaved women used sexually by their Christian owners, he did not penalize the behavior of slaveholders who demanded sex from their slaves.[73] In the final section of this chapter, where I discuss isolated instances where Christians embodied resistance to slaveholding norms, I return to the question of how to account for Basil's apparent sensitivity to the moral plight of sexually exploited slaves in light of his simultaneous affirmation of the rights of slaveholders.

Ambrose

Not all Christians shared Basil's reasoning that a woman who was coerced to have sex against her will should not be considered culpable of wrongdoing. Or at least, many Christians praised women who chose death over rape.[74] Ambrose of Milan excited controversy when he used the resources of the church to redeem Christians who had been captured by pagans; he commented that it was good when "a man is redeemed from death, or a woman from barbarian impurities, things that are worse than death" (*De officiis ministrorum* 2.28). Ambrose lauded the legendary Pelagia of Antioch. Threatened with rape, Pelagia was said to dress herself as for a wedding and then kill herself. The would-be rapists then turned their predatory attention to Pelagia's mother and sisters. The mother and sisters drowned themselves. Ambrose noted that they chose a baptism after which they could not sin (*De virginibus* 3.7.32–37). Ambrose composed a speech for Pelagia that underscored the relationship of liberty to *pudor*: "I die willingly, no one will lay a hand on me, no one will harm my virginity with his shameless glance, I shall take with me my purity and my modesty unsullied. . . . Pelagia will follow Christ, no one will take away her freedom, no one will see her freedom of faith taken away, nor her remarkable purity" (*Ep.* 37). Pelagia died willingly, according to Ambrose, and that death marked her as a freeborn woman. She died with liberty and *pudor* intact.

Ambrose was aware of the sexual vulnerabilities of slaves. Commenting on the story of the patriarch Joseph who was, as a slave in Egypt, the target of his mistress's sexual overtures, Ambrose wrote, "It was not within the power of a mere slave not to be looked upon" (*De Joseph patriarcha* 5.22). Yet, as we have seen, when Ambrose wrote about Abraham and Hagar, he did not express concern for Abraham's injury to Hagar's chastity. Nor did he suggest that Hagar, like Pelagia, should have killed herself to avoid sexual tainting. For Ambrose, Hagar's sin was not a violation of chastity, apparently because he considered her beneath chastity. He alleged that her sin was haughtiness toward her mistress (*On Abraham* 1.4.25). Would choosing death over life have been morally praiseworthy for a slave threatened with rape? That such questions did not arise for most Christian writers attests to their deep-seated habituation to the privileges of free bodies and the vulnerabilities of enslaved bodies. The possibility that a slave woman would be sexually violated against her will did not elicit the horror elicited by the forcible sexual violation of a free woman.

Augustine

Like other Christian theologians who preceded him, Augustine cited the example of Lucretia, but, as Dennis Trout has argued, he did so to challenge the prevalent assumption that forcible sexual violation entailed moral compromise. Reasoning that, if purity could be sullied against a person's will, then purity would rank not among virtues but among bodily goods, Augustine concluded that if a woman, caught "between modesty and logic" (*inter pudorem atque rationem*), was sexually penetrated against her will, she remained as pure as she did prior to the violation (*City of God* 1.17). The blame belonged entirely to the rapist; no part of the blame was imputed to the victim of rape. To make his point, Augustine accused Lucretia of murder. If, that is, Lucretia did not share Sextus's lust, then taking her own life entailed killing an innocent woman. Her guilt as a murderer was mitigated only if she secretly shared Sextus's lust (*City of God* 1.19).

Augustine wrote at the time when attacks on the Roman Empire in the West endangered the personal security of many persons. In arguing that a properly chaste woman should not prefer death to forcible sexual violation, Augustine spoke to the situation of Christian women forced to live with the shame of such violation. But why did God permit chaste Christian women to be molested? Augustine asked women to consider the possibility that their arrogance about their chastity led God to punish them through violation of their bodily integrity, a punishment that nonetheless did not compromise their claims to chastity (*City of God* 1.28). Augustine contrasted conventional conceptions of *pudor* and the proper chastity of a Christian woman. Trout notes that, for Augustine, "Both the heroine's own Livian refusal to be an exemplum for truly unchaste women and her desire to preserve her reputation at any cost revealed the outlines of an ethical system driven by the deeply entrenched imperatives of honor and shame."[75] As I noted in my discussion of Seneca's Hecuba, in Roman habitus *captive pudor* was an oxymoron. Slaves were thus excluded from the ranks of the morally pure, an exclusion that in turn fed an obsession with women's maintenance of sexual purity, as the free woman was defined by her protected body as not a slave. Trout argues that Augustine's "radical retextualization of the story of Lucretia" challenged the traditional values of the Roman elite.[76]

Such a revaluation has significant implications for understanding the moral status of slaves, a significance perhaps subtly recognized by Augustine. He advocated that women, rather than rejoicing in their own sexual inviolability, should sympathize with the lot of the lowly, who were not themselves in a position to so rejoice. Why not? He does not explain, but presumably because women of lower status were not in a position to guard their own somatic integrity: "But what of those whose hearts when questioned answer that they have never been arrogant in their possession of virginity or widowhood or married chastity, but casting their lot with the lowly, rejoiced with trembling at God's gift, and never begrudged anyone equal excellence in sanctity and chastity?" (*City of God* 1.28). Augustine thus hinted that many Christian women denigrated the moral status of sexually exploited slaves. Slavery conditioned Christians so that they accepted the vulnerability of slave bodies as normal even as they equated feminine virtue with chastity, which on standard definitions remained outside a slave's control. Augustine implied that, when elite women were arrogant in their dealings with women of lower status who could not adhere to conventional standards of chastity, God permitted them to be subjected to the same sexual violations routinely endured by slaves. At the same time, in his promotion of a disembodied indifference to rape, Augustine effectively denied the reality of injury in coerced sexual activity.

Changing Habits

How firm was the grip of habitus on moral imagination and practice? Two examples, one from the second century and the other from the fourth.

In a widely circulated early second-century text known as *Apocalypse of Peter*, a seer learns from Christ the fates of the righteous and the wicked. Punishments of the wicked correspond to their transgressions.[77] Even after death, distinctions between free and slave are imagined to persist, habituating resurrected bodies. The seer sees "men and women who chew their tongue without rest while they are punished with eternal fire. These, then, [are] slaves who did not obey their masters. This, then, is their eternal punishment" (11:6–9).[78] The flesh of deceased slaves is spit out by whatever creatures consumed their corpses, their bodies are recomposed, and jaws reconfigured so that resurrected slaves can chew on their own tongues. R. J. Bauckham argues that this is an instance of the "principle that the part of the body which sinned should suffer"; the slaves "disobeyed verbally: they answered back."[79] Dennis Buchholz states, "The punishment implies that the slaves were sassy," and thus perpetuates the slaveholder perspective that insolence is a characteristic servile sin.[80] The good and faithful slave of antiquity was expected to be silent or speak deferentially, as the author of Titus, an epistle traditionally attributed to Paul, insisted: "Tell slaves to be submissive to their masters and to give satisfaction in every respect; they are not to talk back" (2:9). Punishment of slaves in *Apocalypse of Peter* witnesses to the deep hold of the habitus of slavery on Christian moral imagination.

In the fourth century, Lactantius declared that, although some Christians retained the status of slaves, there were ultimately no slaves among Christians: Christians knew one another as brother and sister and as fellow slaves (*Divine Institutes* 7.24.4; 5.15.2–5). Lactantius nonetheless insisted that the status distinction of free and slave should continue to inform everyday behavior. He supplied the example of Archytas. Discovering that his slave overseer had permitted a field to go to ruin, Lactantius reported, Archytas refrained from striking the slave. Archytas was not praiseworthy, Lactantius held. He believed that slaves required punishment to keep them from grosser failings. On the other hand, Lactantius elaborated, if Archytas had restrained himself from expressing his anger at a citizen or equal who offended him, he would merit praise (*Wrath of God* 18). The Christian Lactantius believed that slave bodies benefited from violence. Free bodies neither required nor benefited such punitive pedagogy.

Critics charge that Bourdieu focuses more on ways that bodies perform and perpetuate codes than the ways codes are transformed. Perhaps this criticism should be applied to this chapter. I focus more on ways that bodies participate in and communicate a moral system than on ways that system is transformed. I take this approach not out of deep-seated allegiance to Bourdieu, but because I find scant evidence that, by late antiquity, Christianity altered the everyday corporal dynamics of slaveholding. I conclude this chapter with a few examples from late antiquity where we have evidence, however obliquely gleaned, that some Christians used their bodies symbolically to outrage slavery as habitus and implicitly to challenge the practice of Christian slaveholding. In these few exceptional moments, ancient Christians evinced some awareness of the moral problems intrinsic to the institution of slavery, moments when they brought to consciousness moral discomfort with the habitus that shaped them. The efforts of these Christians were repudiated and suppressed by more powerful figures in the church.

It is important to my argument that these instances of resistance to slavery were embodied rather than written. A few Christians marginalized by the larger church acted out what it might mean for the last to be first and the first to be last, but their actions were condemned rather than debated for their theological merits. Did any Christians in antiquity leave a written record of antislavery sentiments? The closest we come is probably a beautiful homily by Gregory of Nyssa, who lived in the fourth century in Asia Minor. Although Gregory did not set forth a program of reform, he nonetheless anticipates some of the hermeneutical moves of nineteenth-century Christian abolitionists. Gregory's primary scriptural reference was the Genesis creation account, which figures the human person as the master of creation and the image of God (Gen. 1:26). Genesis says, "So God created humankind in his image; in the image of God he created them; male and female he created them." Genesis goes on to say that God gives humanity dominion over the fish of the sea, the birds of the sky, and every living thing that moves upon the earth. Taking his cue from Genesis, Gregory demanded to know what price could be paid for a slave who was himself, by dint of his humanity, lord of the sea and sky. He demanded to know how a scrap of paper could document the sale of a slave who was ultimately an icon of God. The brunt of Gregory's attack was slaveholder arrogance. He did not, however, call for abolition of slavery or even wholesale manumission of slaves, nor did he encourage resistance by slaves to the realities of slavery.[81]

It is noteworthy that Gregory, his brother Basil of Caesarea, and their sister Macrina were at one time in the orbit of Eustathius of Sebaste, whose followers

were condemned by a synod of bishops for their embodiment of Christian principles, including the repudiation of distinction between slave and free.[82]

Eustathius of Sebaste

Eustathius of Sebaste was an influential leader in the origins of monasticism in
Asia Minor in the fourth century.[83] His followers were condemned at the Council
of Gangra, a condemnation that damaged Eustathius's reputation. He nonetheless
remained an influential, albeit controversial, figure. Documents of the Council of
Gangra record but may also caricature the positions of Eustathius and his followers.[84] These partisans allegedly attacked marriage, gender hierarchy, and the
church's access to the offerings of the faithful, as well as the institution of slavery.
Because we do not have any documents written by these partisans, we cannot
assess how accurately their actions are represented, or what theological stances
informed their activism. The list of charges against them can be summarized by
saying that the partisans of Eustathius acted in ways that outraged the habitus of
their world regarding the most basic bodily routines of daily life, including routines related to food and clothing.

The letter composed by the synod of bishops convened at Gangra contends that
Eustathius's followers wear "strange clothes in subversion of the common kind of
clothing." Women disregard custom and "assume men's dress instead of women's
dress and think themselves thereby justified; moreover, on the pretext of piety,
many of them cut short that form of hair which is proper to women." These errant
Christians fast on Sundays, "despising the sanctity of the free days, whereas they
make light of the fasts ordained among the churches and eat on them." Some are
alleged to be vegetarians. This is not a complete catalog of accusations, but all
accusations pertain to behavior rather than theology. As Susanna Elm notes, "they
were accused because they took the Scriptures too literally; Eustathius taught nothing that does not have a firm basis in the New Testament" (*pace* Elm, except vege-
tarianism).[85] Indeed, the bishops' charge that the disciples of Eustathius "condemn
the rich who do not forsake all their possessions" might equally apply to Jesus.[86]

Apparently, those who were slaves among them left their masters, "withdrawing
from their masters and despising them, presuming on their strange dress."[87]

Canon III of the Council of Gangra stipulates that anyone who counsels a slave
to treat a slaveholder with contempt, to render fainthearted service to a slaveholder,
or to flee the slaveholder is to be cursed. The Council of Gangra connected this
challenge to slavery with a challenge to habitus: slaves adopted peculiar dress
rather than the mode of dress customary for slaves, and this violation of sumptuary
norms in turn provoked contempt for slaveholders, a contempt so profound that
some Christian slaves abandoned their owners. The incident illustrates the centrality

of habitus to the maintenance of the practice of slavery. The incident also hints that some Christians in late antiquity found the practice of slaveholding to be incompatible with the gospel. Apparently urging slaves to reject their subordination as slaves, they enacted this challenge, as they enacted their other challenges, by outraging habitus. The institutional church, however, reacted out of its deeply inculcated habitus and condemned these apparently vegetarian, protofeminist, antislavery Christians.

I have argued that social location is known in the body and that such deeply habituated corporal knowledge is rarely held up to conscious moral scrutiny. As Alcoff argues, we become aware of our corporal knowledge at moments when the smooth operation of that knowledge is disrupted. I am therefore fascinated that the Council of Gangra does not record the teachings of the partisans of Eustathius in words. Rather, the Council of Gangra alleges that these strange Christians disrupted the smooth operation of habitus, including the smooth operation of slaveholding habitus. Although the effort is speculative, we may be able to trace Eustathius's influence further through the words and reported deeds of the remarkable family that produced Gregory of Nyssa, Macrina, and Basil of Caesarea.

In his *Life of Macrina*, a reverent account of his sister's life, Gregory records Macrina's influence over her mother's decision to treat the household slaves as sisters. Whether and what kind of manumission is implied is unclear. Equally opaque to me is whether and how the day-to-day lives of the sister-servants changed. Nonetheless, Gregory implies that Macrina shares his own antipathy toward the arrogance of slaveholding. By the time Gregory wrote the *Life of Macrina* he had political, personal, and theological reasons not to mention Eustathius's name—that is, the cloud cast on Eustathius's reputation by the condemnation of his followers at Gangra. In her study of women's ascetic practices in late antiquity, Elm insists that Eustathius's influence remains evident in the life Macrina constructs for herself, including her treatment of (former) slaves as sister-equals.[88]

Basil's relationship to Eustathius's teachings on slavery is especially complex. In his youth Basil actively sought Eustathius's counsel and was known to be associated with him for many years. As Eustathius's political reputation clouded, Basil distanced himself from Eustathius. I argued earlier in this chapter that Basil demonstrated an inchoate sensitivity to the moral dilemma of sexually exploited slaves through his explicit recognition that they should not be penalized for their coerced sexual activity. I suggest that we tentatively locate this sensitivity in the context of the formative influence of Eustathius. I have also mentioned that, along with his awareness of the moral double bind of sexually exploited slaves, Basil supported the rights of slaveholders in his *Longer Rule*. This support was articulated in a climate of reaction against Eustathius. As Anna Silvas explicitly notes of Basil's elaborated rule, "New measures appear that are clearly related to the concerns of

Gangra: slaves are to be received only with the consent of their masters, otherwise they must be returned. The only exception is if their allegiance to God is at risk (*Longer Rule* 11)."[89] I propose that we have the hint of possible murmuring among a family of theologically sophisticated Christians—who at one time were in dialogue with Eustathius—about the wrongs of slaveholding and the cost of slavery to the enslaved. That shadowy evidence is accompanied in Basil's *Longer Rule* by a record of reaction against the real-world implications of such sentiment.

The partisans of Eustathius were not the only Christians in late antiquity to embody resistance to slaveholding norms. In North Africa, the Circumcellions were reported to outrage slaveholding habitus, but in their case, violently.

The Circumcellions

Like the partisans of Eustathius in Asia Minor, the roughly contemporaneous Circumcellions of North Africa acted in ways that outraged the habitus of slavery while practically freeing at least some slaves from their owners. The Circumcellions moved on the fringes of the Donatist Church, which conceived of itself as the true Catholic Church. Imperially aligned Catholics rejected that claim. We know of the Circumcellions only from the writings of Catholics determined to impugn their adversaries. Brent D. Shaw cautions that much of the evidence of the Circumcellions derives from sources outside North Africa with no claim to credible knowledge.[90] However, allegations that the so-called Circumcellions violated the habitus of slaveholding derive from North African sources, the Numidian bishop Optatus of Milevis and Augustine of Hippo.

The Circumcellions are said to have deliberately acted in violation of bodily norms, often violently. For example, Optatus reports that the Circumcellions forcibly "scraped" the heads of Catholic clergy. In his study of violence piously enacted by Christians in late antiquity, Michael Gaddis characterizes this "scraping" as simultaneously "public humiliation, purification, and degradation."[91] By calling attention to outrages against status-dictated bodily norms, accounts of the Circumcellions highlight the importance of habitus to the maintenance of the slave system. The Circumcellions, Optatus tells us, made the roads unsafe. "Even the safest journeys could not take place, because masters, thrown out of their vehicles, ran in servile fashion before their own retainers, who were sitting in their masters' place. By the verdict and bidding of those men the conditions of master and slave were transposed" (*Against the Donatists* 3.4). On Optatus's view, this is an outrage rather than a prophetic fulfillment of Jesus' words: the last shall be first, and the first shall be last.

Augustine's recollections of the Circumcellions are similar. "What master was there who was not compelled to live in dread of his own servant if he had put himself under the guardianship of the Donatists?" (*Ep.* 108.6.18).[92] With violence and threats of violence, the Circumcellions destroyed documents that detailed ownership of slaves, a practical measure. However, the Circumcellions also engaged in symbolic violence, ludic violence, violence with no apparent goal except the expression of outrage at the status quo, at the habitus. (If we had documents composed by the Christians known as Circumcellions, we might be able to reconstruct some coherent purpose behind their reported behavior.) What bothered Augustine was not violence per se, but violence directed at respectable bodies. Respectable bodies were habitually exempt from violation. Respectable bodies were regularly entitled—and even expected—to mete out violence against subordinate bodies. Augustine writes, "Certain heads of families of honorable parentage, and brought up with good education, were carried away half dead after their deeds of violence, or bound to the mill, and compelled by blows to turn it round after the fashion of the meanest beasts of burdens" (*Ep.* 184.4.15). Although a reputation for violence clings to the Circumcellions rather than their adversaries, they were violently suppressed by the more powerful, better organized, and better equipped forces of the imperially aligned church.

We do not know what motivated the Circumcellions. Their actions, however, hint that they found the practice of slaveholding to be incompatible with the gospel. They enacted a symbolic challenge to slavery by outraging habitus: by seating slaves and forcing masters to run like slaves after their own chariots, by hitching slaveholders to mills and whipping them so that they turned the mill. Were these actions unethical? Were these actions any more unethical than requiring slaves to run after their owners' chariots, requiring them to carry their mistresses' litters, or hitching slaves to mills?[93]

Conclusion

In "Mama's Baby, Papa's Maybe: An American Grammar Book," literary critic Hortense J. Spillers examines the legacy of slavery as incarnated in the lives of African American women. She writes memorably that through "*theft of body*" Atlantic slavetraders committed "high crimes against the *flesh*."[94] Although slav in antiquity were at times forced on long and harrowing journeys to market, th damned and damaging rite of New World slavery known as the Middle Passag was not part of ancient Mediterranean systems of slavery. I nonetheless believe that slaveholders in antiquity perpetrated innumerable crimes against the flesh. Slavery was known in the body. Freedom, too, was known in the body, but that bodily knowledge of freedom was learned in daily interaction with servile bodies.

As Alcoff observes, we typically become conscious of what our body knows at moments when such knowledge is disrupted. Neither the partisans of Eustathius nor the Circumcellions left written accounts of their own actions or motivations; we can only glimpse their outrage through the reciprocally outraged accounts of their ancient opponents. I would argue that the responses of those opponents reveal discomfort and even moral umbrage catalyzed by actions that disrupted the smooth operations of what bodies knew about maintaining the dynamics of the slave system. However, such knowledge did not precipitate self-critical epiphanies on the part of Christians who benefited from slavery. Rather, ecclesiastical authorities employed the forces at their disposal to restore the operations of the ordinary and thus to keep the routinized embodiment of slavery beneath the level of consciousness and outside the purview of moral reflection.

4

Mary in Childbirth

Besides, what is admirable beyond the power of thoughts or words to express, He is born of His Mother without any diminution of her maternal virginity, just as He afterwards went forth from the sepulcher while it was closed and sealed, and entered the room in which His disciples were assembled, the doors being shut; or, not to depart from every-day examples, just as the rays of the sun penetrate without breaking or injuring in the least the solid substance of glass, so after a like but more exalted manner did Jesus Christ come forth from His mother's womb without injury to her maternal virginity. . . . Such was the work of the Holy Ghost, who at the Conception and birth of the Son so favored the Virgin Mother as to impart to her fecundity while preserving inviolate her perpetual virginity.
—Catechism of the Council of Trent, 1.3.2

To be female in this place is to be a wound that cannot heal.
—Toni Morrison, *A Mercy*, 163

In the second and early third centuries, Christians read competing stories in the body of Mary in childbirth. Some Christians claimed that Mary experienced no pain and that the birthing process did not split open her body. They implied that her hymen remained intact and that she was surprised to find a newborn infant in the room with her. *Odes of Solomon* 19, a hymn replete with imagery of the maternal fecundity of God, evokes a painless birth. In *Ascension of Isaiah*, Mary gives birth so quickly that the appearance of the child startles her. The *Protevangelium of James*, a work obsessed with Mary's purity, supplies the vivid image of Salome's finger, singed as she probes Mary's postpartum vagina. Scholars sometimes stress what are seen as common points in an emergent Marian tradition.[1] As we will see, although these texts suggest that Mary's body is unperturbed by childbirth and that the condition of her body is theologically meaningful, the meanings they implicitly ascribe to her remarkably easy childbirth differ.[2] Tertullian too views the condition of Mary's body in childbirth as theologically meaningful. However, he denies that Mary retains her virginity *in partu*, that is, while she births her child. He emphasizes the filth in which Jesus wallowed during gestation and the splitting open of Mary's body in childbirth. Tertullian even reminds us, with distaste (or does the distaste belong to the reader?), of the afterbirth.

Jane Schaberg, Beverly Gaventa, and Mary Foskett have, in different ways, enriched our understandings of early traditions related to the virginal conception. I will not repeat their arguments here.[3] The extraordinary manner in which Mary is said to have conceived Jesus concerns me less than the character, alternately reported as extraordinary and as ordinary, of her pregnancy and childbirth. What stories are told by Mary's childbearing body? Is Mary's delivery of her child bloody? What about the afterbirth? Is Mary's body marked by the emergence of her child into the world? Are Mary's genitalia, her organs of generation, configured as pudenda, organs of shame? What does the newly born Madonna know in her body? In whatever ways Mary's body is understood to be like or unlike other women's bodies, these vivid accounts of her childbearing derive their force from broader cultural understandings of the stories told by women's bodies. I am primarily interested in the bodily narratives incorporated in ancient Christian texts. But those ancient tales resonate today. I thus consider some ways that ancient discourses on childbirth intersect with more recent discourses, themselves complex and at times self-contradictory.

Pamela Klassen argues in her study of contemporary American women who choose to birth their babies at home that no birth is completely natural.[4] Childbirth is a practice structured by habitus, as Marcel Mauss notes in his seminal essay on techniques of the body.[5] Following Mauss and Bourdieu, Klassen conceives of habitus as "the socially formed body that seems 'natural' and that allows persons to act within their culture without needing to think twice."[6] Taking a cue from Mauss and Klassen, I situate ancient stories and poetic images of Mary birthing Jesus in the context of ancient cultural practices and understandings. Sources for reconstructing those practices and understandings range from rabbinic writings to Greco-Roman medical treatises. While I continue to draw on approaches to corporeality derived from Bourdieu and Mauss, my theoretical focus broadens to include Maurice Merleau-Ponty's treatment of the human body as an expressive space, "our general medium for having a world."[7] In childbirth, a woman's body is a matrix, a medium. For both Tertullian and Merleau-Ponty, flesh is not only or ultimately an obstacle to knowledge and communication—with God, with other persons—but a space necessary for knowledge and even for communion. This chapter is a meditation on that insight.

Pictures from the Delivery Room

Mary does not suffer in becoming a mother, at least not in the visual heritage of Western Christianity since the Renaissance. An earlier artistic tradition that depicted a postpartum Madonna reclining near the manger was displaced in the fourteenth and fifteenth centuries by another convention of representing the nativity.[8] Since the Renaissance, Mary has been conventionally depicted kneeling beside the manger. She is not enervated by blood loss or exhausted from lack of sleep. She is not lying in bed, as her mother Anne is conventionally depicted in childbirth scenes. Nor is she seated on a birthing stool supplied by a midwife, nor is she propped on another woman's lap, a midwife squatting in front to receive the child.[9] The artistic tradition that supplies so few clues regarding Mary's posture in childbirth is richer in its representations of other events in her life. Aided by that tradition, I can envision other moments in Mary's transition to maternity: a slip of a girl defers to the power of the angel Gabriel; the round-bellied old woman Elizabeth embraces the round-bellied young woman Mary; a ripe Madonna opens her bodice so her plump babe may fix his sweet lips to her rosy flesh. Walking through museum galleries, I find it hard to believe that the luminous, angel-favored maiden menstruates; that the expectant mother is woken at night by an urge to urinate; that the milk of the new mother is delayed, or that when her son cuts teeth he bruises her tender flesh. (As I stand in front of a Flemish portrait of a healthy Madonna, perhaps I can believe that the smile playing across her face is coaxed by the pleasure of a mouth sucking a nipple.)

Artists do not paint the birth itself, just as they do not paint the resurrection itself. Those who have read the *Gospel of Peter* may visualize the moment of resurrection, the improbable moment when Christ, who seems, according to the *Gospel of Peter*, to have burgeoned to cosmic proportions while he gestated in the dank interior of the cave, is led from the tomb, his head disappearing above the skyline (10.39–40). Thankfully, perhaps, this apocryphal image did not enter the Western visual canon. The moment when Jesus bursts from his tomb is outside the conventional artistic repertoire.[10] For different reasons, although we can easily picture the bloody head of Jesus in a crown of thorns, we cannot so easily picture the bloody head of Jesus at the moment when he crowns. We can picture the mother's face lengthened in grief at her son's death, but we cannot so easily picture the mother's face contorted in pain as her body heaves to expel her son into the world. Much less can we steal a look between the mother's legs to see Mary's labia distend in a gory variant of Gustave Courbet's *L'Origine du Monde*. (Would the viewer stare in horror or gratitude?) The old masters of European painting inherited a theological tradition in which Mary, the new Eve, escaped labor pains. As a result they would have been unlikely to paint Mary straining and grunting to birth the Holy Child. But neither do we find paintings of a smiling Joseph lifting an unbloodied child from between the gently spread legs of a girl, the girl nakedly prepubescent, the child untraumatized by passage through the beatific birth canal. Jesus' birth, like his resurrection, eludes visual representation.

Not surprising, you may say. Childbirth is not a frequent subject of artistic representation. Prying apart the virgin's legs to inspect her perineum reeks of prurience. Is this necessarily the case? Artistic reticence about depicting Mary in childbirth does not extend to reticence about depicting Jesus' genitalia. As Leo Steinberg has shown, when Renaissance artists represented the infancy or death of Jesus, they accorded unusual attention to his genitalia. Steinberg writes that "one must recognize an *ostentatio genitalium* comparable to the *ostentatio vulnerum*, the showing forth of the wounds."[11] He argues that descriptive naturalism, often bandied about by art historians to account for works that portray the infant Jesus touching his penis or his grandmother Anne fondling the infantile male member, is an inadequate explanation for these depictions.[12]

Steinberg offers a theological interpretation of artists' fixation on the flesh dangling between the dimpled thighs of the Christ Child. He argues that, by drawing viewers' attention to the infant's genitalia, Renaissance artists stressed the humanity of Christ. Painters and sculptors thus expressed the incarnational theology ascendant in their day.[13] Given their fascination with anatomy and their commitment to humanism, why did Renaissance artists shy away from the subject of Jesus' birth? Perhaps because the tradition that Mary gave birth without labor pains, well-codified by the Renaissance, is potentially in tension with an understanding of Jesus as fully human and hence with the teaching of the incarnation. Alternatively, perhaps Renaissance artists were so taken with the easy and antiseptic birth of the undeniably male babe in the wildly influential visions of the fourteenth-century Birgitta of Sweden that representations of Mary lying abed seemed grossly carnal.[14] In Birgitta's vision, the virgin instructs the visionary, "I was in such a state and gave birth in such a manner as you have now seen: on bended knee, praying alone in the stable. For I gave birth to him with such great exultation and joy of soul that I felt no discomfort when he went out of my body, and no pain."[15] In any case, while Renaissance artists invite the viewer to peek at the Christ Child's naked member and draw the viewer's attention to the penis of the crucified Christ, which is, oddly, often uncircumcised, they keep his mother decently covered.[16]

Talking Bodies

However prurient and out of keeping with the later tradition of Christian visual arts, Christian authors writing in the second and early third centuries invited their readers to contemplate what happens "down there" when Mary gives birth.[17] The *Protevangelium of James* is our earliest source for a number of Marian pieties, including, for example, the name Anna or Anne for her mother. The *Protevangelium* features a scene that, like the scene of Jesus' emergence from his mother's womb or the scene of the resurrected Lord emerging from the tomb, failed to become part of the artistic canon. I am thinking of the scene in which Salome's finger is incinerated when she attempts to thrust it into the postpartum vagina of Mary.[18] Tertullian, in contrast, insists that Jesus' birth terminates Mary's claim to virginity, where virginity is construed to require physical intactness. Both Tertullian and the author of the *Protevangelium of James* are charged by modern commentators with bad taste.[19] In his history of the early church's estimations of Mary's virginity, for example, Hans von Campenhausen notes that Tertullian describes the medical details of the birth "with repellant plainness."[20] Walter Burghardt accuses Tertullian of a "pathological delight in assembling the less attractive details" of childbirth.[21] In a commentary on the *Protevangelium*, H. R. Smid judges that "the author shows an obscene interest in the physical constitution of Mary."[22] Scholars of Christian origins have thus shared the reticence of artists about Mary's physical condition in childbirth, a reticence that applies whether Mary is represented as hermetically sealed or as broken and dripping.

I introduced artistic conventions for representation of the virgin mother in part to highlight the peculiarity of early Christian voyeurism about Mary's body. Tertullian and the author of the *Protevangelium* differ on the question of whether Mary was physically altered in the act of giving birth, but they both find the question to be theologically significant. Today the question of whether, given a choice, Mary would have opted for epidural analgesia does not engender lively theological discussion. Contemporary theologians exhibit little interest in Mary's storytelling body. The parameters of such investigation, including the assumption that women's bodies bear stories as well as babies, nonetheless recur in contemporary discourse.

Eve Ensler's *Vagina Monologues*, for example, based on interviews with hundreds of women from diverse backgrounds, emerged as a performance phenomenon in the late 1990s. In order to raise awareness of violence against women and to raise funds for organizations that work against such violence, women on college campuses across the United States organized readings for Valentine's Day, rechristened V-Day. Ensler's script rests on the conceit, compelling to her audiences, that bodies communicate, or, more precisely, that female genitalia communicate. The script draws on her interviews with more than two hundred women. "If your vagina could talk, what would it say?" she asks.[23] Contemporary sensibilities eschew ascription of theological meaning to Mary's parturient body. Contemporary sensibilities nonetheless treat the bodies and body parts of contemporary women as expressive media. (Men's bodies and body parts are likewise treated in distinctive ways as expressive media in contemporary culture.)

Ensler's closing monologue narrates her reactions to the birth of her granddaughter, a birth she witnessed. The monologue focuses on the role of the vagina in moving a child into the world. Ensler characterizes the vagina as a pulsing heart.

In part the comparison between vagina and heart is physical. Both vagina and heart are red. Both vagina and heart are said to expand and contract, to stretch and bleed. Ensler additionally extends metaphoric attributes of the heart to the vagina. The vagina—like the heart—is said to ache, to forgive, and to sacrifice.[24] Ensler thus sentimentalizes the vagina as a subject. Edward Schillebeeckx, a Catholic theologian influential at the Second Vatican Council, meditates on Jesus' death: "As the most beautiful creation of his redemptive death, Mary is the person for whom Christ shed his redeeming blood most liberally and with the most fervent sacrificial love."[25] The tradition that Mary retained her virginity *in partu* denies her vagina the opportunity to bleed and stretch and sacrifice for her son. No wonder, for he is to bleed and stretch and sacrifice for her.

The story told through the generations is that women suffer labor pains because Eve ate the forbidden fruit. Because Eve obeyed the serpent, God punishes her: "I will greatly increase your pangs in childbearing/in pain you shall bring forth children" (Gen. 3:16). The Catechism of the Council of Trent elaborated the implications for Mariology: "To Eve it was said, 'In sorrow shalt thou bring forth children.' Mary was exempt from this law, for preserving her virginal integrity inviolate she brought forth Jesus the Son of God without experiencing, as we have already said, any sense of pain."[26] The view that Mary birthed Jesus without pain appears in the second century. The typology of Mary as the New Eve also appears, in various accounts, in the second century. Patristic texts that represent Mary as the antidote to Eve do not refer to labor pains, however, and patristic texts that state or imply that Mary gave birth without pain do not allude to the Genesis narrative. As I argue later in the chapter, in the second and early third centuries the story that the sinless Mary was exempt from the punitive pain visited on the sinful Eve was not yet written on Mary's storytelling body. In the earliest Marian traditions, the virgin mother may not know sin in her body. However, neither is she said to know sinlessness.

Theological representation of the birthing of Jesus as pain-free has become less prominent in recent decades, in part because of theological shifts associated with Vatican II and with the rise of feminist theology. Elizabeth Johnson's *Truly Our Sister: A Theology of Mary in the Communion of Saints*, a significant feminist contribution to Mariology, is informed by an apostolic letter by Paul VI, *Marialis Cultus*, which stresses that Mariological veneration should be guided by the biblical portrait of Mary and by ecumenism. Ecumenism reinforces the theological priority of the New Testament corpus, which does not probe Mary's body, rather than the tradition of the church, which does.[27] Johnson offers a critique of interpretations of the Catholic doctrine of the Immaculate Conception that have separated Mary from the vicissitudes of postlapsarian human life. Johnson rejects interpretations of Mary that imply, in Johnson's words, that Mary "had special privileges that enabled her to negotiate the troubles of life effortlessly in a world whose historical struggle was not her own."[28] Mary knew sexual desire, Johnson insists. Did she experience labor pains? Johnson does not refer explicitly to the tradition that Mary's delivery of Jesus was free from pain. She neither rejects the tradition nor attempts a feminist interpretation of it. Genesis 3:16, God's pronouncement that Eve would bring forth children in pain, is not among the scriptural texts she engages. Johnson does not ask what Mary's childbearing body knows.

The Birthing Body in Pain

The reception history of Genesis 3:16 suggests that, through women's physical suffering in childbearing, pain plays a condign role in a divine juridical economy. Along with changing theological trends, the changing habitus of childbirth in industrialized nations has reduced the impact of this tradition.[29] Women today have the option of minimizing pain in labor and delivery, not because they are sin-free or because of the grace of God, but because of advances in anesthesiology. The understanding that pain in childbirth serves as evidence for God's judgment on human sinfulness becomes too convoluted for many to sustain. The Jesuit Karl Rahner, another theologian strongly associated with Vatican II, makes this point explicitly. He assures the reader that seeking pharmacological relief for labor pangs is "morally lawful."[30] Yet even today, some women enunciate perspectives on labor pain that echo older views. A friend, a physician assistant in New York City, reports encounters with women whose teenage daughters conceive outside of marriage. When it comes time for delivery, the soon-to-be grandmothers try to prevent the soon-to-be mothers from receiving pain relief. "She has to learn her lesson," they say. Under these circumstances, labor pain continues to be interpreted as both pedagogic and punitive.[31]

During the nineteenth century, pain slowly came to be conceptualized primarily as a purely physical problem that called for medical amelioration. The use of anesthesia in both surgery and childbirth excited considerable debate over the course of the century. Some who opposed anesthesia in childbirth argued that bearing pain ennobled a woman. Others based their opposition on, variously, the dangers and the intoxicating properties of ether. Others believed that women who knew in their bodies the sinfulness of Eve should also know the penalty Eve paid.

For some, the right of the patient to consciousness during both surgery and childbirth was an ethical consideration. Moved by the voices of their patients, physicians who advocated anesthesia likewise saw their position as ethical. Ariel Glucklich argues that nineteenth-century debates over the ethics of anesthesia require us to revisit Elaine Scarry's widely influential views on pain. For Scarry, pain is typified by the pain of torture. She argues that pain strips the sufferer of his or her voice. However, nineteenth-century opponents of anesthesia in surgery and childbirth insisted that the patient in pain retained his or her voice and that anesthesia rather than pain stole the voice. Advocates of anesthesia agreed. Glucklich writes, "Numerous physicians discussed their feelings of empathy for the squirming and crying patient who suffered excruciating pain under the knife and proclaimed it a higher ethical stance to eliminate pain than to allow the patient to have his (screaming) voice."[32]

While early controversies over surgical anesthesia have been resolved in favor of painless surgery, controversies over pain relief in childbirth continue to crop up. Guidelines on clinical management of obstetric anesthesia developed by the American College of Obstetricians and Gynecologists (ACOG) note, "There is no other circumstance in which it is considered acceptable for a person to experience pain, amenable to safe intervention, while under a physician's care." With a nod to the parturient's wishes, the guidelines presume the advisability of anesthesia during childbirth: "Pain management should be provided whenever it is medically indicated."[33] For ACOG, pain during delivery does not tell a story. Pain, which is a medical problem to be solved, is neither communicative nor expressive.

But this view is not universally held. A view held by more midwives than allopathic practitioners posits labor pain as having positive value for the birthing mother. Midwives typically balance concern about the potential risks anesthesia poses to both infant and mother with respect for a woman's desire for pain control measures. Many midwives also understand pain to convey important information to the laboring woman about the progress of parturition. Some midwives also speak of spiritual benefits of pain. Among the perceived benefits of what many midwives call the "good pain" of labor, midwife Nicky Leap enumerates, "Pain marks the occasion. . . . Pain develops altruistic behaviour in babies; Pain heightens joy; Pain as transition to motherhood; The triumph of going through pain."[34] Glucklich summarizes the position advocated by these midwives. Childbirth pain "strengthens, so they assert, the woman's sense of identity, her ability to situate herself within nature and her social and spiritual world."[35] The women who participated in Pamela Klassen's study of women agree with these midwives. Klassen writes, "Their insistence that physical pain in childbirth need not always be interpreted as suffering that requires obliteration through drugs is grounded in an embodied conviction that pain can also generate propitious forms of power, and in some cases, community."[36] According to Klassen, women who give birth at home claim that they know joy, power, and connection through their bodies.

Even some who seek humane and woman-centered approaches to pain relief ultimately perceive endurance of pain as beneficial. Elisabeth Bing influenced several generations of childbearing American women through her advocacy of the Lamaze method, which emphasizes relaxation through breathing. In a 2000 interview, Bing looked back on changes in obstetrics over the course of her life-time. When Bing began working, the use of scopolamine, twilight sleep, was common on delivery floors. In part because of Bing's work, women today are more likely than their mothers to remember their childbirth experiences. A challenge today, Bing says, is the widespread use of epidurals to minimize childbirth pain. Bing muses, "As one of the doctors said to me, 'Elisabeth, all of our patients are smiling now.' This has brought me personally to ask the questions, 'Who am I to say that they shouldn't have that crutch? Why should they have to work so hard?' I was looking for some very good reasons why somebody should not accept help that is comparatively safe." Bing concludes that the underlying problem is the pathologization of a normal and healthy process. "There is nothing accepted anymore by the medical profession that childbirth is part of a woman's life, of her inner experience, or of her development. Even with regard to the pain—there is no satisfaction achieved because the woman does not have to work for anything. We've minimized the sense of achievement one obtains when mastering a difficult experience."[37] Bing thus implies that the corporal knowledge a woman gains through the pedagogy of painful childbirth is knowledge that should be valued.

In his treatment of Mary's virginity, Karl Rahner considers not only whether to uphold the traditional Mariological doctrine of virginity *in partu* but also, more profoundly, what it might mean to speak of virginity *in partu*. Holding physicality to be essential to personhood, he cannot treat as theologically irrelevant physical questions related to Mary's birthing of her child. However, he invites reconsideration of basic elements of the doctrine of virginity *in partu*, including reconsideration of the meanings most frequently associated with pain in childbirth. His remarks anticipate the arguments of Glucklich and Klassen in suggesting that pain, especially the pain of childbirth, may be constructive as well as destructive (as, all agree, it frequently is). Perhaps one might argue, Rahner notes, that pain as "an element of a beneficient process can only be felt as painful by a human being who is subject to concupiscence [i.e., not Mary], because only such a one [i.e., the rest of us] will feel the apt experience as contradictory to his basic attitude, and hence painfully and strangely unintegrated."[38] Even so, he suggests, whoever would like to argue that Mary bore her child without pain should consider certain questions:

> But he still must ask himself does he know so exactly what pain is, and when and in what measure pain is really an expression of sin and not that of a healthy nature and an exuberance of life. Does he know well enough how pain is constituted, with its purely physiological components *and* its basic spiritual attitude, so that he can be asked how he understands painlessness, in view of the complexity of the concept of pain? Has the physiological element been changed, or the personal interpretation, which is an *intrinsic* element of the pain which is experienced? He must ask himself whether for instance a pain which serves life can, from the anthropological and theological point of view, be simply ranked with pain caused by hostile attack and moral misdeeds.[39]

Strange as it may seem to speak of the "basic spiritual attitude" of pain, many women who participated in Klassen's survey voice similar sentiments.

Invoking something akin to Rahner's "pain which serves life," Glucklich and Klassen independently argue against Scarry's view of pain as a necessarily isolating experience. For Scarry, pain disrupts communication and severs the person in pain from her or his community. Glucklich challenges Scarry's reliance on torture as a paradigm for understanding other experiences of pain. (He also notes that the techniques of the torturer are not confined to the infliction of pain.) He argues, "Religious pain produces states of consciousness, and cognitive-emotional changes, that affect the identity of the individual subject and her sense of belonging to a larger community or to a more fundamental state of being. . . . [P]ain strengthens the religious person's bond with God and other persons."[40] I will return to Glucklich's analysis of religious pain in my discussion of the *Ascension of Isaiah*.

Glucklich acknowledges that pain can isolate a person. However, he holds, religious persons who interpret their own pain as positively meaningful often find that pain enhances rather than diminishes their ability to empathize. In her study of women who choose to give birth at home without anesthesia, Klassen reaches similar conclusions. She acknowledges that, for some women who choose to deliver their babies in congenial home settings, surrounded by family, friends, and even the family dog, pain can be, as Scarry characterizes it, isolating. Nonetheless, Klassen observes that for most home-birthing women, "the pain or pleasure of childbirth did not feel like a solitary experience. Instead, the bodily rigors of childbirth open them up to connection, be it with children, friends, midwives, spiritual powers, or husbands."[41]

"In pain you shall bring forth children," God tells Eve in Genesis (3:16). As important as this teaching has been, both for theologians and for childbearing women, Glucklich and Klassen demonstrate that other meanings may attend pain in childbirth, a conclusion whose relevance for Mariology Rahner anticipated. Women's experiences in childbearing are framed by multiple discourses and practices. Medical discourse and practice treat pain as a problem to be solved. Midwifery treats labor pain as pedagogic and at times even transcendent. Moreover, Ensler is not alone in a romantic, sentimental treatment of women's childbearing bodies as subjects. Finally, the discourse of childbirth pain as condign punishment still scars many women. As I will argue regarding Tertullian's conflicted views on childbearing, people often participate in contradictory discourses without conscious appreciation of contradictions among those discourses. These competing discourses and associated practices affect the ways that childbearing bodies are socially read. Moreover, these discourses and associated practices affect the ways women experience their bodies in childbirth: what they know in their bodies.

Klassen writes, "Birth sticks with a woman, remaining in her bones and flesh as an embodied memory long after the body has left her womb."[42] In what ways did

Christian theologians understand the birth of Jesus to stick with Mary? What knowledge did theologians imagine to linger in Mary's bones and flesh after Jesus, either peacefully or in a bloody show, left her womb?

The New Eve

What do we know about Eve's body? We know that her creation reconfigured Adam's body, but that tells us more about Adam's body than about Eve's body. We know that, denied access to the fruit of the tree of life, her body was mortal and thus corruptible. We also know that Eve's childbearing, occurring after she listened to the serpent, was painful. The pain was punitive. Through that pain Eve knew God's displeasure in her body. Heritable, Eve's pain in childbearing was transmitted through many generations—until, despite continuing attempts by humanity to provoke God's displeasure, introduction of anesthesia eased women's pain in childbearing, a medical remedy for the ill effects of human sinfulness.[43] The question of whether Mary experienced pain in childbearing emerges by the second century. It is routinely assumed that even the earliest references to a painless nativity should be read in the context of Eve's sentence to labor pains. The purpose of this section is to challenge that assumption. The question of whether Mary experiences pain in delivering Jesus is not even the most prominent physical detail of the nativity for early Christian writers. They are more concerned with whether her genitalia remain intact and whether the delivery is messy than they are with whether she suffers labor pains.

The idea of a painless birth appears in several ancient Jewish writings.[44] These sources do not link painful birth with Eve's sinfulness, at least not in an explicit or straightforward manner. The source that comes closest to doing so is 2 Baruch. Perhaps composed in the late first century, 2 Baruch looks forward to the restorations of the messianic age. 2 Baruch images the messianic age as an epoch without warfare or strife, an epoch in which wild beasts will nurture human beings. In that context, 2 Baruch promises, "And women shall no longer then have pain when they bear/Nor shall they suffer torment when they yield the fruit of the womb" (73:7). While the passage does not associate painless childbirth with the redemption of sin, it does associate painless childbirth with restoration of a primordial paradise, a return to an Edenic state.

In the *Jewish Antiquities* Josephus suggests that Moses's mother delivered him without pain. The painless delivery is said to be a confirmation of God's promises to the prayers of Moses's father (2.218). Josephus does not single out Moses's mother as unusually righteous, much less sinless.[45] Rather, the father's prayer is prompted by his fear that, if his pregnant wife bears a son, the son will share the fate of other Israelite male babies and be killed. God's response to the prayer is the easy delivery of the child. Because Moses's mother does not cry out in pain, she does not attract attention to the birth; the couple is able to hide their son for several months. These brief passages from 2 Baruch and Josephus establish that in the early decades of the Christian movement references to painless childbirth circulate among Jews, yet those references are open to multiple interpretations. They do not point in any obvious way to Eve, the first woman to sin and the first woman said to know in her body the painful penalty for sin.

The only passage from the Hebrew scriptures to announce a painless birth emphasizes rapid delivery of progeny. A prophecy of Isaiah reads, "Before she was in labor she gave birth/before her pain came upon her she delivered a son/Who has heard of such a thing?" (66:7–8a). Isaiah does not speak to the guilt or innocence of a human mother, nor does he refer to sin or its redemption, nor does he evoke return to Eden. Rather, his emphasis in this passage is on rapid restoration and vindication of the people of Israel. Although he alludes to a painless birth, his emphasis is not the painlessness of the delivery so much as its speed. "Shall a land be born in one day?/Shall a nation be delivered in one moment?/Yet as soon as Zion was in labor she delivered her children" (66:8b). Promising that troubles will not long endure, Isaiah buoys Israel.

The text was familiar to Christians who evoked the image of Mary delivering her child without pain. Irenaeus writes, "Concerning His birth, the same prophet says in another place, 'Before she who was in labour brought forth, and before the pains of labour came, there came forth delivered a man child,' he proclaimed His unlooked-for and extraordinary birth of the Virgin."[46] Irenaeus includes the quotation in the midst of a series of other citations from Isaiah, all of which, on Irenaeus's view, establish Jesus as the fulfillment of prophecy. Although Irenaeus elsewhere argues that Mary looses the knot first tied by Eve, he does not connect the Eve-Mary typology to painless birth. Rather, his purpose in suggesting that Mary delivers Jesus without pain is to suggest that the nativity fulfilled Isaiah's prophecy of a fast, easy delivery. Irenaeus emphasizes the unexpectedness of the birth of a child to a virgin. In accordance with prophecy, that unexpectedness was intensified by the speed of the delivery.

The *Odes of Solomon* and *Ascension of Isaiah* are likely the first works to suggest that Mary birthed Jesus without pain. Dating these works is difficult. Most often dated to the second century, they are sometimes dated as early as the late first century or as late as the third century. Scholars with a primary academic association with biblical studies stress the closeness of the *Odes of Solomon* to hymns from Qumran and to Johannine literature. On this basis they tend to date the *Odes of Solomon* to the early second century, although some entertain earlier dates.[47] However, Hans J. W. Drijvers argues that the *Odes* incorporate both philosophical terminology and anti-Marcionite elements that militate against such early composition. On this basis he dates the *Odes* to the third century.[48] Like the *Odes of Solomon*, the *Ascension of Isaiah* is usually dated to the early second century, with some scholars entertaining dates in the late first century.[49] The narrative of the birth of Jesus in *Ascension of Isaiah* 11 appears only in an Ethiopic recension. If the *Ascension* is a composite document, the nativity traditions could be a later addition.[50] However, Jonathan Knight argues for the literary integrity of the *Ascension*. He insists that the Marian material belongs with the rest of the composition. He notes that chapters 3 and 11 share significant imagery of an ascending and descending revealer.[51] As we will see, the nativity scene in the *Ascension of Isaiah* is compatible with a docetic Christology. Knight finds deletion of (apparently) docetic material more plausible than addition of such material.[52] *Ascension of Isaiah* 11 and the *Protevangelium of James* share several peculiar narrative details, including a description of Mary as virginally intact postpartum (although the two works represent that intactness differently). Because of these shared elements, George Zervos posits a first-century nativity source used by extant second-century sources.[53] Although the dating of the *Odes of Solomon* and *Ascension of Isaiah* is not crucial for my argument, I follow the majority of scholars who agree that versions of the relevant texts are in circulation in the first half of the second century.

Virgin Ears

Dating the first extant and explicit comparison between Eve and Mary is simpler than dating the first extant and explicit suggestion that Mary delivered Jesus without pain.[54] Justin wrote his *Dialogue with Trypho*, generally taken to be the first articulation of the Eve-Mary typology, in the mid-second century.[55] According to Justin, the virgin Eve birthed disobedience and death because she listened to the serpent. The virgin Mary birthed faith and joy because of the message Gabriel delivered (*Dialogue with Trypho*, 100). Justin was the first but hardly the last theologian to be captivated by Eve's ear, an alluring orifice of seduction. How did Eve come to know sin in her body? The devil spoke to her. Or perhaps sang: The tradition of *conception per aurem* reached an irresistible apogee with an image conjured in the fifth century by Proclus of Constantinople. He envisioned Eve, still in paradise, swaying to the devil's melodies.[56] Ancient theologians saw Mary's ear, too, as an orifice of seduction. In Justin, as I have noted, we first encounter an inchoate version of this comparison.

Irenaeus develops the Eve-Mary parallel along the lines initiated by Justin. He writes, "Just as, once something has been bound, it cannot be loosed except by undoing the knot in reverse order, even so the first knots were untied by the [undoing of the] second ones, and, inversely, these last free the first." So, he concludes, "the knot of Eve's disobedience was untied by Mary's obedience. What Eve bound by her unbelief, Mary loosed by her faith" (*Against Heresies* 3.22). Like Justin, Irenaeus presents the stories of Eve and Mary as parallel tales of aural seduction. "Eve was seduced by the word of the angel and transgressed God's word, so that she fled from him. In the same way, [Mary] was evangelized by the word of an angel and obeyed God's word, so that she carried him" (*Against Heresies* 5.19).[57] Justin and Irenaeus are more interested in what grows in Mary's ear, an ectopic conception, than in what grows in her belly. In the second century, the Eve-Mary analogy thus develops independently of traditions related to Mary's puerperal experience.

Like Justin and Irenaeus, Tertullian is taken with virgin ears. He further develops the conceit of verbal insemination. A deadly word insinuated itself into Eve, he writes, and a life-giving word entered Mary. In dialogue with an implied interlocutor, he continues, " 'But Eve, on that occasion, conceived nothing in her womb by the devil's word.' Yes, she did. For the devil's word was to her a seed, so that thenceforth she should be abject and obedient, and should bring forth in sorrows" (*Carn. Chr.* 17). Tertullian thereby invokes Genesis 3:16, with its reference to Eve's cursed childbearing. The comparison does not lead him to the conclusion that Mary escaped labor pains. Instead, he continues the passage by comparing Eve's fratricidal progeny with Mary's fratrisalvific progeny. Indeed, for Tertullian, the image of Mary as the new Eve is consistent with a bloody, painful childbirth. As we will see, in reading Mary's parturient body Tertullian accords greater attention to the splitting open of her genitalia and to what he sees as the filth of gestation than he accords to the pain she experiences in childbirth. Nonetheless, he does not deny that Mary experienced pain in bringing forth her son. Indeed, he criticizes Marcion for holding such a view (*Marc.* 4.21).

The Syriac poet and theologian Ephrem composed in the fourth century. His poetry is thus too late to help us piece together the earliest traditions about Mary in childbirth. I nonetheless draw attention to some passages from Ephrem's hymns because they confirm that acknowledgment of the pangs Mary must have suffered in childbirth is consistent both with an emphasis on mystical dimensions of Mary's pregnancy and with further elaboration of the Eve-Mary parallel. As I argue later in this chapter, Tertullian stands out for his vehement insistence on the messiness of Mary's birthing of her son. In this he contrasts with Ephrem. Tertullian refers to Jesus' "ten months torment" in the womb (*Marc.* 4.21). Ephrem offers a different view of Jesus' dwelling in Mary's womb:

> While His body in the womb was being formed,
> His power was constructing all the members.

> While the fetus of the Son was being formed in the womb,
> He himself was forming babies in the womb.
> Ineffectual as was His body in the womb,
> His power in the womb was not correspondingly ineffectual.[58]

Ephrem shares Tertullian's fascination with the seductive and seducible ears of virgins. Ephrem writes:

> Just as from the small womb of Eve's ear
> Death entered in and was poured out,
> so through a new ear, that was Mary's,
> Life entered and was poured out.[59]

Mary's aural conception healed the long human earache precipitated by Eve's otologic vulnerability.

Perhaps surprisingly, Ephrem, like Tertullian, acknowledges that Mary suffered labor pains in birthing Jesus:

> The First-born entered the womb, but the pure one perceived not.
> He arose and emerged with birthpangs, and the fair one felt Him.
> Glorious and hidden His entry; despised and visible His emergence,
> since He is God at His entry, but human at His emergence.[60]

Burghardt claims that, among the Eastern fathers, Ephrem is "incomparably sensitive to the implications of the Eve-Mary analogy."[61] However, those implications do not require Ephrem to deny that Mary felt birth pangs as she felt her son descend into the world he had created.[62]

The Eve-Mary analogy and the tradition that Mary gave birth without experiencing pain emerge and circulate independently. Conceding that the church fathers did not explicitly link the tradition of Mary's painless birth to deliverance from the punishment imposed on sinful Eve, Rahner nonetheless supposes that such a link permeates patristic thought. He writes, "It is therefore safe to consider that the background of their theological propositions was their understanding of Gen 3.16, even though it is not cited expressly."[63] This assumption, against which I have argued, has prevailed among generations of scholars, priests, and, painfully, parturient women. Once adduced, the traditions are mutually reinforcing, but reliance on the Eve-Mary analogy is not evident in second- and third-century references to a painless nativity. Early references to the Eve-Mary parallel are distinctively epistemological. A diabolical word enters Eve and she knows sin. The Word enters Mary and she knows redemption. When we presume easy recourse to the Eve-Mary parallel to explain the earliest references to Mary's painless birth, and to explain them away, we are deaf to other stories Mary's body tells. We foreclose other possible interpretations of what the virgin mother knows in her body.

Odes of Solomon 19

The rumor that Mary gives birth without pain surfaces in *Odes of Solomon* 19, a hymn that evokes rather than narrates the virgin birth. The hymn relies on dissonant gender imagery. The Father's breasts are milked. Mary gives birth like a man. The dissonance of the gender imagery invites the reader or singer of the hymn to transcend narrative or linear logic. This is not a poem that grounds its claims on historical warrant. We should therefore ask whether the poet expects the reader to apprehend as historical fact its image of the mother birthing her son without the aid of a midwife. What sense does the painless birth make in the imagistic world created by the odist? Susan Ashbrook Harvey writes, "*Odes of Solomon* 19, depending on how it is dated, is not only one of our earliest references to the virgin birth, but specifically one of the earliest to highlight the significance of painlessness in Mary's birth of Jesus (the undoing of Eve's punishment from Gen. 3:16)."[64] I disagree. The *Odes of Solomon* is a sequence of hymns where ignorance rather than sin requires defeat. On my reading, then, the evocation of Mary's pain-free and purposeful childbearing does not resonate with the punitive pain that Eve condignly experiences in childbearing. Recourse to Eve's punishment as an explanation for the significance of painlessness in Mary's birthing of Jesus deters more careful diagnosis, a second opinion, of the stories Mary's body tells.

In J. H. Charlesworth's translation, *Odes of Solomon* 19 reads:

[1]A cup of milk was offered to me, and I drank it in the sweetness of the Lord's kindness.
[2]The Son is the cup, and the Father is He who was milked; and the Holy Spirit is She who milked him;
[3]Because His breasts were full, and it was undesirable that His milk should be ineffectually released [=without purpose or cause]
[4]The Holy Spirit opened Her bosom, and mixed the milk of the two breasts of the Father.
[5]Then She gave the mixture to the generation without their knowing, and those who have received it are in the perfection of the right hand.
[6]The womb of the Virgin took it, and she received conception and gave birth.
[7]So the Virgin became a mother with great mercies.
[8]And she labored and bore the Son but without pain, because it did not occur without purpose [or cause].
[9]And she did not require a midwife, because He caused her to give life.
[10]She brought forth like a strong man with desire [or: will], and she bore according to the manifestation, and she acquired according to the Great Power.
[11]And she loved with redemption, and guarded with kindness, and declared with grandeur. Hallelujah.

Sin is not mentioned in the *Odes of Solomon*.[65] Rather, the *Odes* suggest that humanity is chained by the darkness of ignorance. Humanity does not require forgiveness of sin. Instead, humanity requires enlightenment. As a result, in the *Odes* Jesus' death is a moment of enlightenment rather than a payment for sin. Jesus spreads out his arm on the cross and dies, but death does not contain him. The I-figure who speaks in *Odes of Solomon*—presumably Jesus—declares, "I did not perish although they thought it of me" (42:10b). Does this escape from mortality divide the crucified one and humanity? No. Escape from mortality unites the crucified one with his followers, who also defy death (42:11–12, 14a).

Just as the Savior's immunity to death distinguishes him from his enemies, so does his birth. In *Odes of Solomon* 28, the I-figure announces:

> [17]And I did not perish, because I was not their brother, nor was my birth like theirs.
> [18]And they sought my death but did not find it possible, because I was older than their memory; and in vain did they cast lots against me.
> [19]And those who were after me sought in vain to destroy the memorial of Him who was before them.

Thus in *Odes of Solomon* 28—as in *Odes* 19—the birth of the Savior is notable. However, in *Odes* 28 the notable quality of that birth is not signified through puerperal experience. Rather, what distinguishes the birth is that the I-figure claims a form of preexistence, a preexistence that ultimately entails his ability to evade death and to bring his followers with him.[66]

Thus within the *Odes of Solomon* the Savior is both preexistent and the generated product of the divine Father's lactating breasts.[67] Harvey notes that in the *Odes* the Father is not the only masculine figure whose bosom brims with sweet milk. In *Odes of Solomon* 8, the I-figure, the Savior, declares, "I fashioned their members, and my own breasts I prepared for them, that they might drink my holy milk and live by it" (12). Moreover, feminine characterizations of divine activity are apposite not only for the Father but also for the Spirit. Dwelling in the Spirit is described as life in the womb, for example, and the Spirit is said to birth believers, imagery that plays on the feminine gender of the word "spirit" in Syriac.[68]

As Harvey has shown, *Odes of Solomon* 19 stretches the limits of gender imaginary. She writes, "[I]n Ode 19, gender is played with for all participants in the salvation drama, both human and divine. Roles are reversed, inverted: no one is simply who they seem to be. More accurately, everyone is *more* than they seem to be—Mary is more than a woman in what she does; the Father and the Spirit are more than one gender can convey in the effort to glimpse their works."[69] Mary is more than a woman in that she gives birth "like a man." What it means for Mary to give birth "like a man" requires explication.[70] In *Odes of Solomon* 19, the virgin birth is said to be painless, thus eliminating need for a midwife; purposeful, not without cause or purpose; and the result of will—left ambiguous is whether the willfulness belongs to Mary or to God. I argue that Mary is like a man in her willful ability to endure a painful situation in order to achieve an end or purpose.

My argument builds on the work of Cornelia Horn, who understands the masculinity of the virgin in *Odes of Solomon* 19 in relation to the text's construction of the virgin as active. Noting that *Odes* 19 associates the virgin with active (rather than passive) verbs, Horn comments that "the virgin, or more precisely the womb of the virgin, is the active party."[71] Horn argues that *Odes* 19 provides an explicit rationale for the painlessness of the birth in its specification that the birth was not without purpose. As Horn translates, "because she was not [acting] in vain."[72]

In "Taking It Like a Man: Masculinity in 4 Maccabees," Stephen Moore and Janice Anderson argue that in 4 Maccabees, as in other texts of the era, the hallmark of masculinity is mastery: mastery of others, mastery of self. In the course of their persuasive argument, Moore and Anderson amply demonstrate that mastery of the self is perhaps most spectacularly evident in mastery over physical pain. True, the mother in 4 Maccabees performs her exemplary masculinity through triumph over the psychological torture of watching her sons' brutal deaths, but her sons in turn demonstrate their exemplary masculinity through triumph over physical pain.

This code of masculinity was widespread in the ancient Mediterrean world. I could multiply examples, but here I simply focus on the exemplum of the Roman matron Arria, whose denial of pain strengthened her husband Caecina Paetus. For his part in sedition Paetus was sentenced by Claudius to end his own life by the dagger, but he lacked the courage or manliness to act. Arria took the sword from Paetus's hands, thrust it deep into her own breast, and then removed it. As she returned the sword to Paetus, she spoke her dying words to assure him, "It does not hurt, Paetus."[73] As in *Odes of Solomon* 19, painlessness and purposefulness are linked. Arria shows her husband what it means to be a man, through an act of will. *Odes* 19 tells us that Mary's childbearing was without pain. *Odes* 19 also tells us how to interpret that painlessness. Like a man with a will toward self-mastery, Mary gives birth without acknowledging pain. Like the matron Arria, the virgin of Ode 19 might say, "It does not hurt."[74]

Warning against static interpretations of later Syriac literature, Sebastian Brock warns of a "tendency, frequently to be observed in the history of religions, to take as literal truth what was originally intended to be the language of symbol, poetry, metaphor, *midrash*, myth (in the good sense of the word), or whatever one may like to call it."[75] *Odes of Solomon* 19 does not offer a full-fledged account of the nativity but an imagistic interpretation of the significance of that birth. The painlessness of the birth makes sense within an ancient worldview where endurance of pain correlates not with immunity to sin but with valorous masculinity. The hymn plays against gender binarism to meditate on a birth that confounds other binaries: the binary of divine and human, for example, and the binary of life and death. In *Odes of Solomon* 19, the virgin's corporal knowledge is not limited by the usual episte-mological categories. The reader of the hymn is invited to participate in the virgin's surprising knowledge of divinity.

Ascension of Isaiah

Pamela Klassen describes birth as "a passage that brings into being two new iden-tities: a baby and a mother."[76] Let us push this claim further. Birth is a passage that introduces two new bodies into the world, the body of the baby and the body of the mother. As the mother pushes out the afterbirth, the gravid body ceases to exist. The woman has a new body, a postpartum body. Some changes are transitional. A sagging midsection tightens when pounds are dropped. Engorged with milk, the mother's breasts are fuller and rounder than they had been before gestation, fuller and rounder than they will be when she weans her last child. By six weeks the uterus fully involutes. Some of the changes mark the mother's body indelibly, though the changes are not always readily apparent. If the woman has birthed her child vaginally, the vagina becomes lax and the cervical os elongates from a round dot to a longitudinal slit. Some changes, such as urine leaking down a thigh or drooping breasts, are unwelcome. Some changes, their inscriptions invaginated, remain occult for years, sometimes forever. All pregnancies scar the uterus.

The visible changes of pregnancy communicate something about a new moth-er's identity to the world around her. Moreover, through what her body has learned a woman differently engages the world. Arguing that epistemic capacity depends on the body, Merleau-Ponty names the body as "that knowledge-acquiring appara-tus."[77] That knowledge-acquiring apparatus, the newly born mother's body, carries her existence, her new identity. A body's knowledge is hard-won, often acquired through traumata. Writing in a postpartum persona, Julia Kristeva identifies child-birth as a corporal loss that is simultaneously corporal gain. Meditating on how a woman's body is changed when her offspring makes the transition from womb to wider world, Kristeva muses about her "removed marrow, which nevertheless acts as a graft, which wounds but increases me."[78] How to interpret the insignia of childbirth varies from one society to another and even from one moment of a wom-an's life to another. Nonetheless women who bring children into the world rou-tinely describe themselves as changed, not only by the presence of offspring in the world, but also by the physical experience of pregnancy and labor. As we turn to the *Ascension of Isaiah*, a text that limns Mary's body as unchanged by childbear-ing, one question to consider is what it might mean for a body to erase its own markings, for a body to escape suffering, not necessarily suffering in the sense of enduring pain, but suffering in the sense of experiencing.

According to the *Ascension of Isaiah*, after a pregnancy of at least two months Mary gives birth to a child so quickly that she is astonished to find herself in a room with him. The nativity is narrated in the context of a vision of the prophet-seer Isaiah. Within Isaiah's vision, the birth itself is described as a vision of Mary and Joseph. According to that vision within a vision, when Mary is found to be with child, Joseph plans to divorce her quietly. He is stopped by an angel. Joseph and Mary live together for two months, during which time Joseph preserves her virginity. In M. A. Knibbs's translation, the text reads:

> And after two months of days, while Joseph was in his house, and Mary his wife, but both alone, it came about, when they were alone, that Mary then looked with her eyes and saw a small infant, and she was astonished. And after her astonishment had worn off, her womb was found as (it was) at first, before she had conceived. And when her husband, Joseph, said to her, "What has made you astonished?" his eyes were opened, and he saw the infant and praised the Lord. . . . And a voice came to them, "Do not tell this vision to anyone." But the story about the infant was spread abroad in Bethlehem. . . . [M]any said, "She did not give birth; the midwife did not go up (to her), and we did not hear (any) cries of pain." And they were all blinded concerning him; they all knew about him, but they did not know from where he was. . . . And I saw, O Hezekiah and Josab my son, and say to the other prophets also who are standing by, that it was hidden from all the heavens and all the princes and every god of this world. And I saw (that) in Nazareth he sucked the breast like an infant, as was customary, so he would not be recognized. (11:1–17)

In this vision within a vision, the newly delivered mother has the body of a nulligravida. What does such a body know? How does the pain of childbirth resemble other pain, or is the pain of childbirth unique? In answering these questions, I suggest we begin by reading other bodies in the *Ascension of Isaiah*, including the body of the crucified one—known as the Beloved—and the visionary tortured body of Isaiah. I argue that the strangeness of the virgin's body has more to do with the author's rejection of body as locus of identity—and knowledge—than with a fixation on preservation of virginity *in partu*.

Although we begin by deciphering the corporal grammar of the *Ascension of Isaiah*, its logic will not foreclose our discussion. The image of the maternal body that erases its own history raises questions that cannot be answered within the framework of the text. "Yes or no," Merleau-Ponty demands, "do we have a body—that is, not a permanent object of thought, but a flesh that suffers when it is wounded, hands that touch?"[79] For Merleau-Ponty, the chiastic quality of touching is essential to corporeality. In short, we cannot touch without being touched; we cannot be touched unless we touch. By extension, a woman cannot bring a child out of the flesh of her body into the flesh of the world without being changed—without being touched, without being wounded. How does bearing Jesus into the world change Mary? Does Mary have, in Merleau-Ponty's formulation, a body? In the *Ascension of Isaiah*, what does the virgin mother know in her body?

The Body of Isaiah

Against Merleau-Ponty's insistence on the significance of a body's history for that body, the *Ascension of Isaiah* offers a strange vision of Mary's body. Nonetheless, Mary's body is not so strange in the context of that work. Like other bodies in the *Ascension*, Mary's body negates its own history. The *Ascension* is organized around a vision of the prophet-seer Isaiah. In the vision, the prophet-seer is transported through seven heavens. In the seventh heaven he stands before the throne of God, whence he witnesses the Beloved descend through those same seven heavens. He witnesses the Beloved's crucifixion and his triumphant return to the throne of God. In light of this visionary experience, Isaiah predicts his own execution.

The reader encounters the body of Isaiah both in Isaiah's visions and in the narrative of his visionary experiences and martyrdom. Little is said of Isaiah's conduct during his execution. Even as Isaiah is slowly slaughtered by being sawed with a wooden sword, he is absorbed in a vision. As the sawing begins, the diabolical leader of the false prophets, Belchira, demands that Isaiah speak on Belchira's behalf. Isaiah rejects the demand. He declares that nothing can be taken from him but his own skin. How does the text understand a body such as Isaiah's? Consideration of bodies in the *Ascension of Isaiah* requires a taxonomy of pain and silence.

As we have seen, endurance of pain was a hallmark of Greco-Roman masculinity. So in 4 Maccabees the brothers and their virile mother are described as exemplars of manly virtue.[80] To heighten the impression of their fortitude, the tortures endured by the sons are adumbrated: "She [the Maccabean mother] beheld the flesh of her children melting in the fire and their toes and fingers scattered on the ground, and the flesh of their heads right down to the jaws exposed like masks" (15:15). No such gruesome summary accompanies *Ascension of Isaiah*'s repeated but curt references to Isaiah's death. The text's emphasis is not on a Stoic endurance of pain, nor on endurance of pain as a crucible of masculinity. Like Jesus in the canonical Gospels, the apocryphal Isaiah remains silent while tortured. However, Isaiah's silence in the *Ascension* does not reverberate with the humility of the canonical Suffering Servant. Nor can the apocryphal Isaiah's silence be assimilated to the silence of Scarry's prototypical torture victim, a Philomela who reverts to "a state anterior to language, to the sounds and cries a human being makes before language is learned."[81] Each silence resonates with its own story.

The *Ascension of Isaiah* suggests that in visionary experience the mind, intellect, or consciousness separates from the body. Somehow separated from his body's painful experiences, Isaiah is silent: "And while Isaiah was being sawed in half, he did not cry out, or weep, but his mouth spoke with the Holy Spirit until he was sawed in two" (5:14). This separation of mindfulness from corporeality is consistent with the text's description of the visionary experience that leads to Isaiah's death. As Isaiah prophesies, a door is heard opening. Isaiah falls silent. He breathes and his eyes remain open, but his mind—or intellect or consciousness—is lifted from his body or skin.

Within Isaiah's elaborate vision, the status of bodies or flesh is ambivalent. The seven heavens are not places for physical bodies, yet Isaiah insists on the spatiality of the heavens. (As I note in chapter 1, Mark Johnson argues that because human beings are embodied our imaginations are ineluctably shaped by the experiences of bodies existing in space. Hence the ubiquity of spatial metaphors, including metaphors related to verticality, to the relationship of center to periphery, and to movement.) For example, in the first five heavens angels are divided between those on the left and those on the right of the throne. The increasing glory of the heavenly beings is apparent in their visages.[82] In the seventh heaven Isaiah sees Enoch and other scriptural saints, stripped of their garments of skin, dressed now in garments of glory. As Isaiah ascends through the first six heavens he is physically transformed to reflect greater and greater glory. His ultimate transformation in the seventh heaven is deferred, presumably until he exchanges garments of flesh for garments of glory after death.[83] Not yet stripped of his garment of skin, Isaiah nonetheless hovers apart from the world of flesh. Separated from his body, the prophet-seer envisions astral beings who possess spatiality and radiant glory but lack physicality. The most important journey of Isaiah's life is surely his visionary journey to the throne of God in the seventh heaven. This journey leaves no traces on his earthly body.

In the scene of Isaiah's execution a similar understanding persists of the distinction between body and person. While his body is being sawed, Isaiah is elsewhere. Absorbed in a vision of the Lord, he does not even see his executioner. Glucklich's account of religious pain offers a context for understanding this displacement. Glucklich writes:

> The more irritation one applies to the body in the form of pain, the less output the central nervous system generates from the areas that regulate the signals on which a sense of self relies. Modulated pain weakens the individual's feeling of being a discrete agent; it makes the "body-self" transparent and facilitates the emergence of a new identity. Metaphorically, pain creates an embodied "absence" and makes way for a new and greater "presence."[84]

Perhaps the author of the *Ascension of Isaiah* intuits that extreme physical pain has the potential to promote a subjective experience of reintegration, an experience signified by the sidereal metamorphosis Isaiah undergoes in the fatal vision. To rephrase, drawing on the imagery in the *Ascension of Isaiah*: In an earlier vision, Isaiah experienced a series of glorious transformations as he ascended to the seventh heaven, but he retained his garment of skin. As he undergoes a brutal execution, his transformation encompasses the loss of his garment of flesh in preparation for donning the garments of the upper world.

The Body of the Beloved

In Isaiah's vision, the infant Jesus suckles merely to maintain the secret of his identity. The text does not specify whether the breast at which he suckles belongs to his mother. Darrell Hannah differentiates Jesus' gratuitous feeding from Jewish accounts of angels who only appear to ingest and drink because they are incapable of doing so. Hannah notes that in the Gospel of Luke the risen Jesus establishes that he is not a ghost by eating fish, fish whose nutritive value is superfluous for the risen Lord.[85] Clement of Alexandria holds more strongly that Jesus ate not because of caloric needs but to keep others from speculating on his identity. Neither Luke nor Clement nor the *Ascension of Isaiah* denies that Jesus' body was composed of flesh and bones. All three ascribe peculiar qualities to Jesus' body (in the case of Luke, to Jesus' risen body).

Another peculiarity of the body Isaiah envisions for the Beloved is its shape-changing nature. As the Beloved descends through the heavens, he takes the form of the beings of each realm without altering his essential identity. Isaiah is told that on earth "they will think that He is flesh and is a man." While the vision does not call into question the enfleshment of the Beloved, the body of the Beloved is nonetheless incidental to his identity. His deceptive flesh does not register his story.

Qualifications about the degree to which Jesus truly becomes flesh do not appear in the five explicit references to the Beloved's death. These references occur both in Isaiah's vision and in the narrative framing of that vision. Persecution, torments, crucifixion, and burial are presented as bodily and real, despite the metamorphoses of the Beloved who descends.[86] Karen King notes that, in a number of texts commonly characterized as docetic, it is said that Jesus suffered, died, and was buried. "But at the same time," King comments, "the flesh is not the true self and is not destined for salvation."[87] (I treat King's arguments at length in chapter 1.) In the *Ascension of Isaiah* Jesus really suffers in crucifixion, but his corporeality is not tied to his true identity. As he descends through the seven heavens he metamorphoses into the forms of the angels and devils of each realm. His metamorphosis induces heavenly misprision. On his ascent he is recognized, presumably not in garments of flesh. Each realm now acknowledges his glory and worships him. Isaiah's glorious transformations suggest that at least some others may share in this capacity for astral metamorphosis. Both Isaiah and Jesus suffer and die, but their physical sufferings do not define them. Although their corporal sufferings may occasion epistemological breakthroughs, the kinds of knowledge valued do not include ordinary kinds of corporal knowing. The flesh is not the true self and is not destined for salvation. In the *Ascension of Isaiah* the self is not ultimately a body, a key point in understanding the text's representation of Mary as a parturient who knows nothing of birth in her body.

Nulliparous Maternity

In the *Ascension of Isaiah* the birth and death of the Beloved are narrated in visions of Isaiah. In the vision of the birth, the people of Bethlehem comment that Mary did not cry out during delivery. Although most scholarly references to the nativity in the *Ascension* focus on its painlessness, I do not think painlessness is central to the nativity account. Mary's silence does not convey the purposeful transformation of pain implicit in the imagery of *Odes of Solomon* 19, nor does it suggest the kind of visionary alienation from physical pain that accompanies the death of Isaiah by wooden sword. In the *Ascension of Isaiah* the birth is so quick that Mary is surprised by the appearance of the child. Mary simply does not feel any pain. While the text does not quote Isaiah 66:7, I believe the words of the canonical prophet shape the vision attributed to the prophet-seer:

> Before she was in labor she gave birth
> before her pain came upon her she delivered a son
> Who has heard of such a thing?[88]

As I note earlier in this chapter, Irenaeus quotes this verse in a concatenation of references to the prophecies of Isaiah fulfilled in the person of Jesus. For the author of the *Ascension of Isaiah*, Mary's brief pregnancy and preternaturally speedy parturition announce the fulfillment of prophecy.

In Isaiah's vision of the nativity, a voice describes the birth itself as a vision. About this vision Mary and Joseph are told, Be mum. Throughout the *Ascension of Isaiah* the prophet-seer emphasizes the hidden identity of the Beloved, a theme evident in the description of the birth of the Beloved. We may discern in the vision attributed to Isaiah the influence of the canonical prophet, who wrote,

> He had no form or majesty that we should look at him
> nothing in his appearance that we should desire him. (53:2b)

The people of Bethlehem were blinded regarding the identity of the babe, about whom rulers of earth and heaven remained ignorant. Even the infant's suckling at the breast is an element in the occult scheme. The baby nurses lest it become known that his body has the ability to sustain itself without nutrition. In this hushed context, both the mother's silence during birth and the abrupt involution of her womb preserve the secret identity of the Beloved. Conflicting voices debate the circumstances of the birth. Even the powers that rule the heavens and the earth are baffled.

The *Ascension of Isaiah* relies on Mary's body in childbirth to convey the secret story of the Beloved, a story predicated on the Beloved's obscure entry into the world and ultimate translation to glory. At the same time, as we have seen, the text insists that bodies are not true selves, to echo King's formulation. Bodies are not destined for salvation. In making this assertion we should recall the work's visionary framing. Isaiah's body is transformed, but in a vision. The metamorphosis of the Beloved's body is reported in the context of a vision. Finally, both at the outset and conclusion of the nativity account, the reader is reminded of the visionary framework. Does the author of the *Ascension of Isaiah* expect the reader to take the seer's visions as a historical account? To put it crassly, does the author actually believe that Mary was astonished to find herself in the room with the beloved neonate, or that her womb instantly reformed itself as the womb of a nulligravida? In reading the bodies in the *Ascension*, we usefully recall the playfulness of symbolic and imagistic language. For a work that denies the finality of bodies, the *Ascension* returns repeatedly and variously to somatic themes. The body of the virgin simultaneously tells the story of messianic fulfillment of prophecy and mutes the proclamation of that story.

But in the *Ascension of Isaiah* Mary's body is stranger still. In the fourteenth century, the young Birgitta of Sweden experienced a vision of the virgin birth that in some details recalls the *Ascension*. Recounting her vision, Birgitta wrote, "[S]o sudden and momentary was that manner of giving birth that I was unable to notice or discern how or in what member she was giving birth. But yet, at once, I saw that glorious infant lying on the earth, naked and glowing in the greatest of neatness. His flesh was most clean of all filth and uncleanness." Birgitta reported, "[T]he Virgin's womb, which before birth had been very swollen, at once retracted; and her body then looked wonderfully beautiful and delicate." The virgin pressed the infant to her breast, and as she did so she took his umbilical cord in her fingers. The cord fell away, and from it, Birgitta reports, "no liquid or blood went out."[89] As in Birgitta's later vision, in the *Ascension of Isaiah* the nativity is so sudden and spontaneous that neither Mary, nor Joseph, nor the reader can discern how the babe appears in the room. In both the *Ascension* and Birgitta's vision, the body of the postpartum virgin disguises her corporal history as her womb instantly involutes. As soon as Mary delivers the babe, we learn in the *Ascension*, "her womb was found as formerly before she had conceived."

For most women, six weeks elapse before the uterus fully returns to its prepregnancy size and position, a period of time which, perhaps coincidentally but nonetheless curiously, roughly corresponds to the forty days that many cultures prescribe as a period of confinement to the house, a period of restriction from sex, and even, in some cultures, a period with its own special dietary regimen.[90] In antiquity, changes wrought by pregnancy were as poorly understood as other dimensions of

internal anatomy. Pliny imagined the architecture of a uterus to include two cavities. The comparatively better informed physician Soranus understood the uterus
as a single cavity. He taught that the uterus of a virgin was smaller than the uterus
of a woman no longer virgin and that the uterus of a mother remained larger than
the uterus of a woman who had never been pregnant.[91] Given the vagaries of ancient
understandings of female anatomy, I am overly clinical to insist that the text implies
that Mary's uterus returned to its earlier size and position, or that Mary's vagina
tightened up, or that her cervix was not distended by the passage of the child. Perhaps the author simply means to suggest that Mary's belly no longer sagged. The
details do not matter. The author denies that Mary's body is marked by childbirth.
Natal knowledge does not stick in her flesh or bones. Her body rewrites itself to
erase the history of her pregnancy, a rewriting that to some theologians has seemed
glorious, but to me appears as a poignant denial of maternal knowing.

You, reader, may be devoted to the Sisyphean task of erasing the marks of experience from your body. Toward that end you may spend hours sweating on an ellip-
tical trainer or grunting as you hoist free weights. But as Merleau-Ponty argues, a
body makes possible a world of experience, an argument that the *Ascension of
Isaiah* at once denies and curiously affirms. In the *Ascension*, bodies are envisioned as disposable and inessential, yet Isaiah can only envision astral travel spa-
tially. Bodies are hard to escape. Harder still is imagining what a world without
bodies might be. Several generations of women escaped the pain of childbirth
through scopolamine, which induced twilight sleep. The women experienced the
pain of childbirth but had no memory of it. But they likewise could not remember
the birth of their child. So in the *Ascension of Isaiah*. Mary has no knowledge of
childbirth. She only knows that the child has arrived. Her body experiences pregnancy but reforms itself to deny that experience. The *Ascension* has been read as a
straightforward docetic text. On this reading Mary gives birth painlessly because
her child lacks corporeality. I offer a different reading. The fleshy baby drinks milk
and grows into a man who will be tortured and killed. But in this text bodies are not
true selves. The text's construction of the maternal body is consistent with its construction of the bodies of the prophet-seer and of the Beloved. These are bodies that
shed their histories. The knowledge prized by the visionary—and, one infers, by
the author of the text—is not corporal knowledge.

Protevangelium of James

While Mary plays a minor role in the *Ascension of Isaiah*, the *Protevangelium of
James* is Mary's book, and Mary's birthing of Jesus is the climax of the tale. The
Protevangelium opens with the despair of the childless couple Joachim and Anna.

Angelic annunciations to both Anna and Joachim presage the birth of Mary, who from birth is protected from anything impure. Joachim and Anna bring their daughter to live in the Jerusalem temple when she is three. She lives there until age twelve, the anticipated age of menarche. The priests dote on her, but purity concerns prompt them to hold a contest to choose a widower to serve as a guardian, or perhaps a husband, for her; the text equivocates on whether the widower is to shelter or to wed the girl as she buds into puberty. The chosen widower is Joseph, who is depicted as the father of children from his previous marriage. Just as the angel of the Lord announced to Anna that she would bear a child, the angel of the Lord announces to the virgin Mary that she will bear a child.[92] Birth as well as conception is to be notable. Mary asks the angel, "If I conceive by the Lord, the living God, will I also bring forth as every woman brings forth?" "No," the angel replies, "the power of God will overshadow you." In the Gospel of Luke these words refer to Mary's conception of Jesus. In the *Protevangelium of James* they refer to the birth of Jesus.[93] The story told by Mary's laboring body is to differ from stories told by other women's bodies as they labor to bring children into the world.

Confused by the angel's visit, Mary travels to visit her cousin Elizabeth, who is pregnant with John the Baptist. When Joseph returns home after an extended absence, he learns of his ward-wife's pregnancy. In despair, he compares himself to Adam, deceived by his wife, and Mary to the transgressing Eve. An angel appears to assure him that the pregnancy is the work of the Holy Spirit. When the temple priests learn of the pregnancy they are outraged. Although Joseph and Mary protest their innocence, the priests infer Joseph has enjoyed sexual relations with his precious charge. The text again equivocates on the nature of the alleged infraction. Was Joseph obligated to announce the consummation of his marriage? Or was he supposed to keep Mary as a virgin? The priests administer to Joseph and Mary a version of the biblically prescribed test of bitter waters. Unharmed by drinking the potion, Joseph and Mary pass the test. Joseph and Mary are en route to Bethlehem for the census when Mary feels the stirrings of labor. While the text does not stress the painfulness of labor, neither does it caution against interpreting the labor as painful; whether Mary suffers the curse of Eve does not concern the author.[94] Joseph leaves Mary alone in a cave while he seeks a midwife. Joseph and the midwife return to see the cave fill with light. When the light recedes, the baby appears and immediately suckles at his mother's breast.

The amazed midwife ventures out. She encounters a certain Salome, who is not otherwise introduced to the reader.[95] Salome swears that in order to test Mary's virginity she will extend her figure into Mary's *physis*, her genitals, more specifically, her vagina. The midwife warns Mary of the impending test and stands by as Salome pokes a finger into Mary's *physis*. Salome's finger is set on fire, but the blessed neonate amiably heals it. After Herod learns from the pilgrim wise men of the birth of the king of the Jews, he orders the slaughter of all infants. Herod sends attendants to the temple to ask where Zechariah has hidden his wife, Elizabeth, and their child, John the Baptist. Zechariah remains silent. Herod's forces slaughter him. The narrative ends with the image of the temple altar, which had escaped pollution by the menstrual blood of the temple virgin, stained by the blood of Zechariah.

Like the *Ascension of Isaiah*, the *Protevangelium of James* suggests that Mary remains virginally intact after a sterile delivery of her infant, a delivery seemingly devoid of placenta and meconium. Pointing to common elements in the nativity scenes in the *Ascension* and *Protevangelium*, George Zervos argues that both texts expand a first-century nativity source. Common elements adduced by Zervos include attribution of Davidic lineage to Mary, absence of a midwife during delivery, and, most memorably, the claim that Mary is physically unaffected by childbirth.[96] While I am struck by the fact that two works in circulation in the second century sketch an apparently bloodless nativity and a Mary unmarked by childbearing, I have no opinion as to whether these traditions develop independently, whether one text is dependent on the other, or whether, as Zervos plausibly argues, both works build on an earlier source. In writing about early Marian traditions, scholars often conflate differences to stress commonalities among accounts. J. K. Elliott, for example, writes, "The Ascension of Isaiah 11 written early in the second century has a similar account of the birth to that found in PJ [*Prot. Jas.*] . . . Ignatius, *ad Eph.* 19, implies virginity *in partu*, and the Odes of Solomon 19 also shows knowledge of this."[97] (I do not see why Ignatius's comment that the mystery of Mary's virginity was hidden from the prince of this world should be taken as an allusion to preservation of *virginitas in partu*.) Unlike Elliott, I focus on differences rather than similarities between the *Ascension* and the *Protevangelium*. In the *Ascension*, as we have seen, bodies shed their histories. In that work Mary's body at once proclaims and confounds the good news of the birth of the Beloved. The bodies of the *Protevangelium* do not share the idiosyncrasies of the textual bodies of the *Ascension*.

In reading the *Protevangelium*, I highlight two peculiar qualities of Mary's parturient body. First, Mary's body in childbirth brings to a climax the *Protevangelium*'s obsession with purity, blood, and pollution. Second, Mary's postpartum intactness implies an ethical and aesthetic judgment on bodies, specifically on orifices that gape in childbirth. Mary's body is exceptional in ways that imply other women's bodies are intrinsically shameful. I argue that in the *Protevangelium* Mary is protected not only from sexual activity but also from the stain of menarche. Mary's body is tightly bounded, neither tacky with menses and lochia nor stretched by her child's emergence into the world.[98] Unlike other babies, Jesus is not battered and traumatized by his birth. The reader infers that newborn Jesus does not redden as his lungs bellow. Rather, he glows. The otherworldly light he brings to the world he brings first to the cave where he is born. The strangely clean and proper bodies of Mary and Jesus imply horror at the abject dependency native to those born of women, a horror that derives from a simultaneous repugnance from and attraction to the prospect of dissolution of identity. Mary becomes mother without blood, but not, perhaps curiously, without milk.[99] The midwife watches as the baby draws his mother's teat into his mouth and sucks. Denied genital insignia of motherhood, Mary leaks news of her maternity from her virginal breasts. Unlike menses, unlike the fluids and solids unleashed in parturition, milk does not pollute.

In reading Mary's exceptional body in the *Protevangelium of James*, we should be attentive to discharges, both the discharges of menstruation and the discharges of childbirth; to lactation; and to the sanctity of Mary's genitalia. Just as the *Protevangelium* implies that the Jerusalem temple is a sacred space that should not be polluted by womanly fluids, so the text implies that Mary's body is a sacred space. Mary's womb is Jesus' prenatal sanctuary. It should not be sullied by the usual sordid byproducts of femininity.

Fluids

According to the *Protevangelium of James*, Mary's twelfth birthday moves the priests to consider her future abode. She could no longer live in the Jerusalem temple, which was off-limits to menstruating women. Purity laws forbade entrance to the temple complex to menstruating women; to women who had given birth to sons within the past forty days or daughters within the past eighty days; and to men who had a recent seminal ejaculation, whether voluntary or involuntary. But how central is biblical law to the *Protevangelium*'s formulation of purity concerns? Tim Horner argues that the *Protevangelium* may derive from a Jewish-Christian community.[100] Certain elements in the story militate against that conclusion, including the idea that even a prepubescent female child could reside in the temple and dance on its altar. Horner nonetheless argues that the *Protevangelium* reflects the kinds of concerns that surface in the Mishnah and thus is likely to be the product of a post-temple Jewish-Christian community.

For example, Horner adduces as evidence the timing of the toddler Mary's delivery to the temple. According to the *Protevangelium*, when Mary turns two, Joachim suggests to Anna that they bring her to the temple. Anna asks to wait until Mary is three. Horner observes that the Mishnah assumes that females whose virginity is disturbed before three can physically regenerate themselves as virgins while females whose virginity is disturbed after age three cannot. For that reason, as I noted in chapter 3, females who had been enslaved and freed prior to that age could be considered virgins, whereas females who had been enslaved at any point past their third birthday could not be considered virgins. Horner argues that Mary's sojourn in the temple begins when she is three so that the priests can vouch for her virginity.[101]

In making his argument, Horner overlooks a more straightforward explanation of Anna's hesitation to deliver Mary to the temple when Joachim first suggests they do so. The story of the once-barren Hannah who dedicates her firstborn son Samuel to the temple serves as a model for the once-barren Anna who dedicates her only child Mary to the temple.[102] According to 1 Samuel, Hannah waited to wean her son before she surrendered him to the temple (1:21–23). In light of Hannah's delay in parting from her firstborn, a parallel Horner ignores, it seems arcane to explain Anna's delay in parting from her firstborn by recourse to a Mishnaic verdict on the qualifications of virgins.[103] Like the majority of scholars, I understand the *Protevangelium of James* to have at most a tangential connection to the versions of Jewish Christianity that flourished in the second century.

I locate the purity concerns of the text more broadly in the context of concerns with purity in Greco-Roman habitus, which of course encompasses Jewish and eventually Christian concern with purity. Archaeological remains of pagan temples include rules posted for admission and behavior, the equivalent of signs posted at modern swimming pools that regulate admission and use of sites. Many pagan temples forbade access to those who had recently been sexually active or attended funerals, to postpartum women, and, albeit less frequently, to menstruating women. Some temples barred entry to all women or to all premenopausal women, exclusions that effectively excluded menstruants. Susan Cole argues that these restrictions derive from a strict separation of distinctively human activity from sacred precincts. Thus, Cole holds, behavior or conditions associated with "birth, defecation, sexual intercourse, and death" were out of place at temples and shrines.[104]

Joan Branham offers an alternative explanation for the separation of menstruants from sacred precincts.[105] Quoting Heinrich von Staden's observation, "Words are not the only bearers of meaning. Matter, too, is a matrix of meanings, and as such it invites interpretation," Branham launches an investigation into "the meaning and figuration of blood."[106] (Later in this chapter I return to von Staden's treatment of matter as a matrix of meaning.) Of particular concern to Branham are the bloody discharges of menstruation and parturition. She argues that ancient Mediterranean societies excluded bloody women from sacrificial quarters because menses and lochia were seen as powerful forces that competed and potentially interfered with the agency of sacrificial blood. Biblical law, for example, treated blood shed in childbirth and blood shed in sacrifice as purifying. Both in Aristotle and in the Hippocratic writings we find comparisons of menstruants and parturients to sacrificial victims.[107] Branham draws attention to the exclusion of the pubescent Mary from the Jerusalem temple in the *Protevangelium of James*. Arguing that the

Protevangelium's Mary illustrates the extent to which Christianity will intensify an earlier Jewish exclusion of women from sacred space, Branham exclaims, "Here, even the bloody Mother of God has the power to pollute the bloody House of God."[108]

The sacrificial blood finally shed on the temple's altar belongs not to a conventional ritual victim but to Zechariah when he is slaughtered by Herod's men. "Take my life," Zechariah says. "The Lord, though, will receive my spirit because you are shedding innocent blood at the entrance to the temple of the Lord" (23:7). After the murder, one of Zechariah's fellow priests enters the temple and sees the bloody altar. A voice announces, "His blood will not be cleaned up until his avenger appears" (24:5). When the other priests enter the temple, Zechariah's blood has been turned to stone. The blood of menarche deferred, blood still soaks through. Branham argues that the menstruating Mary is kept from the altar so that her discharge will not complicate the power of the temple's sacrificial system. I argue that not only is the pubescent Mary kept from the altar, Mary herself is kept from the taint of blood. She does not imbibe her mother's milk until her mother is purified of her own childbearing blood. Although the text is ambiguous, Mary seems to conceive Jesus before menarche. Finally, not only is the childbirth scene presented antiseptically, but, in light of Anna's delayed suckling of Mary, Mary's immediate suckling of her child implies that Mary was not sullied through childbirth. I develop each of these points in turn.

MENSES

I argue that in the *Protevangelium of James* Mary is spared the pollution of menstruation. How old is Mary when she conceives Jesus? Mary leaves her residence in the temple before she menstruates. She is twelve years old. She goes to live in Joseph's home. Curiously, Joseph immediately leaves to work on construction projects. Within the text, Joseph's absence protects Mary's reputation. He cannot be identified as the father of Mary's child. His absence nonetheless leaves Mary—who since birth had been attended by virgins and fed by angels—oddly alone and unprotected. Mary and other virgins are invited to spin thread for the temple veil, but we otherwise have no indication of time passing. Home alone, Mary receives a visitor, the angel who delivers the surprising news of Mary's pregnancy. In short, Mary arrives at Joseph's home as a prepubescent girl and soon learns that she is pregnant. I thus infer that Mary moves from prepubescent girlhood to pregnancy without bleeding.[109]

A counterargument is evident in the text. Some copies of the manuscript indicate that Mary is sixteen when she conceives. Other copies indicate that she is fifteen, while still others indicate that she is twelve. Inconsistency in the manuscript

tradition suggests that scribes copying the manuscript were puzzled by the suggestion that Mary was sixteen or fifteen at conception. In his commentary H. R. Smid
remarks, "We can hardly assume that some three years have passed."[110] Perhaps the
simplest explanation is scribal error: in Greek the numeral 12 could easily be confused with 15 or 16.[111]

The temple priests accuse Joseph of violating his trust by fathering Mary's
child. The charge that Joseph is the father of Mary's child would be nonsensical if
he had been away from home for several years. Thus in his commentary Ronald
Hock suggests that twelve is the most probable age "if the charge against an absent
Joseph is to be plausible."[112] Despite manuscripts that imply Mary was fifteen or
sixteen when she conceived, the thrust of the narrative requires that Mary conceive her child soon after her departure from the temple, that is, when she is still
prepubescent.

Why separate Mary from menses and lochia, from gynecological and obstetrical
discharges? As I argue later in this chapter in my discussion of Tertullian, menses
and other corporal effluvia were treated as shameful. The child so pure that her feet
should not touch the ground should not leave reddish-brown stains. Shaye Cohen
has argued that in biblical and early rabbinic practice, pollution had no moral
valence. Pollution associated with gynecological, obstetrical, and seminal discharges was a fact of life that happened to everyone. Pollution required a bath, not
repentance.[113] Nonetheless, for the association of gynecological and obstetrical
fluids with shame and degradation in Greco-Roman culture, we need look no further than Tertullian, who insists on his culture's harshly negative associations with
bodily fluids even as he transforms those associations. The horror evoked by menses is vividly rendered by Pliny, who views menstrual fluid as a monstrous substance that turns wine, crops, metal, and dogs bad (*Nat.* 7.13.63–67). Mary's body
is clean and dry in the *Protevangelium* because the effluvia associated with fertility
and childbirth evoked horror and visceral shame.[114] In popular discourses of Greco-
Roman antiquity, shame was an emotion at the nexus of ethics and aesthetics. The
good and the beautiful were thought to converge. So were the bad and the ugly. The
argument that feminine discharges carried negative moral weight in Greco-Roman
antiquity will be elaborated when we turn to Tertullian.

MILK

Unlike other distinctively female fluids, milk frequently connotes purity. For
example, Pliny—who recoils from the allegedly corrosive effects of menstrual
fluid—imputes marvelous therapeutic powers to human milk, said to cure fevers
and, applied topically, to relieve ocular pain (*Nat.* 28.21.72). In the *Protevangelium
of James*, until the time that Mary leaves the temple at twelve, she consumes

nothing common or impure, subsisting first on milk and later on food from an angel's hand—a diet that Pieter van der Horst proposes would not produce excrement.[115] However, although the *Protevangelium* ultimately signifies Anna's motherhood through lactation, Anna does not immediately offer a breast to her daughter. The *Protevangelium* states, "After her [Anna's] days were completed, Anna cleansed her discharge of blood and gave her breast to the child and gave her the name Mary" (5:9–10). The sequence is clear, albeit improbable. Anna does not suckle Mary until the mother's prescribed days of purification are completed. According to Levitical law, a woman who gave birth to a boy underwent forty days of purification and a woman who gave birth to a girl underwent eighty days of purification. While Mary could easily have nursed at the breast of a wet nurse in Joachim's household, which the *Protevangelium* depicts as wealthy, Anna's ability to lactate after eighty days is dubious.[116] Verisimilitude is not a goal of the author. Nor, given the author's uncertain acquaintance with Judaism, should we assume that he is versed in the fine points of biblical purity laws, including the duration of the purification period. Perhaps a shorter period is vaguely intended.

In violation of what is now recognized as the nutritional value of colostrum, some ancient medical writers advised women who had just delivered babies to delay nursing their infants.[117] Soranus was the most influential of these experts. Soranus advised that women wait twenty days before allowing their children to feed from them. According to Soranus, early milk is cheesy, raw, and thus hard to digest. Furthermore, he continues, the milk of new mothers "is produced by bodies which are in a bad state, agitated and changed to the extent that we see the body altered after delivery when, from having suffered a great discharge of blood, it is dried up, toneless, discolored, and in the majority of cases feverish as well" (*Gynecology* 2.18). In her study of social practices governing the care of newborns in the ancient world, Susan Holman infers that Soranus's goal was to distance the child from "the socially murky realm of its mother's unstable body."[118] If no other woman were available to nurse the baby, Soranus suggested the baby could consume honey mixed with goats' milk for three days before imbibing mother's milk. Even then, he urged, the mother should first give her breast to an adolescent to suck the first thick milk. As a last resort, he advocated that the newly delivered woman should manually express her breasts to discharge what was seen as cheesy and barely digestible colostrum.

That the author of the *Protevangelium of James* could have been familiar with some practice that required postpartum women to postpone nursing their children is thus conceivable. However, the *Protevangelium* links Anna's delay in nursing her infant to the days of her purification. Why imply that Anna abstains from nursing her child during her days of purification, an otherwise unknown precaution against pollution? I believe that the answer can be found in the context of ancient understandings of the circulation of bodily fluids. Milk was widely understood to be processed uterine blood. Tertullian offers a succinct formulation of this standard idea. He writes that "the veins pay over into the teat that cess of the lower blood, and in the course of that transfer distill it into the more congenial material of milk," incidentally conveying his customary—albeit complex—repugnance toward uterine fluids (*Carn. Chr.* 20). If milk is processed uterine fluid, then the milk of a woman who has not been purified after childbearing may be seen as imperfectly sanitized. (I will explore the complexity of Tertullian's attitude toward childbearing bodies later in this chapter.)

I argue that for the author of the *Protevangelium of James*, as for Soranus, a woman who has recently labored and delivered a child was seen as an uneasy source of nourishment. I suggest that the *Protevangelium* preserves Mary's purity by insisting that she does not even sip from her mother's breast while it could be tainted by the uncleanness of birth. As soon as Mary begins to nurse from Anna, the relationship between lactating mother and her child is celebrated. The description of the child's first birthday party notes that, after Mary met the priests, who were guests of honor, Anna took her to the bedroom that was the child's sanctuary to nurse her. Anna's joyful song on the occasion concludes with the comment, "Hear this, twelve tribes of Israel: Anna nurses a child!" (6:13). While Anna waited until her blood was purified to give her breast to her child, Mary does not wait. As soon as Jesus is born he reaches for his mother's breast. Thus I infer that the *Protevangelium* implies that Mary is spared what must implicitly be viewed as the polluting stains of lochial discharges in childbirth. She is implicitly spared the stains of mucus and blood and amniotic fluid, spared the urine and excrement often released in childbirth. Anna abstains from nursing until her days of purification are complete, but Mary has no need to abstain. The birth of Jesus does not pollute her.[119]

In the *Odes of Solomon*, milky breasts adorn the Father's bosom. However strange we may find this image, milky breasts adorning a virgin's bosom are also an oddity, a point picked up by some ancient theologies. For example, Ephrem celebrates the mystery of overflowing virginal breasts:

> Mary acquired by You all the attributes
> of married women: conception within her
> without sexual union, milk in her breasts
> not in the usual way. You have suddenly made
> the parched earth into a source of milk.[120]

Unlike Ephrem, the author of the *Protevangelium of James* does not pause to marvel at the wonder of virginal lactation. While the *Protevangelium* denies Mary genital insignia of maternity, her breasts attest to her corporal knowledge of what it is to be a mother, a knowledge of exceptional purity.

Wholeness

When Salome extends her fingers into Mary's vagina, what does she find, other than fire?

The text does not say. Mary's physical intactness is taken as a sign of an enduring virginity, but the nature of that physical intactness is not probed. (The author of the *Protevangelium* lacks Salome's exploratory fervor.) The *Protevangelium* teases the reader to ask what happens between Mary's legs during childbirth, then frustrates the reader's curiosity. Does Salome find an intact hymen? A tight vagina? No traces of blood, no dregs of placenta? The assumption that an intact hymen was the necessary and sole sign of female virginity was not universally held in antiquity. Moreover, a virgin was not universally understood as a person who had not experienced sexual intercourse.[121] In classical Greek sources, for example, *parthenos*, virgin, primarily designates the social status of a girl who does not yet have a husband or a child. In a different vein, Pliny claims that the menstrual blood of a woman who has lost her virginity through age has especially powerful properties. Pliny's woman who has lost her virginity through age seems to be a woman who has reached menarche without first experiencing intercourse.[122] Thus in some Greco-Roman sources a virgin was not necessarily understood to be sexually unexperienced nor was an intact hymen presented as the unique sign of a virgin. In the *Protevangelium*, however, Mary's genitalia, untouched by husband or apparently by son, communicate her existential status. Although we are not told the specifics of Mary's physical condition—the thin membrane of the hymen undisturbed, an os free from abrasions, an absence of bodily fluids that would blur interior and exterior—her physical condition has moral valence.

In *For Fear of the Fire: Joan of Arc and the Limits of Subjectivity*, Françoise Meltzer offers an extended analysis of the treatment of Joan by generations of male theorists. Meltzer addresses corporeality and women's subjectivity. She argues that the alleged mysteriousness of woman, a mysteriousness that seemingly distances her from subjectivity, derives from female anatomy. Located inside the body, female sexual organs escape the regime of visuality. Meltzer relies on the virgin birth in the *Protevangelium* as an exemplary case: Mary gives birth in a cave, where the vision of would-be onlookers—the midwife and Joseph—is occluded by a cloud. Meltzer writes, "The cave, acting as a literal metaphor of the miracles of *both* virginity and virgin birth, combined with the great cloud and blinding light, conspire to make all sight impossible. What the midwife has 'seen,' then, which convinces her of the miracle, is that the birth has been unseeable."[123] More broadly, Meltzer argues, female virginity fascinates because the corporal effort to attain a woman's virginity in some sense disturbs and ends that physical state of being outside perception of the senses. Virginity is extrasensual, that is, invisible and untouchable. Seen and touched, virginity ceases to be. In the *Protevangelium*, however, Mary's virginity is represented as extrasensual in a different sense. The senses, seeing and touching, do not destroy her virginity because her virgin state can be neither seen nor touched.

Salome informs the midwife that she will not believe in the mother's virginity unless she digitally explores Mary's *physis*. In her warning to Mary to ready herself, the midwife refers to the examination as an *agon*, an appellation that characterizes the exam as adversarial. Salome extends her finger into Mary's *physis*, wherein the hand combusts. J. K. Elliott translates *physis* as "condition" (Salome "tests" Mary's "condition"). Ronald Hock abstains from translating *physis* directly. In Hock's translation, before Salome inserts her finger "into Mary," she says, "[U]nless I insert my finger and examine her, I will never believe."[124] The Greek is blunter. In everyday usage *physis* refers to genitalia, most often female genitals, the vulva or vagina. Noting that lexica typically ignore or downplay this common usage, John Winkler observes that referring to a vulva as *physis* is a usage alien to literary style but at home in the writings of "physicians, pharmacists, veterinarians, farmers, omen-readers, [and] dream-interpreters."[125] Foskett, who follows Winkler in translating *physis* as "genitalia," observes, "Just as Mary's ante-partum *parthenia* [virginity] is evidence of her moral virtue, her post-partum *parthenia* serves as an expression of a bodily integrity and physical purity that does indeed defy nature."[126]

As we will see, Tertullian insists that the law of the opened body governs Mary's delivery of Jesus. In the *Protevangelium*, Mary's body is governed by the law of the closed body: existential integrity is assimilated to physical integrity. Mary's corporal condition is presented as inseparable from the purity of her character. Salome's finger in flames marks Mary's closed body, Jesus' prenatal sanctuary, as sacred space. Come no closer, for you transgress a holy place. Her vulva is out of bounds.

Insisting that he upholds the church teaching that Mary retained her virginity *in partu*, Rahner raises a series of questions about the presuppositions of the teaching, questions that are relevant when we try to imagine what Salome's finger finds:

> [W]hat is really included in the concept of "bodily integrity" and what does it imply? . . . Is, for instance, the normal expansion of the genital passages in a completely healthy birth to be considered a breach of "bodily integrity"? Will anyone have the courage to maintain this categorically? Are any of the processes of normal birth to be placed under the rubric of "injury" or "damage" (*corruptio*)? And if so, what has been damaged? The "virginity" or a bodily "integrity," "soundness"?[127]

Rahner holds that embodiment is essential to personhood. He perceives the body as precisely "the spirit of man in space and time."[128] He is committed to reading Mary's parturient body as a locus of her unique communication with the world and with God, but at the same time he refuses to endorse views that disparage the goodness of other women's bodies, the goodness of womanly being in space and time.

Will I give birth like other women, Mary asks her angel guest. Salome's finger bursts into flames when she tries to learn the answer. As Meltzer notes, "[T]he 'evidence' for Mary's virginity is not an intact hymen but the miracle of punishing disbelief."[129] Commentators on the scene sometimes note a similarity between Salome's gesture and the gesture that the Johannine Jesus invites Thomas to make: Stick your finger into my side.[130] The similarity lies in the desire to extend a curious finger into a messy hole in order to test a claim: in John, a claim about the resurrection; in the *Protevangelium*, a claim that a virgin has given birth. Yet the tests differ. If Thomas accepts the invitation, as I imagine he does, his curious finger probes an open and gaping hole.[131] Salome's finger probes an orifice that is, if not sealed, then defensively clenched. The Johannine scene affirms the tactile quality of resurrected flesh, affirms, that is, that resurrected flesh can be touched. The scene in the *Protevangelium* repudiates touching. Mary's body not only retains its virginity. Her virginity, her body, is untouchable.

Tertullian

Tertullian, the Carthaginian theologian who in the late second century was the first Christian to compose in Latin, insists on a different body for the virgin mother. The virgin bleeds. She is split open. Her body bears a hard-won knowledge of maternity. The Gospel of John proclaims that Jesus was born "not of blood or of the will of the flesh or of the will of man, but of God" (John 1:13). In his treatise *On the Flesh of Christ*, Tertullian attempts to correct readings of this verse that would deny the substance of Jesus' flesh. Tertullian writes that "the denial that he [Jesus] was born of blood [does not] involve any repudiation of the substance of flesh, but of the material of the seed, which material it is agreed is the heat of the blood, as it were by despumation changed into a coagulator of the woman's blood" (*Carn. Chr.* 19.3). The view that the fetus is a cheesy byproduct of menstrual fluid, curdled and coagulated by the active seed of the male, was a widespread ancient belief with an Aristotelian pedigree. According to Tertullian, Jesus could not have come into being without his mother's menstrual fluid. Rather, Tertullian holds, what John 1:13 wishes to deny is the materiality and sanguinity of the male seed. In making this argument Tertullian has to contend with the Greco-Roman view that the bloody discharges of gestation and childbirth are polluting and degrading, a view that he at first seems to repudiate but on which he ultimately relies.[132] In what follows, I argue that in the writings of Tertullian we find a vexed engagement with a worldview that insists that the curdling of menstrual blood into human life is a filthy process that tells us something important about what it is to be flesh. Indeed, for Tertullian, Christ's humanity is contingent on the dirty blood of his mother's womb and his violent separation from that womb.

Tertullian introduces Mary's body because Marcion and other theological predecessors, whom he treats as rivals, make claims about the nativity. Tertullian disputes these claims in vituperative tirades. According to Tertullian, Marcion denies the corporeality both of Jesus' flesh and of the nativity. Therefore Tertullian repeatedly and explicitly discusses Mary's childbearing body. Tertullian understands Christ's humanity to require that Mary's puerperal experience was as messy as that of any other mother. He refuses to treat Mary's childbearing experience as distinctive from the childbearing experience of any other woman—except, he claims, that Mary's body is more deeply marked than other women's bodies by what he represents as the violence of childbearing.

In a survey of patristic writings concerning the Virgin Mary, Luigi Gambero singles out Tertullian for placing unusual stress on "the identity between the flesh of Christ and the flesh of Mary."[133] That identity is crucial to my argument. On my reading, Tertullian insists that grounds for the shame of Christ derive from the conditions Christ endured in utero. I argue that through this insistence Tertullian implicitly recognizes what Elizabeth Grosz calls "the debt that the flesh owes to maternity."[134] Grosz uses this phrase in the course of a critique of Merleau-Ponty's phenomenological orientation toward flesh. Grosz argues that in developing his analysis of chiastic touching, Merleau-Ponty simultaneously relies on that debt and recoils from it.[135] The mother's womb is a matrix of touching and being touched. The touch belongs to neither mother nor child. Rather, the touch precedes, enables, and infiltrates the child's sentience and sense of self. The chiastic touching of pregnancy is the origin of corporal knowing. For Tertullian, this touch is clogged with impurities. Significantly, however, in conjunction with the intimate violence of birth this polluting contact is essential to Christ's redemption of the flesh.

Competing Corporeal Discourses

Tertullian derives his understanding of parturition both from medical sources and from everyday knowledge (or perhaps better: everyday prejudice). The educated male elites of the Roman Empire comprised a ready audience for anatomical and therapeutic disquisitions. Male householders regulated access of household members to medical services and thus required some version of scientific knowledge to control members of their households.[136] With his systematic acquisition of a storehouse of potentially useful information, for example, Pliny exemplifies the elite Roman male.[137] Tertullian exceeds many of his Roman peers—albeit not Pliny—in his medical competence.[138]

In his treatise *On the Soul*, Tertullian acknowledges his debt to the physician Soranus, a first- or second-century Greek author of a work by the same name.[139] Tertullian also quotes a wide range of other medical writers, although we do not know whether he knew their works directly or as mediated through Soranus.[140] While it is unclear whether Tertullian was directly familiar with Soranus's treatise on gynecology, he exhibits familiarity with views on women's bodies that are associated with Soranus, who is known for his clinical approach to women's bodies, an approach that attempted to purge medical practice of prejudice and superstition.[141] Precisely because Soranus perceived amulets and other charms to be therapeutically indifferent, for example, he had no objection to women in childbirth clutching them. He observed that such behavior might calm a woman and ease the delivery of her child.[142]

Despite Soranus's apparent influence on Tertullian, the theologian was not free from the habitus of his day, including its popular prejudices. The competing discourses in which Tertullian participated led him to positions at times inconsistent with one another. We find evidence of such inconsistency in the conflicting accounts Tertullian provides of the respective contributions of the mother and the father to the child's body. As I note above, in his treatise *On the Flesh of Christ* and in other writings, Tertullian echoes a widespread belief that "the human body comes into existence by the sperm of the father solidifying the [menses] of the mother."[143] Elsewhere, however, Tertullian argues that the father is the source of the embryo; on this view, the mother's womb is a mere depository for the sperm.[144] Tertullian expresses these competing views in works that are roughly contemporaneous. He seems unconcerned about the inconsistency between the two positions he espouses, that is, between the position that a woman contributes sanguinary stuff to the embryo and the position that a woman functions merely as vessel. In his commentary on Tertullian's *On the Soul*, Jan H. Waszink reasons that Soranus's influence leads Tertullian to embrace the position that the mother contributes nothing materially to conception, even though Tertullian does not consistently abandon his earlier position.[145]

Tertullian's tolerance for scientific inconsistency is compatible with the paradoxes that characterize his theology and the contrary statements that inflect his rhetoric. In his monograph on Tertullian as "first philosopher of the West," Eric Osborn describes Tertullian's paradoxes as "both a personal habit and part of his Stoicism." He writes that the reader finds in Tertullian's treatise *Against Marcion* "a consistent claim that antithesis is essential to the ways of God and to the world which he has made."[146] In my view, Tertullian's reliance on paradox and acceptance of contradiction should be understood in the context of habits of discourse that were widespread in the ancient world. That ancient writings are rife with inconsistencies is noted by philosopher Pierre Hadot (whose work was important for Foucault's reading of ancient philosophy). Hadot comments on the obsession of modern scholars with consistency: "One could compile a whole anthology of complaints made against ancient authors by modern commentators, who reproach them for their bad writing, contradictions, and lack of rigor and coherence."[147]

On Hadot's view, this tolerance or even fostering of contradiction and paradox is related to the goals of ancient writers. He argues that the writings of ancient philosophers—including the writings of Stoics and Jews and Epicureans and Christians—were designed not as ends in themselves but as spiritual exercises. In approaching Tertullian from this vantage point, my goal is not to solve his paradoxes, to identify a still point in a turning world. Rather, my goal is to understand where Tertullian is trying to bring the reader through paradox. Of immediate relevance is what Virginia Burrus calls "the productive tension of [Tertullian's] paradoxical embrace of shame."[148]

Earlier in this chapter I surveyed the competing corporeal discourses that shape the childbearing experiences of women in the twenty-first century. In Tertullian's writings on the nativity, I suggest that we similarly hit upon a concentration of competing corporeal discourses. An adept in the discourses of science and medicine, Tertullian nonetheless shares the popular Greco-Roman preoccupation with the perceived dirtiness and shamefulness of women's interiors. He appropriates the vocabulary of Roman law to express the commonplace notion of woman as property by dint of sexual possession. He has studied the discourses of Marcion and Valentinus, discourses widely characterized as "anti-body." All these corporeal trajectories are presupposed and transformed in Tertullian's rhetoric, shaping his affirmation that flesh is at once despicable and beloved. As we will see, the graphic tale Tertullian reads in Mary's body derives its intensity from these colliding discourses.

Filth

Tertullian begins his treatise *Against Marcion* with invective as he describes Marcion's homeland, Pontus, which lies on the south shore of the Black Sea. There, Tertullian claims, the sun never shines. The people are barbaric. Even the women "have lost the gentleness, along with the modesty, of their sex. They display their breasts, they do their housework with battleaxes, they prefer fighting to matrimonial duty" (1.1). As Tertullian reaches a climax, he avers that, despite all the other deficiencies of the place, "The most barbarous and melancholy thing about Pontus is that Marcion was born there" (1.1). The reader quickly realizes that Tertullian will cast his dispute with Marcion in extreme terms. In graphic detail, Tertullian then taunts his opponents with what he treats as sordid and distasteful details of Mary's delivery of Christ into the world.

Tertullian launches an extended barb against Marcion by stating a position that he attributes to his bête noire: "Even a real nativity of God is of course a thing most disgraceful." Tertullian thus challenges the absent Marcion:

Use all your eloquence against those sacred and reverend works of nature, launch an attack upon everything that you are: revile that in which both flesh and soul begin to be: characterize as a sewer the womb, that workshop for bringing forth the noble animal which is man: continue your attack on the unclean and shameful torments of childbearing. . . . And yet, when you have pulled all those things to pieces, so as to assure yourself that they are beneath God's dignity, nativity cannot be more undignified than death, or infancy than a cross. (3.11)

What is Tertullian's rhetorical strategy? He refuses to separate Mary's body from the bodies of other childbearing women or Jesus' flesh from the flesh of other human beings. If Marcion reviles the location and conditions of Jesus' birth, Marcion reviles the location and conditions of his own birth. Tertullian represents Marcion's views so vividly that he animates them. In *Saving Shame: Martyrs, Saints, and Other Abject Subjects*, Burrus comments on a related passage from Tertullian's treatise *On the Flesh of Christ*: "Painting a vivid scene of gestation and birth, Tertullian performatively invokes the abjection of flesh, even as he skillfully displaces the defensive affect of shame onto others."[149] She continues, "Rhetorically throwing all of this bloody mess into the face of Marcion . . . [Tertullian] addresses him challengingly: 'You detest a human being at his birth; then how do you esteem anybody?'"[150]

But how does Tertullian differentiate his position from Marcion's? "You characterize as a sewer the womb," Tertullian writes, "that workshop for bringing forth the noble animal which is man" (*Marc.* 3.11). Tertullian offers two contrasting images of the womb. In one image, the womb is characterized as a workshop, a sacred factory, for producing the human person. I infer that in the image of womb as workshop we may detect the influence of Soranus. Like Soranus, Tertullian here views the female body clinically, apart from a visceral response against the imaginary of the dark female interior. On the other hand, the image of womb as sewer is attributed at least initially to Marcion. Yet linkage of the unclean and the shameful recurs throughout Tertullian's repeated references to childbearing. For example, as we have seen earlier in the chapter, Tertullian commented on the results of Eve's transgression, "[T]he devil's word was to her [Eve] a seed, so that thenceforth she should be abject and obedient, and should bring forth in sorrows" (*Carn. Chr.* 17). Here Tertullian explicitly connects the painfulness of childbearing with abjection. Because of her transgression, Eve is to know sorrow and degradation in her body. In arguing against Marcion Tertullian at least temporarily repudiates the view that women's reproductive capabilities are repugnant, but he does not consistently hold this view.

The association between women's reproductive systems and sewers, between organs of gestation and organs of elimination, is a common association in both popular and some medical sources from Greco-Roman antiquity. Although at first Tertullian seems to reject the association of womb with sewer, he reiterates and ultimately relies on related comments about the shameful filthiness of gestation and childbirth to clinch his affirmation of human flesh. Osborn comments that Tertullian "feels and redefines Marcion's antitheses."[151] Tertullian's celebration of flesh only succeeds emotionally if flesh celebrated is flesh reviled.

As I note above, despite Tertullian's engagement with a worldview that imbues women's reproductive organs with the stench of excrement and its attendant corruption, he is simultaneously engaged with a measured approach to women's bodies, an approach that resonates with the scientific tone of Soranus. So, for example, in *Against Marcion*, where Tertullian's language in places teems with the filthiness he attributes to the womb, he nonetheless refers in a matter-of-fact fashion to the woman with the flow of blood who reaches out to touch Jesus in the New Testament Gospels (Matt. 9:20–22; Mark 5:25–34; Luke 8:43–48). Without recoiling or grimacing, Tertullian argues that the woman had not broken the Levitical law, which regulates contact with menstruants (cf. Lev. 15:19–24).

Tertullian proposes that "the injunction in the law is concerned with that ordinary and customary flux of blood at menstruation or childbirth, which proceeds from natural functions—not such as proceeds from ill health. She however had an issue caused by ill health" (*Marc.* 4.20). According to Levitical law, in fact, the woman with the flow of blood would not have polluted Jesus, albeit for a different reason than that adduced by Tertullian. Although Jewish men and women in a state of ritual impurity were forbidden to enter the temple precincts, their behavior was not otherwise restricted.[152] A woman with an abnormal flow of blood was known as a *zavah*. According to Leviticus, a *zavah* could be touched, but by Tertullian's day rabbinic opinion was moving in a different direction. According to the Mishnah, a woman with an irregular flow of blood could communicate impurity by touching.[153] (Would Tertullian have been familiar with the Jewish practices of his day? Blake Leyerle argues convincingly that he would.[154] In this case, however, Tertullian gets a fine point wrong.) In Tertullian's nonjudgmental response we may again detect the influence of Soranus, who elaborates dispassionately on the distinction between menstruation—which he regards as normal but nonetheless inessential for women's health—and diseased varieties of gynecological flux.[155]

Neither Marcion nor Tertullian innovates the cloacal construction of the womb. Associations between women's reproductive systems and sewers, between organs of gestation and organs of elimination, recur in ancient writings, including magical texts and medical writings (although not the writings of Soranus). In some contexts the uncleanness of the human body seems to be concentrated in women's poorly understood cavities. In Hippocratic literature, for instance, women's genitalia are both a source of pollution and especially susceptible to pollution. Heinrich von Staden argues that in Hippocratic sources the association of women's reproductive systems with excrement is the motivation for reliance on animal dung to treat gynecological disorders, a prescription more remarkable because animal dung is not prescribed for men by Hippocratic writers.[156] (Later writers, however, occasionally prescribed excrement for men. For example, a mouse dung lotion was prescribed to treat baldness, presumably by fertilizing the barren scalp.)[157] While the early writings of the Hippocratic corpus date to the fifth or fourth century B.C.E., they were widely circulated and influential throughout antiquity. The Hippocratics urged that dung and urine should be smeared on women's bodies, consumed by women as medicine, and formulated into pessaries and douches.[158] Uterine troubles seemed especially amenable to such *Dreckapotheke*. Von Staden suggests that Hippocratic dung prescriptions are likely derived from magic practices that also use excrement to counter pollution.

Ann Hanson acknowledges that von Staden has identified an unusual tendency in Hippocratic protocol. However, she attributes the prevalence of dung treatments to qualities of dung such as heating and drying. These qualities might be considered especially conducive to curing the kinds of maladies to which women were thought to be prone, maladies stemming, it was believed, from a female tendency to excessive moisture.[159] While Hanson downplays the repellant qualities of excrement, both she and von Staden demonstrate a strong association of urine and excrement with wombs, an association evident in the writings of the Hippocratic corpus. Hanson comments, for example, that the "exclusive use of urine in medicaments for the uterus and the anus may have been influenced not only by the anatomical similarity of these two bodily conduits and their anatomical proximity in the female body, but also by the roles each conduit played in evacuation."[160]

The continuing influence of the Hippocratic corpus is evident in the writings of Celsus, who wrote in the first century for elite Roman men. Celsus drew on and modified earlier medical teachings, including Hippocratic teachings.[161] Celsus goes well beyond the Hippocratic association between gynecological discharges and other forms of human waste. Von Staden observes that "in both therapeutic and pathological contexts, [Celsus] tends to compare the adult female vagina and the *os uuluae* to the male anus."[162] Although Julie Laskaris argues that Roman therapeutic practice does not foreground Hellenic phobias about women and dirt, the association of women and dirt hardly disappears, as is evident in both Celsus and Tertullian.[163]

The image of womb as sewer—attributed to Marcion and vivified by Tertullian—thus resonates with a rich set of discursive associations where moral judgment and physical repugnance are intertwined. Although Tertullian attributes the image of womb as sewer to Marcion and although he is conversant with nonjudgmental discourses about gynecological discharges, the identification of women's reproductive abilities as filthy and shameful is ultimately affirmed in the course of Tertullian's celebration of the flesh. The gutter talk that Tertullian ascribes to Marcion is presupposed by the structure of Tertullian's argument, the emotional wallop of which relies on Tertullian's expectation that his audience will share with him the association of women's anatomy and reproductive function with dirt and shame.

Degradation and Redemption

In discussing the nativity, Tertullian seems to lose sight of reproduction as a sacred and reverend work of nature and the womb as a workshop for production of that noble creature, the human person. When Tertullian returns to the topic of the nativity in *Against Marcion*, he begins by quoting Jesus. "Whoever will be ashamed of me," Jesus says, "of that person I will be ashamed" (Mark 8:38; Luke 9:26). Tertullian asks: how could Marcion's incorporeal, unborn Jesus credibly speak such words? Without flesh and without the sordid business of birth, Marcion's Christ would give no one grounds for shame. Tertullian's Christ does.

At this point in his argument, Tertullian no longer repudiates the view that conditions of birthing are shameful. Instead, the denouement of his argument is predicated precisely on that view. "Yet ground for shame does not attach to any Christ but mine," writes Tertullian, "whose whole life was so much a matter of shame that it lies exposed even to the taunts of heretics, who . . . complain endlessly of . . . the squalor of his birth and babyhood, and even the indignity of his flesh" (4.21). Marcion's Christ does not share in the human condition, a condition defined, it seems, by muck. Tertullian writes:

> He [Marcion's Christ] was not conceived in a womb. . . . [H]e was not set free after ten months' torture [*cruciato*], nor was he spilt upon the ground through the sewer of a body, with a sudden attack of pains along with the uncleanness of all those months, nor did he greet the daylight with tears or suffer his first wound at the severing of his cord . . . no question thereafter of his wallowing in uncleanness in a mother's lap. (4.21)

In what ways could life in utero be conceived as torture? Tertullian's characterization of the experience of gestation as torture combines several elements that are still twinned in contemporary torture techniques. The torture of life in utero includes both humiliation and pain, the humiliation of contact with human filth coupled with presumed physical pain, as the fetal body is contorted for months in the womb, which is thus figured as a cramped, fetid prison cell.

As Judith Perkins recognizes, "Tertullian acknowledges the repulsion that maternal birth processes would evoke; indeed, he uses this common reaction to dispute the legitimacy of Marcion's Christ."[164] Perkins argues that for Tertullian the corporeality of Christ's incarnation revokes the shame associated with the maternal body. On my reading, however, Tertullian's project implies ambivalence: for Tertullian, the incarnation intensifies rather than resolves the paradoxes of the flesh, the paradoxes inherent in being a body. Although Tertullian begins his diatribe on the nativity by distancing himself from the notion that the womb is a foul chamber, he ultimately revels in Christ's share in what he characterizes as the degrading ugliness of birth. Because of Christ's gestation in squalor—a physical squalor that evokes ethical squalor—he is born with full knowledge of the human condition.

In his treatise *On the Flesh of Christ*, Tertullian offers a parallel treatment of what he graphically pictures as the squalidness of Christ's birth. Here too invoking an absent Marcion, Tertullian challenges:

> Beginning then with that nativity you so strongly object to, orate, attack now, the nastinesses of genital elements in the womb [*spurcitias genitalium in utero elementorum*], the filthy curdling of moisture and blood [*humoris et sanguinis foeda coagula*], and of the flesh to be for nine months nourished on that same mire [*carnis ex eodem caeno alendae*]. (4.1)

The fact of the afterbirth is evoked for its repulsiveness: "You shudder, of course, at the child passed out with his afterbirth, and of course bedaubed with it" (4.1). Vocabularies of moral deficiency and human waste overlap with the vocabulary of gestation and birth. Tertullian describes the prenatal environment as a latrine. (As pregnancy progresses, the fetus's urine does in fact supply an increasing percentage of amniotic fluids, a clinical fact that English allows us to relay without reference to moral corruption.) For Tertullian, the fetus wallows in and feeds on shit. Tertullian's vocabulary evokes moral decay as well as shame: *Spurcitia, foeda, caeno*. In English as well our words for uncleanness double as expressions for shame, sexual judgment, and ethical lapses. A dishonest transaction makes us feel dirty. We tell dirty jokes and complain about dirty politicians. Shame is an emotion at the nexus of ethics and aesthetics. The revulsion at maternal interiors conveyed by Tertullian—whether or not he claims that revulsion as his own—spills into the suggestion of moral degradation. Wombs are dirty places, and womb bearers are dirty people.

Why does Tertullian wallow in the filthiness of flesh? My assessment differs from that of Perkins. In her insistence that Tertullian understands Christ to have "annulled all the shame associated with the body," Perkins implicitly holds Tertullian to a standard of consistency that I argue is at odds with the intellectual climate that shaped him and alien to his paradoxical mode of argumentation.[165] Yes, Marcion insists on the shamefulness of flesh, maternal and all; yes, Tertullian condemns Marcion; but in the end, despite that condemnation, Tertullian embraces rather than repudiates the shamefulness of flesh. For Tertullian, flesh not only seems degraded; flesh is degraded, yet in the same breath redeemed.

In working through this analysis, I weighed another possible explanation for Tertullian's mire-wallowing, an explanation that, while it does not ultimately satisfy me, nonetheless helps clarify what is distinctive about Tertullian's argument. In an essay on Marcus Aurelius, Hadot returns several times to Marcus's habit of itemizing the gross and repulsive. Hadot quotes Marcus: "Just like your bath-water appears to you—oil, sweat, filth, dirty water, all kinds of loathsome stuff—such is each portion of life, and every substance."[166] Marcus's habit of dwelling on what is abhorrent extends even to the conception of usually pleasant experiences as repellant. Marcus writes, "These foods and dishes . . . are only dead fish, birds, and pigs; this Falernian wine is a bit of grape juice; this purple-edged toga is some sheep's hair dipped in the blood of shellfish; as for sex, it is the rubbing together of pieces of gut, followed by the spasmodic secretion of a little bit of slime."[167] Hadot concludes that through such rehearsals Marcus "wants to emphasize that the transformations of matter, qua natural processes, are necessarily accompanied by phenomena which *seem to us* to be repugnant, although in reality they too are natural."[168]

Like Marcus Aurelius, Tertullian is shaped by Stoicism. Could his rehearsal of the sordid details of life in utero be designed to bring the reader to an appreciation of the processes of natural generation, degeneration, and regeneration that govern all life? As I have argued, Tertullian participates in competing discourses without demonstrating great concern for resolving the inconsistencies among those discourses. An educated man, a philosopher, Tertullian acknowledges the body as part of the natural order and in that context conceives of the uterus as a sacred workshop. A sacred workshop, however, does not require redemption by Christ. In the end, Tertullian is interested not in the natural processes that inform flesh but in the transformation in flesh effected by Christ's incarnation and resurrection. Because this transformation will not be fully realized until humanity shares in Christ's resurrection, the sordidness of the flesh is not yet annulled.

The Resurrection of the Pudenda

The sordidness of corporeal interiors continues to be a problem for Tertullian as he expounds on the resurrection of the flesh. This resurrection will transpire when human flesh is spit up from the guts of fish and the crops of birds and "the peculiar gluttony of time itself" (*Res.* 4). He claims his opponents cite the existence of digestive and reproductive organs as evidence against the resurrection of the body. Tertullian tells us that his opponents demand, "Then what of the appurtenances of the flesh? Will these all again be necessary to it, and particularly food and drink? And will it have to breathe with lungs and heave in its intestines and be shameless with its shameful parts and have trouble with all its members?" (*Res.* 4). Tertullian contends with the shamefulness of bowels as well as the shamefulness of genitals.

He likens vulva to craw and reels with disgust at both, despite his repeated asser-
tions that the disgust belongs properly to his opponents. "Now I have expressed
this somewhat decently," he writes, "out of respect for my pen: but how much
license is given even to foul-speaking, you may find out for yourselves in these
people's discussions" (*Res.* 4).

His opponents mock: are we to be raised with our gullets and pudenda? As
usual, Tertullian returns an equivocal response. He attempts to uphold a clinical
attitude toward bodies while tacitly conceding an organic abhorrence of ordinary
bodily functions:

> The lower parts in man and in woman are perforated—so that there, you say, the lusts
> may be in motion: why not rather that the excreta may be filtered? Also, women have
> within them a place where the seed may be garnered: why not where there may be a
> diversion of the overplus of the blood, which the less energetic sex has not the strength
> to throw off? (*Res.* 61)

At least on Tertullian's view, organs of desire and generation double as organs of
elimination and, for women, as organs designed to ensure physiological soundness.
Yet, even so, Tertullian argues that resurrected flesh will be relieved of the twin
burdens of lust and of fecal production, a condition anticipated in his own day
among those who fasted from food and sex.

Again, Tertullian participates in competing discourses. Defecation is both natural and good. At the same time, however, bodies will be relieved of this natural and
good process when they share in the resurrection. Flesh has a double or perhaps
triple quality: created and beloved by God; corrupt and repulsive; redeemed and
ready for transformation at the resurrection. "So all flesh is grass, which is destined
to the fire," he writes, "and all flesh shall see the salvation of God" (*Res.* 59). With
his own flesh, Tertullian muses, he committed adulteries, and with that same flesh
he now strives for a state of continence. Yet his flesh is the same flesh. Flesh, whose
acquaintance with filth begins in the mother's dirty innards, is the occasion and
condition of redemption.

Theology from the Womb

Perhaps as a result of direct or indirect influence from Tertullian, the third-century
Christian author Origen of Alexandria pictures Jesus' first earthly abode in terms
similar to those Tertullian employs in his charged description of Mary's cloacal
womb. Origen writes in his fourteenth homily on Luke: "In his mother's womb he
saw the uncleanness of bodies. He was walled in on both sides by her innards; he
bore the straits of earthly dregs" (*Hom. Luc.* 14.8). The fetal Jesus almost chokes
on impurities in a cramped womb, an experience that guarantees his knowledge of
the stain of human existence from the day of his birth. Given this vision of Mary's

uterus crammed with occult filth, it is no wonder that in the same homily Origen confirms that Mary needed to participate in the purification ritual after Jesus' birth. Commenting on Luke 2:22, which indicates that at the time for "their" purification Mary and Jesus traveled to the Jerusalem temple, Origen puzzles only about the implicit suggestion that Jesus participated in the purification ritual. "Who are *they*?" Origen asks. "If Scripture had said, 'on account of "her" purification'—that is, Mary's, who had given birth—then no question would arise. We would say confidently that Mary, who was a human being needed purification after child-birth" (*Hom. Luc.* 14.3).

Elsewhere, however, Origen demurs from treating Mary's childbirth blood as though it were mixed with impurities. In his eighth homily on Leviticus, Origen analyzes an injunction from Leviticus: "If a woman conceives and bears a male child, she shall be ceremonially unclean seven days; as at the time of her menstruation, she shall be unclean (Lev. 12:2)." Why does Leviticus specify that a woman's blood is unclean for seven days if she has conceived and given birth to a son rather than sim-ply saying that a woman's blood is unclean for seven days if she has given birth, Origen asks. Aren't the two formulations equivalent? No, he deduces, the formula-tion of Leviticus allows us to understand that the blood of Mary's parturition remained pure. He writes, "For the Lawgiver added this word [conceived] to distin-guish her who "conceived and gave birth" without seed from other women so as not to designate as "unclean" every woman who had given birth but her who had "given birth by receiving seed" (*Hom. Lev.* 8.2). The injunction to purification applies to parturient women, not parturient virgins, Origen avers, relying on a differentiation between the category of woman and the category of virgin: "Therefore let women carry the burdens of the Law, but let virgins be immune from them" (*Hom. Lev.* 8.3).

Here Origen immediately recognizes that he has created a problem for himself. In Galatians 4:4, Paul specifies that Jesus was born of a woman. But what is a woman, what is a virgin? Origen's definition shifts as he explains that Paul refers to Mary as a woman "not because of corruption, but because of her sex" (*Hom. Lev.* 8.3). Origen thus moves from defining "woman" as sexually experienced, in contradistinction to a virgin, to defining "woman" as female, in contradistinction to a man. Origen attempts yet another definition: a virgin can be defined by age and not by sexual experience. Thus, when Paul calls Mary a woman, he refers to her maturity rather than her corruption by sexual experience, a corruption that would require the purification of her blood after childbearing.[169] I will not attempt to rec-oncile Origen's two statements on whether Mary's blood was impure after the ges-tation and birth of Jesus. What is clear, I think, is that Origen regards the lochial pollution of ordinary childbirth as symptomatic of a moral stain.

One might imagine life in the womb quite differently. Kathleen E. McVey argues that, in his *Hymns of Paradise*, Ephrem does just that. For Ephrem, McVey argues, life in paradise would be akin to life in the womb or nursing at a breast. In these hymns, McVey writes, "A unique feature of the maternal imagery of nourishment—of wombs and breasts—is that it appears to be effortless both on the part of the one feeding and the one being fed."[170] Both unlike and like Tertullian and Origen, Ephrem demonstrates in his own way what Julia Kristeva describes as the compelling psychic sway of "the desirable and terrifying, nourishing and murderous, fascinating and abject inside of the maternal body."[171] Ephrem's evocations of gestational life as a foretaste of paradise might seem to challenge Luce Irigiray's claim that the God of Christianity is threatened by the intimacy of the womb. For Irigiray, touch rather than vision enjoys a privileged epistemological position. Irigiray writes, "God is always entrusted to the look and never sufficiently imagined as tactile bliss. Who imagines the beyond as an infinitely blissful touch [as opposed to a beatific vision]. Being touched by God, for example. Which is impossible to imagine insofar as God is the counterweight to immersion in intrauterine touching?"[172] Yet ultimately the very rarity of Ephrem's association between the pleasures of gestation and the pleasures of paradise confirms Irigiray's insight.

What story is told by Mary's childbearing body, or by the body of any childbearing woman? Are Mary's genitalia, her organs of generation, configured as pudenda, organs of shame? Does the virgin mother know shame in her body? Tertullian triumphantly notes that the degraded birth Marcion deems beneath Christ is no different from the passage that brought Marcion into the world. You despise the human person during birth, Tertullian generalizes, so how can you love any person? Unlike Marcion, Tertullian continues, Christ loves the person "who was curdled in uncleannesses in the womb, who was brought forth from organs immodest [*pudenda*], who took nourishment from organs of ridicule [*ludibria*]" (*Carn. Chr.* 4.3). While in some contexts the Latin *pudenda* may simply connote a more or less nonjudgmental reference to genitalia, something akin to "private parts," here we must give the word its due: shameful parts. Despite Tertullian's initial evocation of parturition as a sacred and reverend work of nature, he insists on exposing explicitly excremental and shameful associations of pregnancy and childbirth for both mother and child. In this, Mary and Jesus are no different from any other mother and child.

Only by acknowledging these associations is Tertullian able to exploit the full force of Christ's scandalous love for human flesh, a love that leads to the still greater shame of Christ's crucifixion and climaxes in the transformation of that flesh and that shame. Tertullian claims that the shame of crucifixion exceeds the shame of birth. He asks, "For which is more beneath God's dignity, more a matter of shame, to be born or to die, to carry about a body or a cross, to be circumcised or to be crucified, to be fed at the breast or to be buried, to be laid in a manger or entombed in a sepulcher?" (*Carn. Chr.* 5.1). Nonetheless, Tertullian's references to the shame of crucifixion lack the disgusted detail of his references to the nativity. The virginal womb reeks with the shame of being human. After Tertullian demands acknowledgment that Mary's organs of generation are pudenda, organs of shame, he paradoxically insists that Christ was not ashamed to be delivered through Mary's shameful parts. Why? So that Christians might live in the shamelessness of faith.[173]

Intimate Violence

Mary's body opens to tell one other story for Tertullian. The nativity, Tertullian tells us, was an occasion of intimate violence, of sexual violence. According to Tertullian, all childbirth is violence, wounding the mother as well as the child. Mary's body differs from other women's bodies only in that Mary was more profoundly marked by childbirth. If gestation initiates a person to an intimate acquaintance with muck, birth initiates a person to wounding. Just as, we may infer, each person is permanently mired in muck, so each person is permanently marked by the first cut. Before the baby boy knows the pain of the knife slicing the foreskin at circumcision, even before the humiliations of salt bath and swaddling, the baby suffers its first wound: the severing of the umbilical cord.[174] What Tertullian claims Marcion denies is this: that after ten tortured months in utero Jesus departed his mother's womb in a torrent of pain and filth, that as he burst into the daylight he burst into tears, and that his first of many wounds was suffered as he was severed forever from his mother's body.[175] Jesus is saved from the fecal medium of Mary's womb only by the knife. We humans know violence from birth.

Childbirth is violent not only for the child being born but also for the birthing mother. Both mother and child have specific corporal knowledge of violence. Cut, the child leaves the site of violence. The mother *is* the site of violence. Tertullian argues that in Psalm 22 David hymns Christ in conversation with God the Father: you ripped me out of the womb (cf. Psalm 22:9). Tertullian elaborates on the implications of that tearing, emphasizing meanwhile the congress of mother and child. What can be ripped away except that which is joined? Jesus, like any baby, is joined to his mother by the umbilical cord, a cord that belongs at once to mother and to child. The intimacy of a mother's congress with a child is perhaps most evident, and painfully evident, at the moment when that intimacy ruptures. Burrus translates Tertullian, "Even when one strange matter amalgamates with another, it produces such a communion of flesh and viscera [*concarnatur et convisceratur*] with that which it amalgamates, that when it is torn away, it takes with it from the body from which it is torn a certain consequence of the severed union and bond of mutual joining [*coitus*]" (*Carn. Chr.* 20.5).[176] Gestation and childbirth are a kind of intercourse, Tertullian hints, a kind of intercourse interrupted by cutting.

Tertullian, who shares the widespread belief of his day that milk is processed and refined uterine blood, continues (in a passage on which I commented in my discussion of *Prot. Jas.*):

[L]et midwives, physicians, and biologists bear witness concerning the nature of breasts, whether they are wont to flow except at the genital experience of the womb, from which the veins pay over into the teat that cess of the lower blood, and in the course of that transfer distill it into the more congenial material of milk. That is why, during lactation, the monthly periods cease. (*Carn. Chr.* 20.6)

Burrus notes that for Tertullian the bloody separation of child from mother continues to well up in the mother's body, spilling as milk from her breasts. Mary's womb, Tertullian writes, "cannot have possessed blood for the supply of milk without also having reasons for the blood itself, namely the tearing away of flesh which was its own" (*Carn. Chr.* 20.6). Childbirth for the mother is an open wound, spilling over to sate the wounded child's hunger.

The Law of the Opened Body

Tertullian thus interprets Psalm 22 to suggest that Christ sings of his mothers' breasts. He infers that if Christ sings of Mary's breasts he must have nursed from them. Moreover, on his view, the milk that flowed from those breasts must have been an overflow from the primary bloodletting of childbirth (*Carn. Chr.* 20.6). Tertullian presents Mary's body as a sign of contradiction that requires interpretation. Willemien Otten argues that the enfleshment of the Son from virgin flesh is an impossibility that brings Tertullian's long series of paradoxes to culmination and collapse: "in the *signum contradicibile* of Christ's birth of a virgin salvation history ultimately contracts to a point from which there is no escape: the concreteness of human flesh."[177]

Consideration of the logic of this obstinate flesh leads Tertullian to the conclusion that, by being born, Jesus becomes, none too gently, his mother's lover—a conclusion that implies that all childbirth necessitates a sexual moment between child (or, at least, male child) and mother:

[I]f as a virgin she conceived, in her child-bearing she became a wife. For she became a wife by that same law of the opened body, in which it made no difference whether the violence was of the male let in or let out [*de vi masculi admissi an emissi*]: the same sex performed that unsealing. This in fact is the womb [*uulua*] by virtue of which it is written also concerning other wombs: *Everything male that opens the womb [uulua] shall be called holy to the Lord.* . . . Who in a strict sense has opened a womb [*uulua* = vagina], except him who opened this that was shut? For all other women marriage opens it. Consequently, hers was the more truly opened in that it was the more shut. . . . In stating, on these considerations, not that the Son of God was born of a virgin, but of a woman, the apostle acknowledges the nuptial experience of the opened womb [*uulua* = vagina]. (*Carn. Chr.* 23.4–5)

Uulua, which in some cases refers clearly to the uterus and in others has the sense of vagina or—not surprisingly—vulva, comes into widespread use during the empire, but is never as common in literary Latin as in graffiti and epigrams. Throughout *On the Flesh of Christ* Tertullian uses *uterus* and *uulua* interchangeably to refer to the uterus. In *The Latin Sexual Vocabulary*, J. N. Adams proposes that Tertullian's reliance on *uulua* to refer to the uterus—a reliance unusual for a literary source—is an artifact of his use of the Old Latin translation of the Bible, which has a marked preference for *uulua*.[178] The meaning of *uulua* slides from "uterus" in the scriptural quotation to "vagina" in Tertullian's exposition. A woman whose marriage is conventionally consummated has her vagina, not her uterus, opened by her male partner.[179]

Origen, too, glosses Luke 2:23, which designates as holy every firstborn male, by stressing that Jesus uniquely opens Mary's womb. "In the case of every other woman, it is not the birth of an infant but intercourse with a man that opens the womb," Origen writes, and then continues: "But the womb of the Lord's mother was opened at the time when her offspring was brought forth, because before the birth of Christ a male did not even touch her womb, holy as it was and deserving of all respect" (*Hom. Luc.* 14.7–8). As I note above, Origen's exegesis may suggest influence from Tertullian's writings on the nativity. Nevertheless, Origen's treatment of the Lukan text has two important differences from that of Tertullian. First, Origen does not designate Jesus' passage through Mary's vagina as a nuptial act. Second, Origen describes Mary's *uulua* as holy and deserving of distinctive respect, a sentiment at odds with the tenor of Tertullian's representation of her *uulua*.

If Mary's childbearing is her nuptial deflowering, then any experience of childbirth should be construed as a sexual encounter, albeit not ordinarily a deflowering. Moreover, while Tertullian does not represent childbirth as an erotic moment—by which I mean a moment when desire is expressed—he does imply that the erotic encounter of intercourse, at the very least a woman's first intercourse, must be a moment of intimate violence when a man forces his entry to the *uulua*. As in the image of the infant who suffers his first wound by severance from his mother's body, Tertullian's reference to sexual intercourse as an exercise of male force implies violence as a ground for human intimacy—perhaps not a surprising sentiment for a man who so identifies subjection to crucifixion with love and encourages Christians to flock to bloody ends in arenas.[180] Humanity, Tertullian seems to say, originates in violence and gravitates to a destiny of violence, from blood to blood.

By the law of the opened body, Tertullian says, Mary becomes a wife. He thus inscribes Mary into a legal and therefore symbolic register. Sexually possessed by her son, she becomes his property.[181] In the *Protevangelium of James*, Salome's finger ignites when it reaches between Mary's legs; Mary's genitalia are untouchable.

For Tertullian, Mary's pudenda—although Tertullian does not here use that term—are most certainly touchable, touched and therefore owned by her son. What Tertullian deems the violence of sexuality leaves its mark on Mary's opened body. The marks of violence in turn demand interpretation. On Judgment Day, Tertullian tells us, those who crucified Jesus will recognize him by the flesh they marked, "without doubt the same flesh upon which they wrought their savagery, for without it he can neither be nor be recognized as himself" (*Carn. Chr.* 24.4). We will not recognize Mary by her ordinary markings, markings of a violence all mothers share. Still those markings make possible both flesh and word.

What is at stake in Tertullian's treatment of the nativity? Distancing himself from Marcion and influenced both by Soranus and by Stoicism, Tertullian can refer to the womb as "that workshop for bringing forth the noble animal which is man" (*Marc.* 3.11). Benign natural processes of generation, degeneration, and regeneration, however, do not require redemption by an incarnate, crucified, and resurrected God. The body's redemption will not be complete until the body is raised, free from the desires of the flesh, free from desires for food and drink and sexual pleasure. Insisting that Christ is fully flesh, Tertullian also insists on what Grosz calls "the debt flesh owes to maternity."[182] Primed not by vision but by mutual and chiastic touching, "the being touched of the touching," corporal knowing begins in the womb.[183] From his mother's womb, Tertullian tells us, Jesus knows the woundedness and uncleanness of bodies. Although he initially distances himself from Marcion's view that maternal bodies are filthy and degrading places, Tertullian's understanding of the incarnation ultimately requires that he treat the bloody discharges of parturition and childbirth as both polluting and degrading. In order for the incarnation to matter, Mary must know abjection deep within her. For Tertullian, Mary's violated and unclean *uulua* is the matrix of redemption.

Defending the Lady's Honor

I bring this chapter to a close with two anecdotes involving attempts to insulate the virgin mother from dishonor and abjection. One incident takes us back to early modern Spain. The other incident takes us back to Brooklyn on the eve of the third millennium.

Spain, 1522

In his autobiography, Ignatius Loyola, founder of the Society of Jesus—more commonly known as the Jesuits—relates a story that attests to the emotional sway exerted by the virgin's genitalia, which, in Ignatius's eyes, are certainly not pudenda.

Early in his journeys, Ignatius tells us, he encountered a Moor. Both men were mounted on mules. As they rode companionably along they began to chat about Our Lady, as Ignatius calls Mary. The Moor was ready enough to believe that Mary conceived as a virgin, but he denied that she could have retained her virginity through childbirth. Ignatius might not have realized that the Qur'an insists on Mary's virginity but also specifies that she experienced pain in labor.[184] How did the Moor react to the conversation? According to Ignatius, the Moor hurried his mule along, leaving Ignatius behind to stew about the Moor's disrespect for Our Lady.

As a youth, Ignatius had been enamored of books of chivalry, a taste in reading that perhaps influenced his reaction to the Moor. Ignatius tells us that "he thought that he had done wrong in allowing the Moor to say such things about Our Lady and that he was obliged to defend her honor. A desire came over him to go in search of the Moor and strike him with his dagger for what he had said."[185] Uncertain of how to proceed, he allowed his mule to choose its own route. As the route chosen by the pacifist mule diverged from the route followed by the Moor, Ignatius did not resort to violence to defend his Lady. Recounting the incident after many years, Ignatius gives no hint that he regrets the choice of his base steed to pursue the path of peace. Indeed, he recounts the tale with a touch of ruefulness at the headstrong inclinations of his youth.

What attracts my attention to the tale is Ignatius's fierce attachment to the concept of *virginitas in partu*, a concept for which he was willing to charge as a knight into battle—albeit mounted on a mule. For Ignatius, Mary's physical condition was inseparable from her honor; he understood her body to express her moral status. Ignatius was shaped by a tradition that began to emerge in the second century—a tradition that claimed that Mary retained the outward signs of virginity even during labor and delivery.

As we have seen, the twentieth-century Jesuit Karl Rahner asked, could "the normal expansion of the genital passages in a completely healthy birth" be construed as "a breach of 'bodily integrity'? Will anyone have the courage to maintain this categorically?" What is injured or damaged through childbirth, Rahner demanded. His unarticulated answer: nothing. Ignatius, however, might have answered: honor. Purity. In the emotion of shame, ethics and aesthetics intersect. Flesh is shame's fertile ground, its richly manured soil. According to the time-honored tradition Rahner implicitly challenged, a stretched vagina was understood to communicate first-person knowledge of the fallen state of humanity.

Brooklyn, 1999

On the eve of the third millennium, New York City major Rudolph Giuliani excited controversy when he threatened to cut off the city subsidy to the Brooklyn Museum because of the museum's decision to host Sensation, a traveling exhibition featuring the work of young British artists. Especially controversial was a Madonna created by former altar boy Chris Ofili. Incorporating elephant dung, Ofili's *The Holy Virgin Mary* was called "sick stuff" by Giuliani. Then first lady Hillary Clinton stepped into the fray to announce that although she herself would not go to see such depraved art, she opposed any attempt to cut off funding for the exhibition.

Other controversial works were on display, but Ofili's painting became iconic for the exhibition. In an article on Salon.com, Daniel Kunitz extolled Ofili's artful incorporation of dung. "Oh yes, I forgot the dung," Kunitz writes. "By now we all should know that in Africa, where the dung idea came from, elephant droppings carry none of the horrible connotations that shit carries in New York. Before offending us all with his own bullshit, Giuliani might have troubled himself to learn about the sacred nature of pachyderms and their dung in other parts of the world."[186] Emphasizing not Ofili's Nigerian heritage but his identity as a British artist who was born and raised in London, other critics located Ofili's use of excrement in the context of trends in late twentieth-century European art.[187] I note this art historical controversy without attempting to enter into it.

While we may feel ourselves a world away from Ignatius as he defends his Lady's honor, response to Ofili's artwork suggests a fierce urge in our own day to distance the virgin mother from abasement. Clinton's weak defense of the Brooklyn Museum underscores the public's revulsion at imagining the virgin body in conjunction with corporal waste. Even Kunitz's defense of Ofili's work relies on denying the shittiness of shit. In Ofili's *The Holy Virgin Mary*, dung becomes a vehicle for transcendence. In a parallel way, Tertullian stresses what he sees as the abjection inherent in birthing and in being born. He positions this abjection as central to understanding God's sublime love that becomes manifest in the incarnation. Approaching Ofili's Madonna after reading Tertullian, I have no interest in spinning his dung into gold or of looking past the base materiality of the composition. Instead it seems to me that we should insist on the sordid materiality of excrement even as we understand it as an occasion of the sublime.

Conclusion

In their treatments of the virgin birth, both the *Protevangelium of James* and Tertullian draw on a corporal vocabulary that evolves into the aristocratic habitus of early modern Spain. The *Odes of Solomon* 19 and *Ascension of Isaiah* do not emphasize the same corporal vocabulary. Their references to Mary's painless childbirth function on symbolic and visionary levels, evoking other corporal imaginaries: masculinity as mastery over pain, for example, and the accidental relationship of bodies to identity. As we read the earliest references to Mary in childbirth, we are forced to grapple with habituated views of bodies—especially reproductive female bodies—that were widely held in the Roman Empire. We do not have female-authored sources—or more specifically mother-authored sources—that would open windows on the ways that those habituated views affected the corporal experiences of childbearing women. Nonetheless, it is hard to imagine that a woman's being-in-the-world was not informed by cultural discourses. At the same time, the ancient male theologians who invoke, narrate, and analyze Mary's childbearing body thereby invite meditation on what it means to be a body.

I do not share the view of *Ascension of Isaiah* that bodies are subsidiary to identities. I understand bodies as constitutive of identities. Our bodies structure our engagement with the world, what we can know, and who we are. Virginia Woolf wrote that the remaining task for a woman writer is to tell the truth about her experiences as a body. Can we ever tell the truth about being a body? Can we put into words what we know in our bodies? Does every attempt to do so open the wounds of past tellings?

I suspect there is no innocent corporal discourse, just as there is no birth without scarring.

Epilogue

By torture we mean the infliction of anguish and agony on the body to elicit the truth.
—*Digest of Justinian* 48.10.15.41

Christs crucifix shall be made an excuse for Executing Criminals
—William Blake, inscription in the manuscript of *The Four Zoas*

Throughout this book I have attempted to analyze both how bodies are read—the stories bodies tell—and what bodies know. Following philosopher Linda Alcoff, I have viewed the body as, "oddly enough, a kind of mind, but one with a physical appearance, location, and specific instantiation." As Alcoff argues, "We perceive and process and incorporate and reason and are intellectually trained in the body itself."[1] Our skilled bodies know their places in complex social systems and know how to interact with other socially located bodies. However, our bodies are not robots. Social interactions are performances in which our knowing bodies may interpret, reinscribe, modify, or resist our corporal training. At times we bring the implications of our bodily movements and postures to consciousness. We may deliberately raise or lower our voices, stride boldly into a meeting or tiptoe out, aware as we do so of how our bodily habitus is likely to be interpreted. More often, however, we do not think about how loudly our voices are projected or the kind of gait we affect. Our bodies choose.

We do not have access to ancient bodies, but writings from the Roman Empire are attuned to the niceties of embodied moral and social distinctions. I have argued that we should attend to traces of corporal dynamics at play in a variety of kinds of early Christian writings. I have paid special attention to ways that Roman habitus shaped emergent patterns of Christian thought and practice. Early Christians relayed paradigmatic stories that implied rejection of Roman norms of bodily interaction and embodied self-understanding. For example, Christians remembered

137

that Jesus instructed his followers to wash one another's feet, a servile action. Most important, Jesus suffered a humiliating execution that was morally appalling to embodied Roman sensibilities. As a result, Paul could even cite his own history of abuse as a source of knowledge and power parallel to his ineffable astral journeying.

Based on these corporal models, we might expect that Christians would have recoiled from the morally coded embodiment of status distinctions so prevalent throughout antiquity. Not so. Certainly Christians developed new forms of community that deliberately retrained bodies. Christians were said to welcome martyrdom; in large numbers they pursued ascetic disciplines; by late antiquity many Christians joined monasteries that inverted moral understandings of humble bodies. Other Christians who did not follow ascetic ways turned to monks for guidance and healing. This book has not attempted to tell stories of these developments, stories that have been well told by any number of other scholars.

Instead, I have argued that in daily practice the embodied interactions and self-understandings of Christians were subject to the status-conscious corporal pedagogy of the Roman Empire. In instances where Christians brought to consciousness the implications of embodied morality, they had the opportunity to revise their practice, yet in the typical exchanges of daily life the implications of embodied morality transcended—or sank beneath—conscious analysis. I would even argue that the continuing visible presence of bodies perceived as debased—by which I mean bodies perceived both as socially and morally debased—facilitated Christian self-definition.[2] In order to appreciate the heroic self-abasement of wellborn Christians who virtuously chose to abstain from rich foods and regular bathing, for example, it would have been helpful to apprehend the degradation of other bodies deprived by poverty of sound nutrition and a good scrub in the steamy baths. Ascetic virtue neither canceled nor elevated the degradations of poverty.

I have been interested not only in the stories told by bodies but also in the experience of being a body. Social discourses and practices inform corporal experience. One way to phrase this trajectory of my argument would be in terms of subjectivity: socially located experiences of being a body inform a person's subjectivity. For a variety of reasons I have chosen instead to phrase this trajectory of my argument in terms of epistemology: socially located experiences of being a body inform what a body knows. This line of argument has been at the crux of my case studies of Pauline self-representation, the impact of slaveholding on Christian morals, and representations of Mary in childbirth. Aware of possible of abuses such an argument, I have insisted in a multiplicity of ways that we are more than the sum of privileges we have enjoyed and more than the sum of abuses we have endured.

Moreover, while I am centrally interested in ways that gender and social location inform corporal epistemology, my reading of Merleau-Ponty pushes me to think about forms of corporal knowing that exceed—ooze out from—our social locations. That fascination is perhaps most evident in my treatment of Mary in childbirth, where I read male theologians as engaging the tactile quiddity of bodies, or, to put it more colloquially, as bumping up against bodies. In short, while I argue that social location is centrally implicated in corporal knowing, I do not think what I know in my body is exhausted by my location in a social grid. We might think here of contrasting interpretations of fetal life. For Tertullian and Origen, a child is born after enduring months of torture in the fetid prison of the womb; for Ephrem, that same life in utero seems an Eden of ready nourishment and bountiful refreshment. The child who enters the world lacks both interpretive paradigms yet knows something of an occult life she will never be able to put into words.[3]

As there is no innocent reading, Louis Althusser wrote, we must say what reading we are guilty of. Throughout my years of working on this project I have been haunted by the underbelly of my argument, what I call the torturer's logic: the conviction that truth can be beaten out of bodies, that truth can be squeezed from flesh. What has disturbed me—at times prompted me to write in agitation, at other times stalled my work as I stared blankly at the computer screen—has been the realization that the torturer's logic retains its resonance today. In the first chapter I invited the reader to contemplate ways that storytelling bodies of the third millennium mediate our encounters with ancient representations of bodies. What do we know in our bodies? What stories do our bodies tell? How do the stories we tell about our bodies complicate the stories we read in ancient bodies? How do our own experiences of embodied knowing color our expectations regarding the limits and content of what other bodies may know? Thus, for example, in chapter 4 I accord attention to childbearing practices and discourses of the modern era. In a different way, while I have written at length about what bodies know, I have been reminded far too often that intelligence and security professionals—as well as many of my fellow Americans—consider knowledge something that can be exacted by violence from an enemy body. And perhaps should be so exacted, my fellow citizens have been inclined to think, especially if that enemy body speaks a strange tongue and lacks the protections of citizenship.

For an ancient example of such logic at work, we can turn to the scene of Jesus' trial before Pilate. In the Gospel of John, Pilate famously asks Jesus, "What is truth?" Not waiting for a response, Pilate leaves the praetorium to report to the assembly that he finds no evidence of crime in Jesus. The assembly shouts down his offer to release Jesus, clamoring instead for the release of Barabbas. Pilate takes Jesus and scourges him.[4] Roman soldiers shower Jesus with blows as they mock him as king of the Jews. Pilate returns to the assembly to announce that he will bring Jesus out to them so that they may know that he finds no evidence of crime in the battered man (18:38–19:4). I argue that the midtrial beating of Jesus in the

Gospel of John is an instance of judicial torture, which is the understanding of torture operative in the Greco-Roman world. Judicial torture can be defined as torture inflicted neither to punish nor to terrorize—or at least, not primarily to punish or to terrorize—but to elicit testimony or a confession. I argue that although Pilate walks away from the praetorium, he does not walk away from his question, What is truth? As he scourges Jesus he attempts to extract the truth from him.[5]

I have not been able to avoid contemporary examples of such logic at work. As I conclude work on this book, anyone who reads a newspaper is aware of the use of torture by Americans—the military, the CIA—in the so-called war on terror after the September 11 attacks on the World Trade Center and the Pentagon. Yet there has been a kind of willed naïveté among Americans about this torture policy, as though American use of torture techniques were an aberration rather than a long-standing practice among democratic nations. Dirty, but not even a dirty secret. Wearisome: The French in Algeria. The English in Ireland. The Israelis in the West Bank. Americans—and American advisors—in Iran, Vietnam, El Salvador, and elsewhere.[6] This is not the place to rail against American policy and practice. But in light of this sad history, claims about corporal knowing are not anodyne claims.

Nonetheless as I have worked on this project it has been important to me to affirm precisely that bodies are sites of knowledge. In part I have written this book as an effort to think through the diverse phenomena of corporal knowing, to think through what it might mean to say, "she knew in the body." The answer proposed by the torturer is not the only answer. I have argued that other answers are implicit in a variety of early Christian writings. In the epigraph at the head of Chapter 1, Virginia Woolf suggests that no woman has yet managed to tell the truth about her experiences of being a body. There is something welcome about this incompletion. Frustrating the torturer's passion for control as well as for knowledge, the body knows more than it is willing to tell.

Notes

Chapter 1

1. The parallel between the woman's corporal self-knowing and Jesus' self-knowing is pointed out by Collins, *Mark*, 282.

2. Johnson, *Body in the Mind*.

3. Thomas, "'Stop Sinning,'" 14–17.

4. Sontag, *Illness as Metaphor*, 3.

5. Ibid.

6. Ibid., 17.

7. Rieff, *Swimming in a Sea of Death*, 86–87.

8. Sontag, *Illness as Metaphor*, 183.

9. Johnson, *Body in the Mind*, xix.

10. Scheper-Hughes and Lock, "The Mindful Body," 6.

11. Ibid., 25.

12. Among the works I have found helpful as I work through these theoretical questions are Strathern, *Body Thoughts*; Csordas, *Embodiment and Experience*.

13. Scheper-Hughes and Lock locate Bourdieu's influence in the treatment of the social body ("The Mindful Body," 22). In suggesting that Bourdieu helps us analyze "the body politic," I am not registering disagreement so much as emphasis on other parts of Bourdieu's exposition.

14. Gleason, "Truth Contests and Talking Corpses," 305.

15. Alcoff writes, "Marilyn Frye describes the discomfort most people feel when we don't know the sex of the person we are meeting; the discomfort comes not just from some abstract conceptual block but because we don't know how to greet or interact with them, so gendered are our gestures" (*Visible Identities*, 103).

16. Ibid., 114.

17. Ibid., 108.

18. Iris Marion Young's 1980 essay "Throwing Like a Girl: A Phenomenology of Feminine Body Comportment, Motility, and Spatiality" remains essential—albeit dated—reading (in *On Female Body Experience*, 27–45).

19. Alcoff, *Visible Identities*, 108.

20. For essential discussions, see Byron, *Symbolic Blackness*; and Buell, *Why This New Race?*

21. Alcoff, *Visible Identities*, 92.

22. Judge, *Social Distinctives*, 57.

23. Brilliant, *Gesture and Rank*, 9.

24. Gleason, *Making Men*; Gunderson, *Staging Masculinity*.

25. Schmitt observes that Cicero has company in his explicit attention to the morality implicit in bodily comportment appropriate to social status and gender. He locates Cicero at the start of a tradition that stretches, via Seneca and Tertullian and Ambrose—the last of whom reproduces large sections of Cicero's *On Duties* in his own writings—through medieval scholasticism ("Ethics of Gesture").

26. While I discuss those contributions to the study of Greco-Roman bodies that are most immediately relevant, there are, not surprisingly, others, for example, Lateiner, "Nonverbal Behaviors"; Newbold, "Non-verbal Communication."

27. Roller, *Dining Posture*, 8.

28. Ibid., 8.

29. Corbeill, *Nature Embodied*, 1.

30. Ibid., 6.

31. Ibid., 1.

32. Contrast Matthew, where the Canaanite woman does not kneel until after Jesus ignores her and the disciples attempt to dismiss her (10:25).

33. For example, Rhoads likens the leper's act of kneeling before Jesus (1:40) to Jairus's falling on the ground before him ("Jesus and the Syrophoenician Woman," 350).

34. Although I emphasize that gesture is meaningful within a particular corporal vernacular, the gesture of lowering oneself before another may be perennially legible. As I was writing in fall 2008 about the Markan gesture of self-lowering, I was startled to read newspaper accounts of Henry Paulson, secretary of the treasury under President George W. Bush, kneeling before Speaker of the House Nancy Pelosi to beg for her support in a financial bailout scheme. No one seemed in doubt how to interpret the gesture.

35. See the plates in Brilliant, *Gesture and Rank*, 189–195.

36. In Matthew, John says that he is not worthy to carry Jesus' sandals (3:11), and in Luke, John says that he is not worthy to untie Jesus' sandals (3:16).

37. Collins comments that "the only other place in which someone falls on his knees . . . before Jesus is 1:40. . . . In both passages the gesture expresses deference for Jesus and intense petition" (*Mark*, 476). Two points of disagreement with Collins: I do not think there is any perceptible difference between Mark's understanding of the gesture of kneeling and other gestures and postures of self-lowering, such as falling at Jesus' feet. Moreover, note that although the phrasing is different, Mark explicitly represents Roman soldiers kneeling before Jesus (15:19).

38. Matthew, who follows Mark closely in the scene, picks up the detail (27:29).

39. How the reader is to picture the unclean spirits as they fall before Jesus and shout out his identity as Son of God is unclear to me (3:11).

40. The detail that the leper kneels is omitted in some manuscripts.

41. In Matthew's abbreviated version, the hemorrhaging woman does not fall to the ground (9:20–22).

42. Joel Marcus weakens his case with a peculiar argument for parallels between the Markan story of the hemorrhaging woman and the Lukan story of the sinful woman (7:36–50; *Mark 1–8*, 457).

43. Spencer, *Dancing Girls, Loose Ladies, and Women of the Cloth*, 64. Although I disagree with Spencer on this particular point, I find his treatment of women in Mark 5–7 otherwise complex and subtle.

44. With the father the verb is *piptō* (5:22) and with the mother the verb is *prospiptō* (7:25).

45. Joanna Dewey, "Jesus' Healings of Women."

46. Roller, *Dining Posture*, 20.

47. The rich man who seeks counsel on eternal life expresses his deference to Jesus not only by kneeling in front of him but also by running to him (Mark 10:17).

48. Luke 7:8 (cf. Luke 7:1–10; Matthew 8:5–13).

49. Ringe, "A Gentile Woman's Story Revisited," 88.

50. I am convinced by Gerd Theissen's argument that the identification of the Syrophoenician woman as Greek functions as a marker of cultivated and privileged ethnicity that is consistent with an identity as Syrophoenician by descent (*Gospels in Context*, 61–80).

51. As Buell argues, in antiquity race and ethnicity were fluid and complex categories. She writes that the "meaning of ethnicity" does not inhere "solely in fixed criteria such as claims of common descent or territory. Ethnicity/race is a possible (though not necessary) feature of cultural identity, one that is always entangled with and produced in relation with other social concepts and categories" (*Why This New Race?* 45).

52. Donahue and Harrington, *Gospel of Mark*, 237.

53. Rhoads, "Jesus and the Syrophoenician Woman," 351.

54. Donahue and Harrington, *Gospel of Mark*, 237.

55. There is a tendency in English translations to downplay Jesus' response to the petitioner. For example, the New Revised Standard Version reads, "For saying that, you may go," a translation that trivializes the significance of Jesus' capitulation to what he calls the woman's logos. Emphasizing the Syrophoenician woman's appearance in the broader context of Mark 7, Claudia Setzer writes, "We assume that as a Gentile foreigner she does not worry about what goes into her, neither the kashrut nor the ritual purity of the food she ingests. But what comes out of her, her 'logos,' or teaching, identifies her as one who really understands Jesus" ("Three Odd Couples," 77). Setzer in turn acknowledges Joanna Dewey's insistence on the significance of the woman's logos (Dewey, "Gospel of Mark").

56. Pliny, *Nat.* 11.250; noted in Corbeill, *Nature Embodied*, 81. Corbeill's emphasis here is not on the posture of kneeling but on the suppliant reaching toward the knees of the one from whom favor is desired, a gesture that would ordinarily require self-lowering.

57. Here I differ from Collins, who identifies Jesus' throwing himself to the ground primarily as an expression of violent emotion (*Mark*, 67). While the interpretations are not mutually exclusive, in a text where the act of throwing oneself on the ground has frequently been associated with petition, the gesture seems more closely associated with Jesus' desperate petition to his Father.

58. Alcoff, *Visible Identities*, 93.

59. King, *What Is Gnosticism?*, 213.

60. King, *Secret Revelation*, 121–123.

61. Ibid., 124.

62. Ibid.

63. Ibid.

64. Yet there are certainly scholarly works on early Christianity that have shaped my thinking about the experiences of being a body. I hesitate to list them for fear of omitting equally important works. Nonetheless, any such list would have to include contributions by Virginia Burrus, Patricia Cox Miller, and Stephen D. Moore.

65. Csordas, *Embodiment and Experience*, 4.

66. Ibid., 10–12.

67. Csordas's phrasing. Ibid., 12.

68. Merleau-Ponty, "Selections from the Phenomenology of Perception," in Baldwin, ed., *Maurice Merleau-Ponty*, 63–233, esp. p. 123.

69. See, for example, images in La Regina, ed., *Sangue e Arena*, 218, 220.

Chapter 2

1. Martyn, *Galatians*, 568.

2. A view set forth as early as Jerome (*Commentary on Galatians* 3.6.17). For modern bibliography, see n. 94.

3. Martyn, *Galatians*, 568.

4. Moore, *God's Gym*, 28.

5. J. Fitzgerald, *Cracks in an Earthen Vessel*, 43. Andrews has rightly noted that Fitzgerald (among others) "does not describe how any particular type of hardship list differs . . . in function from another type" ("Too Weak Not to Lead," 264).

6. On *andreia*, see Moore and Anderson, "Taking It Like a Man," 253.

7. Bourdieu, *Logic of Practice*, 52.

8. Ibid., 56.

9. Ibid., 69.

10. On the Roman blush, see Barton, *Roman Honor*, 199–269.

11. Bourdieu, *Logic of Practice*, 69–70.

12. We must allow the possibility of varying interpretations not only between ancient communities and modern interpreters but also among Corinthians of varying backgrounds. Cf. Bourdieu, "The Sentiment of Honour," 193–197.

13. See Whitmarsh, *Greek Literature and the Roman Empire*.

14. I am not concerned with the historicity of the incident, but with Luke's location of the incident in an explicitly Roman context. Gaventa cautions against insisting that Paul refers in 1 Thess. 2:2 to the incident familiar from Acts 16 (*First and Second Thessalonians*, 23). Richard argues more absolutely, and less convincingly, against identifying 1 Thess. 2:2 with the incident in Acts 16 (ibid., 78).

15. On Roman and Greek influences in Corinth, see Engels, *Roman Corinth*, passim.

16. Guthrie suggests that "the marks of Jesus would be the scars of persecution. Some of the Galatians had seen those scars" (*Galatians*, 152).

17. Fagan, *Bathing in Public*, 26.

18. Leigh argues that the display of wounds in Roman discourse encodes conflict between persons of higher and lower status ("Wounding and Popular Rhetoric").

19. In his discussion of "tribulation lists" in Paul, Hodgson cites a number of examples of the display of wounds in Greek and Roman literature, but he does not question whether

the use of such battle-scarred imagery to describe Paul's marking by whip and rod is apt ("Paul the Apostle").

20. For additional references to display of war wounds, see Leigh, "Wounding and Popular Rhetoric," passim.

21. Even more broadly, Leigh suggests that it is difficult to cast "anything as typically Greek, Spartan, Roman or whatever in antiquity. Ancient Mediterranean literature reflects common values and expresses these values through anecdotes which are morphologically very similar" (Ibid., 198).

22. See Gunderson, "Discovering the Body," 183.

23. Gleason, "Mutilated Messengers," 66.

24. E.g., Ovid *Metamorphoses* 13.262–267; Diodorus 8.12.1–16.

25. Accusations of predatory libido were a standard element in Roman political invective. Dunkle, "Greek Tyrant and Roman Political Invective."

26. Leigh, *Lucan*, 214–215.

27. Martyn, *Galatians*, 568 n. 73, following a suggestion by W. Klassen ("Galatians 6:17," 378).

28. I intend the term *whippable* to echo an adjective Plautus applied to a slave, *uerberabilissime*, "eminently beatable" (Plautus, *Aulularia*, 633; quoted in Saller, "Corporal Punishment," 154).

29. Saller, "Corporal Punishment," 152.

30. Gleason, "Mutilated Messengers," 59–60.

31. Ibid., 63.

32. Cf. Bauman, *Crime and Punishment*, chap. 4.

33. Saller, "Corporal Punishment," 151.

34. Garnsey, *Social Status and Legal Privilege*, 141.

35. See Fisher, "*Hybris* and Dishonour: I."

36. McCarthy, *Slaves, Masters*, 26. See also Segal, *Roman Laughter*; Parker, "Crucially Funny"; W. Fitzgerald, *Slavery*, 32–47.

37. Roller, *Constructing Autocracy*, 226.

38. See Gleason's discussion of the correspondence between social status and moral character ("Truth Contests and Talking Corpses").

39. For additional examples of such anecdotes, along with analysis of their function in Roman literature, see Leigh, "Wounding and Popular Rhetoric," 210–211.

40. W. Fitzgerald, *Slavery*, 38.

41. Ibid., 27. For an alternate view, see J. Hughes, "*Inter Tribunal et Scaenum*," 184.

42. Athenaeus *Deipnosophistae*, 6.239f; 6.250a.

43. I am indebted to the collection of testimonia to the Spartan flagellation context collected in Kennell, *Gymnasium of Virtue*, 149–161.

44. Kennell notes, "Although death was not common, its mere possibility added a tangible element of risk for the ephebes to confront" (ibid., 74).

45. On self-control as the hegemonic masculine virtue, see Moore and Anderson, "Taking It Like a Man." See also C. Williams, *Roman Homosexuality*, 138–142.

46. See discussions of *Anacharsis, or Athletics* in Whitmarsh, *Greek Literature and the Roman Empire*, 123–125; Branham, *Unruly Eloquence*, 83–102.

47. In enduring beatings, a slave was perceived to embody *patientia* as "the essence of slavery . . . not a testing and assertion of will . . . but a complete absence of will by someone at the rock bottom of the social hierarchy" (Kaster, "The Taxonomy of Patience,"

138–139). On slavery and masculinity, see Glancy, *Slavery in Early Christianity*, 24–29 and 34–38.

48. I regard 2 Cor. 10–13 as a discrete letter, written later than 2 Cor. 1–9 (constituting an earlier letter, or possibly letters). However, that position is irrelevant to my argument in this chapter, which holds even if chaps. 10–13 conclude a longer letter.

49. Selected bibliography: Judge, "Paul's Boasting in Relation to Contemporary Professional Practice," 57–71 in *Social Distinctives of the Christians in the First Century*; Betz, "*De Laude Ipsius* (*Moralia* 539A–547B)"; Forbes, "Comparison, Self-Praise and Irony"; Mitchell, "Patristic Perspective"; Watson, "Paul's Boasting in 2 Corinthians 10–13."

50. Forbes is an exception. See "Comparison, Self-Praise and Irony," 19.

51. Savage, *Power through Weakness*, 63. Selected further bibliography includes Garland, "Paul's Apostolic Authority"; Murphy-O'Connor, *Theology of the Second Letter to the Corinthians*, 115.

52. Against the view that Paul's clandestine getaway from Damascus (2 Cor. 11:32–33) was intrinsically humiliating, Welborn has adduced convincing evidence that clever escapes could be seen not as weak maneuvers but as daring and expedient tactics ("Runaway Paul," 117). I am not, however, convinced by his overall thesis, that in the fool's speech Paul enacts the role of a mime and that particular verses of the fool's speech correspond to particular characters known from mime.

53. I thus disagree with the scope of Watson's contention that Paul "boasts of what is degrading and ignoble: his imprisonments, floggings, whippings, beatings with rods, and being hungry, cold, and naked" ("Paul's Boasting in 2 Corinthians 10–13 as Defense of His Honor," 273).

54. Moreover, in order to espouse the position that, when Paul boasts of himself, he boasts exclusively of things that exhibit weakness (cf. 12:5), one would have to maintain that Paul represents himself as weak when he boasts that he is a Hebrew, an Israelite, a descendant of Abraham, and a minister of Christ.

55. Betz, "*De Laude Ipsius* (*Moralia* 539A–547B)," 388.

56. For a sampling of related positions, see, for example, Best, who writes, "How many untold stories of courage, compassion, and endurance lie behind this list!" (*Second Corinthians*, 114); Danker, who writes that Paul "displays courage" in 11:23–27, "a catalogue of perils . . . which have the net effect of establishing his own personal prestige" ("Paul's Debt," 272, 277); A. Harvey, who writes that "piling on case after case of apparently heroic endurance was a rhetorical device from which Paul may well have drawn perhaps unconscious inspiration" (*Renewal through Suffering*, 99); Malina and Neyrey, who write, "Paul claims superiority to them [his rivals] in terms of his deeds of the body. . . . He actually numbers his beatings . . . to emphasize strength and endurance (*Portraits of Paul*, 58); and Lambrecht, who writes that, in 11:23–33 (and other passages), "Paul was admirably, heroically strong!" ("Dangerous Boasting," 338).

57. A martial context is also implicit, though unacknowledged, in W. Klassen's argument that Antipater's stripping to reveal his wounded (battle-scarred) body helps us better understand Paul's stigmata ("Galatians 6:17").

58. J. Fitzgerald, *Cracks in an Earthen Vessel*, 25.

59. Ibid., 26 n. 97.

60. Ibid., 193; cf. 48.

61. J. Fitzgerald is hardly alone in this oversight. Danker, for example, refers readers to Aeschines's *Against Ctesiphon* on "the receipt of honor for endurance of hardships." The passage to which Danker refers readers involves public inscriptions celebrating soldiers who endured much toil and great dangers while on a successful military campaign (Aeschines, *Against Ctesiphon*, 183–185; Danker, "Paul's Debt," 265 n. 2).

62. Hodgson, "Paul the Apostle," 76–80; Ebner, *Leidenslisten und Apostelbrief*, 118–122 and 161–172.

63. Hodgson, "Paul the Apostle," 76.

64. Hodgson cites Ananus's speech in Josephus's *Jewish War* as "illuminating compara-tive material for Paul's trial lists." Ananus attacks the Jerusalem populace for their compla-cency, specifically mentioning that they did not protest even when flogged. Hodgson writes, "In passing, one will want to note the material agreement with 2 Cor . . . 11:23–29 in the matter of beating." He does not acknowledge that the passage from Josephus stresses the humiliation of being flogged (ibid., 69).

65. J. Fitzgerald, *Cracks in an Earthen Vessel*, passim; Ebner, *Leidenslisten und Apos-telbrief*, 112–115.

66. Saller, "Corporal Punishment, Authority, and Obedience," 152.

67. Bourdieu, *Logic of Practice*, 60–61.

68. Edwards, "Suffering Body: Philosophy and Pain," 254. See also Roller, *Construct-ing Autocracy*, 103–106.

69. Shaw, "Body/Power/Identity," 292.

70. A story well told in Barton, "Savage Miracles"; Barton, *Roman Honor*.

71. See, for example, Barrett, *Commentary on the Second Epistle to the Corinthians*, 297; Furnish, *II Corinthians*, 517; Danker, *II Corinthians*, 182; Thrall, *Critical and Exeget-ical Commentary on the Second Epistle to the Corinthians*, 739–742.

72. "For a high-status person to be subjected to one of these typically 'servile' punish-ments was regarded as singularly damaging to his status" (Roller, *Constructing Autocracy*, 205).

73. Bataille's observation that "no greater drive exists than a wounded person's need for another wound" raises another series of questions—outside the scope of this chapter—about Paul's submission to repeated beatings (*Guilty*, 31). Downing suggests that, after the manner of a Cynic, Paul incited violence against himself (*Cynics, Paul and the Pauline Churches*, 155–156).

74. In this context, Windisch notes that Paul ultimately received 195 lashes (*Der zweite Korintherbrief*, 355).

75. By the first century C.E., the forty lashes seem to have been customarily meted out stopping one stroke short of the fortieth snap of the whip.

76. John Chrysostom's reading of Paul's storytelling body points to the modification of classical bodily hexis in late antiquity. He says that, like a soldier emerging bloody from battle, Paul bears in his body evidence of manly goodness (*andragathia*), so that Paul's exhibition of wounds in Gal. 6:17 is more persuasive than any argument he might make in his own defense. Chrysostom, however, introduces this reading of Paul's body by noting its peculiarity, since in Gal. 6:17 Paul seems to vaunt what is disgraceful (*oneidos*, *Homilies on Galatians* 6.4). Would the Corinthians likewise infer that Paul's corporal markings spell out a martial story? Even after centuries of mounting Christian influence, Chrysostom—who, unlike the Corinthians, has no doubts about Paul's authority—acknowledges the degradation of Paul's bodily appearance.

77. Shaw, "Body/Power/Identity," 303–304.

78. On Paul's choice of and attitudes toward manual labor, see Hock, *Social Context of Paul's Ministry*.

79. Barton, "Savage Miracles," 51–52.

80. P. Hughes, *Paul's Second Epistle to the Corinthians*, 362. Furnish suggests that the superapostles' reference to the weakness of Paul's body may imply sickliness, although he argues that the weakness "is inclusive of more than his state of health" (*II Corinthians*, 478–479); similarly, Hamerton-Kelly, "Girardian Interpretation of Paul."

81. Black, *Paul, Apostle of Weakness*, 136; Hamerton-Kelly, "Girardian Interpretation of Paul," 74; Bultmann, *Second Letter to the Corinthians*, 190; A. Dewey, "Matter of Honor," 213; Thrall, *Critical and Exegetical Commentary on the Second Epistle to the Corinthians*, 631.

82. Danker argues that Paul "lacks personal presence"; he rightly emphasizes the importance of corporal self-presentation in the establishment of authority in ancient contexts (*II Corinthians*, 155).

83. Harrill, "Invective against Paul (2 Cor 10:10)," 211.

84. Harrill bases his argument on 2 Cor. 10:10. He does not track other clues Paul supplies about his body, nor does he explore the credibility of the superapostles' charge, that is, whether Paul's body would have been legible as weak and servile. Following Saller, he notes, albeit briefly, that "the repeated physical abuse of the whip broke down and re-shaped the bodies of slaves, thereby creating in actuality the slave body that ideology required" (ibid., 194–195). He does not acknowledge the relevance of this insight for interpreting the allegation that Paul's bodily appearance was weak. Harrill argues that, in describing his body as weak, Paul defends himself by implicitly taking on the mantle of Odysseus, who disguised himself as a slave by whipping himself and dressing in rags, thereby securing admission to Troy (212; Malherbe, "Antisthenes and Odysseus"). Unlike Odysseus, however, Paul did not flagellate himself. Rather, he was repeatedly and publicly whipped and beaten with rods. He did not choose the persona of a slave. Instead, to first-century eyes, a tale of abasement was legible in his scars, so the superapostles described his whippable body as weak in appearance.

85. Roller, *Constructing Autocracy*, 226.

86. Savage suggests that the charge of somatic weakness is linked to Paul's failure to discipline the community (*Power through Weakness*, 66).

87. Lattey suggests that translation of λαμβάνειν (2 Cor. 11:20) should convey the idea of physical force ("λαμβάνειν in 2 Cor xi.20," 148). Scholarly opinion is divided on the question of whether the superapostles have physically expressed their mastery over the Corinthians, or whether their seizing and slaps are metaphorical. Given the ubiquity of corporal expressions of dominance around the ancient Mediterranean world, even in synagogues and churches, I am persuaded that Paul refers to physical aggression in this verse. My argument, however, requires only that Paul demonstrate—as he does in 11:20—his habituation to a corporal vocabulary associating submission to corporal punishment with enslavement. Against the view that Paul's reference to a slap across the face refers to flesh-to-flesh contact, note that he refers to "your [pl.] face" rather than to "your faces." Those who express ambivalence on the question of whether Paul refers metaphorically to violence include Barrett, *Commentary on the Second Epistle to the Corinthians*, 291; Bultmann, *Second Letter to the Corinthians*, 212; Thrall, *Critical and Exegetical Commentary on the*

Second Epistle to the Corinthians, 717–718. For the view that the violence is metaphorical, see Windisch, *Der zweite Korintherbrief*, 347; Furnish, *II Corinthians*, 497; Danker, *II Corinthians*, 177; Lambrecht, *Second Corinthians*, 190. For the view that Paul refers to physical violence, in particular, literal slaps on the face, see P. Hughes, *Paul's Second Epistle to the Corinthians*, 400; Kruse, *Second Epistle of Paul to the Corinthians*, 193.

88. "When a power-holder's relationship . . . is figured as that of a master in relation to slaves, he is most often said or implied to be imposing corporal punishments of various (typically slavish) sorts" (Roller, *Constructing Autocracy*, 262–263).

89. Although he is prepared to discipline the Corinthians when he returns (13:1–3, 10), he will not do so as a slaveholder. In chaps. 10–13, Paul applies several metaphors to himself that could govern the disciplinary role he foresees for himself. He describes himself as a military commander (10:3–6) and the father of the community (11:2; 12:14–15). J. Fitzgerald notes the importance of Paul's presentation of himself as father of the community for his disciplinary role in 2 Cor. 10–13 ("Paul, the Ancient Epistolary Theorists, and 2 Corinthians 10–13," 196). The whip symbolized the relationship between slaveholder and slave, not the relationship between officer and soldier and certainly not the relationship between father and child (Saller, "Corporal Punishment, Authority, and Obedience in the Roman Household"). A slaveholder subjugated a slave through physical assaults, keeping the slave in a permanent state of dishonor and humiliation. At least in theory, a father sought the good of the one who was disciplined, and an officer sought the good of the company. Thus, although Paul represents the submission of the Corinthians to the discipline of the superapostles as servile, he offers other possibilities for interpreting his own role as disciplinarian.

90. While the superapostles are likely to have followed the standard practice of including labors and hardships in their own boasting—Paul boasts that he has endured "far greater labors, far more imprisonments" (v. 23b)—Paul gives no hint that the superapostles have boasted of beatings.

91. Martyn, *Galatians*, 568 n. 72.

92. While treatments of Gal. 6:17 routinely identify Paul's corporal markings as souvenirs of the hardships of Paul's apostolate, typically with explicit reference to 2 Cor. 11:23–25, Paul's invocation of his talismanic *stigmata* is less frequently adduced as relevant for understanding why Paul boasts of beatings. For the view that Paul's *stigmata* are literal scars from injuries incurred in the course of apostolic ministry, see Moulton, "Marks of Jesus" Burton, *Critical and Exegetical Commentary on the Epistle to the Galatians*, 360–361; Klassen, "Galatians 6:17" Guthrie, *Galatians*, 152; Betz, "στίγμα," TDNT 7.663; Betz, *Galatians*, 324–325; Osiek, *Galatians*, 90; Bruce, *Epistle to the Galatians*, 276; Cousar, *Galatians*, 151; Hamerton-Kelly, "Girardian Interpretation," 74; Harvey, "Forty Strokes Save One," 88; Fung, *Epistle to the Galatians*, 313; Lührmann, *Galatians*, 122; Matera, *Galatians*, 227; Dunn, *Epistle to the Galatians*, 347; Moore, *God's Gym*, 28.

93. Jones argues that slaves were generally marked by tattoos, not brands ("Tattooing and Branding").

94. D. Martin comments that "the purpose for which Paul brings up the marks is to preclude judgments on his actions by outsiders. The only one who legitimately judges a slave is that slave's master" (*Slavery as Salvation*, 59–60; he suggests that the stigmata may have been actual tattoos). See also Bruce, *Epistle to the Galatians*, 275.

95. "Thus, the praetor does not promise an action for every affront in respect of a slave . . . for it is highly relevant what sort of slave he is, whether he be honest, regular

and responsible, a steward or only a common slave, a drudge or whatever. And what if he be in fetters, branded, and of the deepest notoriety?" (*Dig.* 47.10.15.44). Roman law was not uniformly applied throughout the empire; we cannot infer that practices advocated in legal codes conform to social realities. Roman law is, however, a useful index of Roman ideology; what is relevant here is the belief that a branded or tattooed slave was infamous and therefore deserved even less respect of person than other slaves.

96. Martyn, *Galatians*, 568–569. Martyn is following an insight of Güttgemanns, *Der leidende apostel*, 134.

97. As we have seen, scholars deciphering Paul's *stigmata* (Gal. 6:17) frequently allude both to 2 Cor. 11:23–25 and to 2 Cor. 4:10. Those interpreting Paul's boasting of beatings (2 Cor. 11:23–25) refer much less frequently to Gal. 6:17 or 2 Cor. 4:10. Murphy-O'Connor, who writes that in 2 Cor. 11:23–25 Paul "graphically illustrated . . . 'bearing in the body the dying of Christ,'" is an exception (*Theology of the Second Letter to the Corinthians*). See also Forbes, "Comparison, Self-Praise and Irony," 19.

98. Osiek writes that it is likely that Paul's *stigmata* memorialize "the physical effects of his labors and the suffering that he has had to endure in his missionary work . . . or even more specifically to the effects of several beatings (2 Cor 11:23–25). These are physical scars which manifest the dying of Jesus (2 Cor 4:10)" (*Galatians*, 90). On the parallelism of Gal. 6:17 and 2 Cor. 4:10, see also Ridderbos, *Epistle of Paul to the Churches of Galatia*, 228; Betz, *Galatians*, 324 n. 129, 325; Matera, *Galatians*, 232; Dunn, *The Epistle to the Galatians*, 347.

99. In his references to the death of Jesus, Paul does not explicitly mention the ritualized abuse and humiliation Jesus endured as prelude to crucifixion, although he would have known it occurred, if only because flogging regularly preceded execution (cf. Garnsey, *Social Status and Legal Privilege*, 138). Compare Mark 10:33–34 and parallels, where Jesus anticipates that he will be mocked, spat upon, and whipped.

Chapter 3

1. Suetonius, *Gaius Caligula* 26.2; quoted in Roller, *Dining Posture*, 85.
2. Cf. *Oxford Latin Dictionary*, s.v. habitus.
3. Philo, *That Every Good Person Is Free* 9.79; Josephus, *Ant.* 18.1.5 [21].
4. Bourdieu, *Logic of Practice*, 52.
5. Ibid., 56.
6. Ibid., 58.
7. Adair, "'Branded with Infamy,'" 451.
8. Ibid., 456.
9. E.g., Strathern, *Body Thoughts*, 28; Jenkins, *Bourdieu*, 82.
10. Originally published in French in 1936, Mauss's "Techniques of the Body" introduces concepts later developed by Bourdieu.
11. Alcoff, *Visible Identities*, 114.
12. I share Walter Johnson's wariness about scholarship that uncritically attempts to "give slaves back their agency." "On Agency," where Johnson develops these ideas, is worth reading in full. Johnson notes that "the term 'agency' smuggles a notion of the universality of a liberal notion of selfhood, with its emphasis on independence and choice, right into the middle of a conversation about slavery against which the supposedly natural (at least for

white men) condition was originally defined." He contends that social historians of American slavery have too often ended up with "what is more-or-less a rational choice model of human being, and shoved to the side in the process a consideration of human-ness lived outside the conventions of liberal agency, a consideration, that is, of the condition of enslaved humanity" (115). Because discussions of slaves' "agency" are often allied to discussions of their resistance to slavery, Johnson painfully suggests that "the way to begin to sort 'humanity' from 'agency' from 'resistance' is to remain aware of forms of human 'agency' which can in no way be seen as resistant to slavery, specifically collaboration and betrayal" (116).

13. E.g., Strathern, *Body Thoughts*, 28; Jenkins, *Bourdieu*, 79–81.

14. Indeed, despite the tenacious hold of corporal conditioning, habitus does change. An interesting case study is the evolution of middle-class American women's bodily habitus between 1980, when feminist political theorist Young published her now-classic essay "Throwing Like a Girl," and the present day—whatever day that may be as you read this. A shift from a childhood in skirts to a childhood in jeans, the impact of Title IX on the self-identities of girls and women, the opening of (some) boardrooms and (some) pulpits to women: these and myriad other changes affect a woman's sense of body-self and thus the way she inhabits and moves through space. Young is aware of such shifts (see *On Female Body Experience*, 10).

15. J. Martin, *More Than Chains and Toil*, 60. I thank Monique Moultrie for drawing Martin's work to my attention.

16. I initially considered comparative material from the United States in my first article on slavery, "Mistress-Slave Dialectic."

17. This final caveat would, of course, apply equally to the writings of slaveholders and of white abolitionists. Marcus Wood rightly complains of a tendency to single out the writings of slaves and former slaves for "questions about intentionality, control, subversion, and cultural gamesmanship," questions from which white authors are too often exempt (*Slavery, Empathy, and Pornography*, 11).

18. Johnson, "On Agency," 115–116.

19. Douglass, *My Bondage*, 106.

20. Historian Alex Bontemps observes, "Slaves could look to their owners (and to others to whom they were expected to be subservient). Indeed, it was necessary and required that they do so. But it was not expected that they look at them." Glances or stares construed as insolent were a frequent occasion of punishment (*Punished Self*, 13).

21. More ads: A slave "could not 'look at anyone in the face with confidence.' . . . 'apt to turn himself sideways and look down.' . . . 'eyes would shake when you look attentively at her . . . ' 'is apt to turn her face a little to one side and casts her eyes towards the ground.'" We might note that such refusal to meet a gaze is at once self-protective and potentially defiant. Quoted in ibid.

22. Jacobs, *Incidents in the Life*, 79.

23. Douglass, *My Bondage*, 110.

24. Jacobs, *Incidents in the Life*, 45.

25. Hine makes a related observation regarding the American South. "[R]ape and the threat of rape influenced the development of a culture of dissemblance among southern black women. By dissemblance I mean the behavior and attitudes of black women that created the appearance of openness and disclosure but actually shielded the truth of their inner lives and selves from their oppressors" (*Hine Sight*, 37).

26. See Weiler's treatment of the hexis (physical or mental habit resulting in permanent disposition or attribute) informing the bodies of slaves ("Inverted Kalokagathia," 28 n. 87).

27. Douglass, *My Bondage*, 141.

28. See, for example, the important studies of Egerton, *Gabriel's Rebellion* and *He Shall Go Out Free*.

29. Hartman, *Scenes of Subjection*, 8.

30. See further George, "Slave Disguise in Ancient Rome," 48.

31. *Papyrus Wisconsin* 33.

32. For the dialectic of heroism and shame in the arena, see Barton, "Savage Miracles."

33. Against Allard's view that the sufferings of martyrdom, from imprisonment to death itself, leveled the differences between slave and free (*Les Esclaves chrétiens*, 222).

34. Perkins, *Suffering Self*, 105. Although I highlight my differences from Perkins, her work has influenced the direction of my own investigations. Here, for example, although I disagree in specific ways with her readings of Perpetua and Blandina, I am indebted to her more comprehensive argument about suffering and self-definition.

35. *Honeste nata, liberaliter instituta, matronaliter nupta.* Castelli's translation; Castelli calls attention to emphasis on status markers in this description (*Martyrdom and Memory*, 86, 240 n. 76.

36. Saller, "Symbols of Gender and Status Hierarchies," 86.

37. Saller, "Pater Familias, Mater Familias," 197.

38. Perkins, *Suffering Self*, 104–113.

39. See the helpful discussion of Blandina in Harrill, "Domestic Enemy," 249–253.

40. Although the Romans generally expected slaves to be cowardly, their literature also includes tales of slaves whose bravery indicts the cowardice of certain free men. See, e.g, the story of the freedwoman Epicharis in Tacitus, *Annals* 15.57.

41. Tilley, "Ascetic Body."

42. I thank certified social workers Ginger Andrews and Laurie Sanderson for sharing insights from their social work practices.

43. Animals released to devour condemned prisoners were not always eager to go after their assigned prey. For visual evidence attesting to the practice of binding condemned prisoners to posts to be consumed by wild beasts, along with images of trainers attempting to incite the animals to their assigned duty, see the gladiator mosaic from the North African villa at Zliben (Dunhabin, *Mosaics of Roman North Africa*, plates 47–48.

44. Castelli, *Martyrdom and Memory*, 126. I would like to express my gratitude to Carolyn Osiek, who in her invited response to a Bible and Cultural Studies panel at the 2001 meeting of the Society of Biblical Literature first drew my attention to the significance of Blandina for thinking about early Christian attitudes toward slaves and slavery.

45. Perkins, *Suffering Self*, 114.

46. Stowe, *Uncle Tom's Cabin*, 382.

47. Kaster, "Taxonomy of Patience." See also Burrus, *Saving Shame*, 27–28.

48. For related arguments see Clark, "Asceticism, Class, and Gender."

49. Richlin, "Sexuality in the Roman Empire," 353.

50. Ibid., 349.

51. Ibid., 350.

52. Seneca, *Troades* 87–91 (*paret exertos turba lacertos;/veste remissa substringe sinus/uteroque tenus pateant artus./cui coniugui pectora velas,/captive pudor?*). Translation adapted from Fantham, *Seneca's Troades*, 132.

53. Benton argues that, while Seneca sets his tragedy in the charred ruins of Troy, his concerns are those of a first-century Roman nobleman negotiating the loss of power and prestige of Roman aristocrats under the principate ("Split Vision," 33).

54. On expected attire of female slaves in Roman circles, see Olson, *Dress and the Roman Woman*, 42–44; George, "Slave Disguise in Ancient Rome," 42–45.

55. Cf. *Oxford Latin Dictionary*, s.v. pudor.

56. Barton, *Roman Honor*, 202; discussion of *pudor*, 197–269.

57. Noted by Fantham, *Seneca's Troades*, 227; Keulen, *Introduction, Text and Commentary*, 141.

58. On the horror evoked by reduction to slave status, see Briggs, "Can an Enslaved God Liberate?"; Glancy, *Slavery in Early Christianity*, 71–85, 96–101.

59. Seneca, *Controversiae* 1.2, esp. 1.2.3.

60. See *Mishnah Ketubbot* 1:2D, 4C; *Mishnah Niddah* 5:4; Wegner, *Chattel or Person?*, 21–23.

61. In an article that twines investigation into Philadelphia police records with literary analysis, literary critic Toni Irving argues that black women's bodies continue to be treated as less worthy of protection than white women's bodies. After noting that individuals frequently attempt to distance themselves from the stories read in their bodies, Irving raises a question that informs my question of what it would be to know either freedom or slavery in the body. "If, as Merleau-Ponty suggests," Irving writes, "the body is our general medium for having a world, how do black women structure a sexual body in spite of less-than-ideal bodily experiences?" ("Borders of the Body," 85).

62. Jordan, "Body as Reader," 107.

63. Ibid., 114.

64. Gabler-Hover, *Dreaming Black/Writing White*, passim.

65. Jordan, "Body as Reader," 117.

66. For a selection of references, see D. Williams, *Sisters in the Wilderness*, 245–246 n. 2.

67. *Passion of Andrew* 17.

68. Schwartz rightly observes that "the text reflects an aristocratic bias by making Euclia's masquerade as a mistress seem ridiculous, while at the same time valorizing the behavior of aristocrats who shed their privileges" ("From Bedroom to Courtroom," 305). This observation is at odds with her concluding affirmation that the text constructs "a new model for social identity, one in which the distinctions between kin and strangers, free and slave, male and women, become blurred and reorganized" (310).

69. See also Tertullian, *To the Martyrs* 4; *Exhortation to Chastity* 13.

70. Clark, *Origenist Controversy*, 144; for broader context, see 121–151.

71. For the association between servile status and prostitution in the Roman world, see Flemming, "*Quae Corpore Quaestum Facit.*"

72. Allard, *Les Esclaves chrétiens*, 244.

73. Personal communication.

74. For further discussion of Lucretia in early Christian writings, see Trout, "Re-textualizing Lucretia."

75. Ibid., 64.

76. Ibid., 67.

77. On measure-for-measure punishments, see Himmelfarb, *Tours of Hell*, chap. 3; Bauckham, *Fate of the Dead*, 198.

78. Buchholz, *Your Eyes Will Be Opened*, 221.

79. Bauckham, *Fate of the Dead*, 218.

80. Buchholz, *Your Eyes Will Be Opened*, 336.

81. See discussion in Stramara, "Gregory of Nyssa."

82. For the complex relationships between Eustathius and the family of Basil, Gregory, and Macrina, see Silvas, *Asketikon of St Basil the Great*, 56–71.

83. See discussion in Elm, *"Virgins of God,"* 106–136.

84. Holman, "Rich City Burning," 201.

85. Elm, *"Virgins of God,"* 130.

86. Silvas, *Asketikon of St Basil the Great*, 489.

87. Translation from ibid., 488.

88. Elm, *"Virgins of God,"* 135. See also ibid., 57–58.

89. Silvas, *Asketikon of St Basil the Great*, 31.

90. Shaw, "Who Were the Circumcellions?"

91. See citations to Optatus and discussion in Gaddis, *There Is No Crime*, 120 n. 362.

92. For translation and discussion see Frend, *The Donatist Church*, 73–75.

93. Augustine's reaction against such outrages to slaveholding habitus should be seen in the context of his complex view of slavery, in which slavery figures as a punitive dimension of the postlapsarian world. See discussion in Garnsey, *Ideas of Slavery*, 206–219.

94. Spillers, "Mama's Baby, Papa's Maybe," 67.

Chapter 4

1. See, e.g., Elliott, *Apocryphal New Testament*, 49.

2. In an important essay on the concept of *virginitas in partu*, Karl Rahner notes that in these early traditions "the content of the doctrine" varies (*"Virginitas in Partu,"* 149 n. 51).

3. Schaberg, *Illegitimacy of Jesus*; Gaventa, *Mary*; Foskett, *A Virgin Conceived*.

4. P. Klassen, *Blessed Events*.

5. Maus treats both "techniques of birth and obstetrics" and "techniques of infancy" ("Techniques of the Body," 79).

6. P. Klassen, *Blessed Events*, 13.

7. Merleau-Ponty, "Selections from the Phenomenology of Perception," in *Maurice Merleau-Ponty*, ed. Baldwin, 63–233, esp. p. 123.

8. Henrik Cornell refers to the newer style of nativity, in which "the Virgin gives birth to her son in a kneeling position," as "superseding" the older style, which depicts the virgin reclining, or perhaps half-sitting up. "This change from the old manner of representing the birth of Christ took place so abruptly that there is no gradual development to be traced in the pictures" (*Iconography of the Nativity*, 1). See also Hull, "Sex of the Savior in Renaissance Art," 78.

9. Exceptions exist. From the Byzantine period through the late Middle Ages Mary was often depicted lying in bed with her child, and in some of those images she even appears fatigued. For review of the history of representations of Jesus' birth, including images that suggest the birth fatigued the mother, see Schiller, *Iconography of Christian Art*, 1.58–88.

10. The late Rev. Raymond E. Brown, SS, my *doktorvater*, offered this observation in a seminar on resurrection narratives.

11. Steinberg, *Sexuality of Christ in Renaissance Art*, 1.

12. Ibid., 6–8, 171–174, plates 13 and 80.

13. For a view that simultaneously affirms, complicates, and challenges central tenets of Steinberg's thesis, see Bynum, "Body of Christ in the Later Middle Ages," 399–439.

14. Hull argues that the emphasis on the infant Jesus' genitalia is influenced by the visions of Birgitta of Sweden, who stressed the maleness of the infant. Hull contends that Birgitta's visions catalyzed the shift toward representation of the utterly serene Madonna, a Madonna depicted kneeling or standing rather than reclining ("Sex of the Savior in Renaissance Art"). See also Debby, "Images of Saint Birgitta of Sweden."

15. Birgitta of Sweden, *Revelations*, 7.22.2–3.

16. On the oddity of Christ's uncircumcised penis in Renaissance art, see Steinberg, *Sexuality of Christ in Renaissance Art*, 157–159.

17. "Down there," according to Elizabeth A. J. Salzer, PA-C, is how many gynecological patients refer to their genitalia, as in, "I have a pain *down there*."

18. Exceptions include several Byzantine images that feature Salome's burnt finger. See Schiller, *Iconography of Christian Art*, plates 152, 259.

19. Geoffrey D. Dunn summarizes widespread scholarly assessment of Tertullian's pronouncement that Jesus' physical passage through Mary's vagina consummates his marriage to her: "Most commentators have been content to comment negatively about Tertullian's literary style here in terms of its graphic description and poor taste" ("Mary's Virginity *In Partu*," 480).

20. Von Campenhausen, *Virgin Birth in the Theology of the Ancient Church*, 37.

21. Burghardt, "Mary in Western Patristic Thought."

22. Smid, *Protevangelium Jacobi*, 141.

23. Ensler, *Vagina Monologues*, 15–21.

24. Ibid., 124–125.

25. Schillebeeckx, *Mary*, 50.

26. *Catechism of the Council of Trent*, 1.3.2. The 1992 *Catechism of the Catholic Church* teaches that Mary remains perpetually a virgin without speculating on the question of her virginity *in partu* beyond noting that "Christ's birth did not diminish his mother's virginal integrity but sanctified it" (1.2.2.3.2.2 [499–500]).

27. In Protestant theology, treatment of Mary has tended to conform to the outlines suggested by the New Testament writings. The canonical evangelists did not consider questions related to Mary's hymen, labor pains, lactation and afterbirth. Such questions are therefore unlikely to engage Protestant theologians, including feminist theologians. In several works on Mary, for example, Gaventa invites greater attention to Mary. (Along with Gaventa's *Mary*, see Gaventa and Rigby, *Blessed One*.) Although Gaventa introduces readers to patristic references to Mary, she stresses the canonical mother of Jesus. Thus Gaventa, who elsewhere writes of Paul's claim to experience labor pains in giving birth to the Galatian Christian, does not evoke Mary's body in childbirth (see "The Maternity of Paul," 29–40).

28. E. Johnson, *Truly Our Sister*, 131–134.

29. Glucklich, *Sacred Pain*, 16.

30. Rahner, "*Virginitas in Partu*," 159 n. 104.

31. Elizabeth A. J. Salzer, PA-C, personal communication, August 30, 2007.

32. Glucklich, *Sacred Pain*, 188.

33. "Obstetric Analgesia and Anesthesia."

34. From the Web page of "Birth International: Specialists in Birth and Midwifery," accessed January 7, 2007, at http://www.acegraphics.com.au/articles/leap02.html.

35. Glucklich, *Sacred Pain*, 33.

36. P. Klassen, *Blessed Events*, 15.

37. Zwelling, "History of Lamaze Continues."

38. Rahner, "*Virginitas in Partu*," 160.

39. Ibid., 159–160.

40. Glucklich, *Sacred Pain*, 6.

41. P. Klassen, *Blessed Events*, 196.

42. Ibid., 3.

43. On the heritability of original sin, see Rahner: "*Original sin is transmitted through procreation* [emphasis in original]. Not, of course, because there is anything sinful or inferior about the act of procreation. But because it is the plain, simple fact that everyone belongs to this one, particular human race, where everyone is related to everyone else by blood; and this makes a person a member and sharer in what we call original sin" ("The Body in the Order of Salvation," 73).

44. Despite significant differences of interpretation, I am dependent on Hannah, who suggests the relevance of Isaiah 66.7, 2 Baruch, Josephus's *Jewish Antiquities* 2.218, and several later rabbinic texts for the interpretation of Mary's virginity in *Ascen. Isa.* ("Ascension of Isaiah and Docetic Christology").

45. *Pace* Hannah, who leaves the impression that righteous women including Moses' mother are exempt from Eve's punishment, an interpretation that may be unduly influenced by the much later Babylonian Talmud ("Ascension of Isaiah and Docetic Christology," 185).

46. Irenaeus, *Proof of the Apostolic Preaching*, 54.

47. See, e.g., Aune, "Odes of Solomon and Early Christian Prophecy"; McNeil, "Odes of Solomon and the Scriptures"; Brownson, "Odes of Solomon and the Johannine Tradition"; Sanders, "Nag Hammadi, Odes of Solomon, and New Testament Christological Hymns"; Charlesworth, "Odes of Solomon and the Jewish Wisdom Texts."

48. In particular, Drijvers reads *Odes Sol.* 19 as encoding a Trinitarian theology that develops themes not introduced before the end of the second century ("19th Ode of Solomon"; see also Drijvers, "Odes of Solomon and Psalms of Mani").

49. For summary of positions and a balanced argument that the text dates to the late first or early second century, see Catherine Anne Playoust, *Lifted up from the Earth*. I am most grateful to Dr. Playoust for trusting her unpublished manuscript to a complete stranger. Jonathan Knight ventures a more precise date between 112 and 138 (*Ascension of Isaiah*, 9). Relying on possible parallels to literature from Nag Hammadi, Matthew Black prefers a date in the middle of the second century, around the time Justin composed the Dialogue with Trypho ("Gnostic Elements in the 'Ascension of Isaiah'"). For an argument that *Ascen. Isa.* may be a late first-century composition, see Hannah, "Isaiah's Vision in the Ascension of Isaiah." Enrico Norelli dates chaps. 6–11, including the nativity material, to the late first century, and locates the first five chapters in the early second century (cited in Playoust, *Lifted up from the Earth*, 145). Richard Bauckham proposes what seems to be the earliest date for the work as a whole, 70–80 C.E. (*The Fate of the Dead*, 363–390).

50. Composition of *Acts of Peter* represents a *terminus ante quem* for *Ascen. Isa.* 11, as a concatenation of passages on the nativity in *Acts of Peter* cites *Ascen. Isa.*: "We have neither heard her voice, nor has a midwife come in." The citation is nonetheless of little use in dating *Ascen. Isa.* as we lack a firm date for *Acts of Peter*. Although a significant redaction may

exist in the second century, the text of *Acts of Peter* continues to evolve in various ways. See Thomas, "Prehistory of the *Acts of Peter*."

51. Knight, "Portrait of Mary in the Ascension of Isaiah," 96.

52. Ibid., 97.

53. Zervos, "Seeking the Source of the Marian Myth."

54. The author of the *Prot. Jas.* offers a twist on the Eve-Mary parallel. Lamenting that his wife was seduced in his absence, he compares himself to Adam, whose wife was also seduced in his absence (13.1). On this view Mary repeats rather than reverses the sin of Eve.

55. Thoroughness invites a nod to Papias as the possible originator of the Eve-Mary analogy. Burghardt writes, "It is possible that the remote origins of the parallelism may be traced as far back as Papias, Bishop of Hierapolis in Asia Minor, at the turn of the first century. Papias's use of the Eve-Mary analogy, however, is admittedly conjectural and its content is at best insignificant." The text in question is preserved in a fragment of Victorinus of Pettau, and reads, "the Angel Gabriel brought the good tidings to Mary on the day whereon the dragon seduced Eve." ("Mary in Eastern Patristic Thought," 88–89). The problematic attestation from Victorinus, martyred in the time of Domitian, does not significantly affect the argument. With or without Papias, basic comparisons between Eve and Mary might well have circulated before Justin, just as they continued to circulate after he wrote.

56. See Constas, *Proclus of Constantinople and the Cult of the Virgin*, 273–313.

57. Translation adapted from Gambero, *Mary and the Fathers of the Church*, 561.

58. Ephrem, *Hymns on the Nativity* 4.160–162.

59. Ephrem, *Hymns on the Church* 49.7. In Brock, *Luminous Eye*, 33.

60. Ephrem, *Hymns on the Nativity* 21.21.

61. Burghardt, "Mary in Eastern Patristic Thought," 92.

62. Or at least, the Eve-Mary analogy does not *require* Ephrem consistently to deny that Mary experienced pain in childbirth. Compare, e.g., Burghardt, "Mary in Eastern Patristic Thought," 110. Poet and mystic as well as theologian, Ephrem is not bound to the logical argumentation and perspicuous definitions that so often characterize theological discourse. Arguing that Ephrem's reliance on poetry frees him from the temptation "to encapsulate eternal verities and truths in fixed formulae and dogmatic definitions," Sebastian Brock quotes Ephrem himself: "It is not at the clothing of the words/that one should gaze,/but at the power hidden in the words" (*Luminous Eye*, 160–161, from *Hymns on the Church* 28.17). Ephrem's poetry teases out and even participates in the contradictions of a virgin's pregnancy and ultimately of the incarnation, contradictions that are not puzzles to be solved but mysteries to be entered. He shows that even within the corporal imaginary of a particular writer, the virgin's susceptibility to labor pains may be in flux.

63. Rahner, "*Virginitas in Partu*," 161.

64. S. Harvey, "On Mary's Voice," 82 n. 1. (Likewise, S. Harvey writes in "Odes of Solomon," "Her birth is painless, one of the earliest meanings for Mary's 'virgin birth'; being painless, it reverses the curse placed on Eve in Gen 3:16," 93.) In "On Mary's Voice," Harvey notes that proposed dates for *Odes Sol.* 19 range from the late first to the third century. Obviously, if *Odes Sol.* 19 dates from the mid-second century or later, the possibility that the hymnist is familiar with the Eve-Mary analogy increases. I argue more strongly that *Odes Sol.* 19 offers no suggestion that Mary's painless birthing experience had anything to do with sin or sinlessness, an argument strengthened but not contingent on relative dating of texts and traditions.

65. Noted by, e.g., McNeil, "Odes of Solomon and the Sufferings of Christ."

66. For more on the significance of the Savior's death in *Odes Sol.*, see ibid.; and McNeil, "Suffering and Martyrdom in the Odes of Solomon."

67. The appearance of a lactating father in *Odes Sol.* 19 is not unique in Christian literature. As early as Paul's first letter to the Corinthian Christian community, he pictures himself nursing the young congregation: "I fed you with milk" (1 Cor. 3:2a). Gaventa argues that Paul should be seen not as a nursing father but as a nursing mother (*Our Mother Saint Paul*, 41–50). Clement of Alexandria, whose career spanned the late second and early third centuries, refers to the milk of the Father's breast. For Clement, paternal milk is required to nourish the offspring of a virgin, since a virgin's breasts do not produce milk; Clement has in mind the church as virgin. For further symbolism related to "divine milk, breasts, and bosom," see Drijvers, "19th Ode of Solomon," 344.

68. See *Odes Sol.* 28 and 36. For a crucial discussion of gender in *Odes Sol.* and other early Syriac literature, see S. Harvey, "Feminine Imagery for the Divine."

69. Ibid, 126–127.

70. Compare James Lagrand, who argues that Mary "was given grace to transcend normal sexuality in bringing new life to mankind and so became the only human parent, father-mother, of the Son of God" ("How Was the Virgin Mary 'Like a Man'?," 104).

71. Horn, "The Virgin and the Perfect Virgin," 421. I thank Cornelia Horn for her gracious comments on a version of this material delivered at the 2007 Society of Biblical Literature meeting.

72. Ibid., 423.

73. Pliny, *Epistles* 3.16.6; cf. Martial 1.13.

74. What does Rome have to do with Edessa? Or can we invoke Greco-Roman codes of masculinity to interpret Syrian literature? Yes. In the early Christian era, Syria was a crossroads of cultures, its population largely bilingual and culturally oriented toward both East and West. See S. Harvey, "Odes of Solomon," 88.

75. Brock, *Luminous Eye*, 160–161.

76. NB: P. Klassen's formulation makes more sense with respect to a woman's first delivery (*Blessed Events*, 84).

77. Merleau-Ponty, *Basic Writings*, 150.

78. Kristeva, "Stabat Mater," 168.

79. Merleau-Ponty, *Basic Writings*, 254.

80. Moore and Anderson, "Taking It Like a Man."

81. Scarry, *Body in Pain*, 4.

82. Playoust, *Lifted up from the Earth*, 153–169.

83. Himmelfarb, "The Experience of the Visionary," 100–101; cf. *Ascen. Isa.* 7:25.

84. Glucklich, *Sacred Pain*, 207.

85. Hannah, "Ascension of Isaiah and Docetic Christology," 172–181.

86. Ibid., 170–172.

87. King, *What Is Gnosticism?*, 211.

88. I am indebted to Hannah, who suggests the relevance of Isaiah 66:7 for the representation of the virgin birth in *Ascen. Isa.* I disagree with his broader suggestion that "it may be that the Jewish tradition about the reversal of the curse of Eve in the next age originated with a messianic interpretation of this passage from Isaiah. Once established in Judaism it was transferred to Christianity," and taken up by, among others, the author of

Ascen. Isa. ("Ascension of Isaiah and Docetic Christology," 186). I see no suggestion in *Ascen. Isa.* or the other early Christian texts he cites that the painless birth is predicated on the curse of Eve.

89. Birgitta of Sweden, *Revelations* 7.21.10–11, 13, 17.

90. Elizabeth Salzer, PA-C, private communication, September 25, 2006.

91. Soranus, *Soranus' Gynecology*, 1.3.1.

92. "In an Armenian version of the P.J. [*Prot. Jas.*] conception takes place through the ear" (Smid, *Protevangelium Jacobi*, 84).

93. *Prot. Jas.* 11:6–7; Luke 1:35. Briefly discussed in Smid, *Protevangelium Jacobi*, 85.

94. Horn concedes that *Prot. Jas.* "contains indications that Mary may have experienced pressure and stress shortly before giving birth," but also notes that "no pain is recorded as having accompanied the very moment of birth-giving" ("Virgin and the Perfect Virgin," 425 n. 58).

95. Richard Bauckham argues that *Prot. Jas.*'s Salome was known to the tradition as a daughter of Joseph by his first wife and thus a half sister of Jesus ("Salome").

96. Zervos, "Seeking the Source of the Marian Myth," 116–118.

97. Elliott, *Apocryphal New Testament*, 49.

98. See Kristeva, *Powers of Horror*.

99. Kristeva writes, "We are entitled only to the ear of the virginal body, the tears and the breast." She continues, "Milk and tears became the privileged signs of the Mater Dolorosa" ("Stabat Mater," 172–173).

100. Horner, "Jewish Aspects of the *Protevangelium of James*."

101. Foskett also finds in the age references of *Prot. Jas.* "an implicit guarantee of the child's sexual purity and anatomical integrity" (*A Virgin Conceived*, 149).

102. Smid, *Protevangelium Jacobi*, 62; Hock, *Infancy Gospels*, 45.

103. Horner's suggestion is even more far-fetched because the virginity of legitimate daughters raised in Jewish households was assumed by the Mishnah. Although he speculates that by being raised in the temple Mary would be protected from allegations that she had been raised in a non-Jewish home, there is nothing in text or tradition to suggest that such allegations ever surfaced.

104. Cole, "*Gunaiki ou Themis*," 107. Hock briefly suggests that Cole's article is relevant for interpreting purity concerns of *Prot. Jas.* (*Infancy Gospels*, 47).

105. Related is Nancy Jay's classic argument that in patrilineal societies sacrificial ritual simultaneously expiates the stain of maternal origins while powerfully substituting sacrificial blood for maternal blood to integrate the patrilineage ("Sacrifice as Remedy for Having Been Born of Woman"; expanded in Jay, *Throughout Your Generations Forever*).

106. Branham, "Blood in Flux," 53.

107. Ibid., 62–63, 68.

108. Branham, "Bloody Women and Bloody Spaces."

109. In antiquity girls were often married before menarche. If such a marriage was quickly consummated a bride might well become pregnant before her first period.

110. Smid, *Protevangelium Jacobi*, 92.

111. Thanks to Kim Haines-Eitzen, who proposed this possibility to me during a September 2007 meeting of the working group known as LARCNY (Late Ancient Religion in Central New York) at which I presented an earlier version of this chapter.

112. Hock, *Infancy Gospels*, 55.

113. Cohen, "Menstruants and the Sacred."

114. A persistent association. Katherine Park writes of *I segreti delle femine* (*Secrets of Women*), a treatise that circulated in Florence in the fourteenth and fifteenth centuries, "Focusing on menstruation, which it consistently calls an 'illness' (*malactia*), it describes the menses as a corrosive and poisonous fluid, emitted through the eyes as well as the vagina" (*Secrets of Women*, 93).

115. Van der Horst, "Sex, Birth, Purity and Asceticism," 217.

116. Gaventa writes, "Nothing is said of Anna's feeding Mary prior to this rite of purification, although without such feeding the child would surely have died" (*Mary*, 112). The text does not require this conclusion, as reliance on wet nurses was widespread in antiquity.

117. Holman, "Molded as Wax," 85–88.

118. Ibid., 84.

119. Ronald Hock comments that, in contrast to Anna's delayed nursing of Mary, "Mary's immediate feeding of Jesus may emphasize her exceptional purity" (*Infancy Gospels*, 67).

120. Ephrem, *Hymns on the Nativity* 11:4.

121. For complexities of Greek views of virginity, see Sissa, *Greek Virginity*. For clarifications on medical sources see Hanson, "Logic of the Gynecological Prescriptions."

122. Pliny *Nat.* 28.23.85; see D'Angelo, "Gender and Power in the Gospel of Mark," 89.

123. Meltzer, *For Fear of the Fire*, 70.

124. Hock, *Infancy Gospels*, 69.

125. Winkler, *Constraints of Desire*, 217.

126. Foskett, *A Virgin Conceived*, 159, 186 n. 82.

127. Rahner, "*Virginitas in partu*," 161.

128. Rahner, "Body in the Order of Salvation," 84.

129. Meltzer, *For Fear of the Fire*, 71.

130. See, e.g., Vorster, "The Protevangelium of James and Intertextuality," 269.

131. See my discussion in Glancy, "Torture," 131–134.

132. As we will see, the belief that women's "blood" is dirty was widespread and complex in the Greco-Roman world. In Judaism the discharges of menstruation and childbirth were seen more narrowly as polluting. Blake Leyerle has argued convincingly (and importantly) that we find in Tertullian as well as in rabbinic sources a distinction between two types of bloodshed: (1) controlled bloodshed (for the rabbis, circumcision; for Tertullian, martyrdom), which is redemptive; and (2) uncontrolled bloodshed, which is polluting. Instances of uncontrolled and polluting bloodshed include the discharges of menstruation and the discharges of lochial fluids in childbirth ("Blood Is Seed").

133. Gambero, *Mary and the Fathers of the Church*, 65.

134. Grosz, *Volatile Bodies*, 104.

135. In *An Ethics of Sexual Difference*, Luce Irigiray enters into impressionistic dialogue with Merleau-Ponty's phenomenology (151–181; see also Merleau Ponty, *Visible and the Invisible*). What I characterize as Grosz's critique of Merleau-Ponty is in fact part of her lucid exposition and expansion of Irigiray's chiastic commentary on Merleau-Ponty (*Volatile Bodies*, 86–112).

136. Flemming, *Medicine and the Making of Roman Women*, 183.

137. Ibid., 131–136.

138. For a discussion of how Tertullian's engagement with physiological theories of his day affects his exegesis, see Satran, "Fingernails and Hair."

139. For detailed discussion of Soranus's influence on Tertullian, see Jan Hendrik Waszink's discussion in his translation of Tertullian's *De Anima*, 22–38.

140. Of the physicians quoted by Tertullian, all but two are quoted in extant writings attributed to Soranus. As most of Soranus's writings are lost, the remaining two physicians may well have been known to Soranus. See Waszink's notes in Tertullian, *De Anima*, 28–29.

141. Hanson and Green, "Soranus of Ephesus," 1006.

142. Ibid.

143. See Waszink's references to Tertullian in his translation of *De Anima*, 342–344.

144. Ibid., 342–346.

145. Ibid., 346.

146. On paradox as personal habit and as evidence of Tertullian's Stoicism, see Osborne, *Tertullian*, 63; on antithesis as essential to the ways of God, 114.

147. Hadot, *Philosophy as a Way of Life*, 61.

148. Burrus, *Saving Shame*, 57. The influence of *Saving Shame* on my thinking extends beyond the footnotes that pepper this chapter. For example, *Saving Shame* focused my attention on the potential importance of Julia Kristeva's work for thinking through early texts on the parturient Mary. To Virginia Burrus, who graciously shared her manuscript with me, my thanks.

149. Ibid., 53; cf. Tertullian, *Carn. Chr.* 1.2.

150. Burrus, *Saving Shame*, 53.

151. Osborn, *Tertullian*, xvii.

152. I refer to Jewish law as it would have been understood in Jesus' day, when the temple still stood. See Cohen, "Menstruants and the Sacred"; D'Angelo, "Gender and Power in the Gospel of Mark"; Levine, "Discharging Responsibility."

153. *Mishnah Zavim* 5:1. Of the woman with the irregular flow of blood who reaches out to touch Jesus, Charlotte Elisheva Fonrobert writes that even "if we accept Lev. 15 and by extension its mishnaic elaboration as the intertext of the story, and even if we assume that the woman is Jewish," the woman has not committed a transgression. A person touched by a *zavah* would only remain ritually impure until the end of the day. Fonrobert continues, "Rabbinically speaking, the woman of our narrative would only have committed a transgression had she done something that might lead to or initiate sexual contact, which is clearly not the point of the story" (*Menstrual Purity*, 194–195).

154. Leyerle, "Blood Is Seed," passim.

155. Soranus 3.11.

156. Von Staden writes that "it is a stunning fact that ninety-nine percent of all instances of 'excrement therapy' I have found in the Hippocratic writings occur in the gynaecological works" ("Women and Dirt," 12).

157. Hanson, "Talking Recipes in the Gynaecological Texts," 89.

158. Von Staden, "Women and Dirt," 10.

159. Hanson, "Talking Recipes in the Gynaecological Texts," passim.

160. Ibid., 89.

161. Flemming, *Medicine and the Making of Roman Women*, 129–131.

162. Von Staden, "*Apud nos foediora uerba*," 278.

163. Laskaris, "Error, Loss, and Change in the Generation of Therapies."

164. Perkins, "Rhetoric of the Maternal Body," 318. My gratitude to Shelly Matthews, who drew Perkins's work to my attention in her response to a paper I presented at the 2007

meeting of the Society of Biblical Literature. Matthews's comments on that paper ("The Law of the Opened Body: Tertullian on the Nativity") have in various other ways helped me tighten my argument in this chapter.

165. Perkins, "Rhetoric of the Maternal Body," 320.

166. Hadot, *Philosophy as a Way of Life*, 184.

167. Ibid.

168. Ibid., 188.

169. Compare Tertullian's handling of the categories "virgin" and "woman" in *Veiling of Virgins*, as carefully analyzed in Dunn, "Rhetoric and Tertullian's *De Virginibus Velandis*," 16–19.

170. McVey, "Images of Joy in Ephrem's Hymns on Paradise," 69.

171. Kristeva, *Powers of Horror*, 54.

172. Irigiray, *Ethics of Sexual Difference*, 162.

173. As Burrus writes, "Indeed, precisely because his faith in a God enfleshed is shameful, Tertullian can be made shameless. His shameless love of the flesh, mining Christ's own love, is the source of his salvation" (*Saving Shame*, 54).

174. On Marcion's alleged repugnance toward salt baths and swaddling clothes, see Tertullian, *Marc.* 4.21. For a helpful discussion of these child care practices, see Holman, "Molded as Wax." On Marcion's rejection of the notion that the child Jesus endured the pain of circumcision, see Tertullian, *Carn. Chr.* 2.

175. On the severing of the umbilical cord as primal wound, see Tertullian, *Marc.* 4.21.

176. Burrus, *Saving Shame*, 55.

177. Otten, "Christ's Birth of a Virgin," 255.

178. Adams, *Latin Sexual Vocabulary*, 105.

179. Compare the treatment of this section by Dunn, "Mary's Virginity *In Partu*."

180. For Tertullian's glorification of martyrdom, see his *To the Martyrs*.

181. Otten observes, "With the steadfast belief with which he argued in ch. 1 that Christ's human flesh would lay down the law for humanity's bodily resurrection (. . . *dabit legem nostrae resurrectioni*), he doggedly clings here in ch. 23 to the law of the opened body (. . . *ipsa patefacti corporis lege*)" ("Christ's Birth of a Virgin," 256).

182. Grosz, *Volatile Bodies*, 104.

183. "[T]he being touched of the touching" is Grosz's phrase. Grosz summarizes Irigiray's critique of Merleau-Ponty: "More primordial than vision, the tangible is also the necessary accompaniment of the earliest sensations, those in the blackness of the womb" (ibid., 105).

184. Sura 19:16–20. For discussion of Mary in early Islamic tradition, see Stowasser, *Women in the Qur'an, Traditions, and Interpretation*, 67–82.

185. Ignatius Loyola, *Autobiography of St. Ignatius Loyola*, 30.

186. Kunitz, "True 'Sensation.'"

187. See, e.g., Hynes, "Africanizing Chris Ofili?" and Cosentino, "Cosentino Replies."

Epilogue

1. Alcoff, *Visible Identities*, 114.

2. In complex ways this line of argument emerges from my ongoing reflections on Toni Morrison's important work of criticism, *Playing in the Dark*.

3. Of course even in utero one is affected by variables such as maternal access to adequate nutrition.

4. While in a straightforward way the Gospel of John implies that Pilate himself delivered the whipping, it would have been common practice for a ranking official to delegate the task to someone else, possibly to a slave. See discussion in Moore, *Empire and Apocalypse*, 56–63.

5. I explore in detail the implications of this scene in "Torture: Flesh, Truth, and the Fourth Gospel," passim.

6. For an encyclopedic history, see Darius Rejali, who writes, "The puzzle is no longer, 'Does torture persist after the Cold War?' (it obviously does), nor, 'Is torture compatible with democracy?' (evidently they can coexist). It is, rather, 'How is it that democracy and torture can coexist?'" (*Torture and Democracy*, 22).

Bibliography

Note on ancient sources: For quotations from the Bible I have either relied on my own translations or on the New Revised Standard Version. I have generally relied on Loeb editions and translations of Greek and Roman sources. Exceptions are scatted throughout the bibliography. Again, I have at times modified the printed translations slightly, especially where those translations obscure the point I am arguing.

The Acts of Andrew and the Acts of Andrew and Matthias in the City of Cannibals. Ed. Dennis Ronald MacDonald. Atlanta, GA: Scholars, 1990.

Adair, Vivyan. "'Branded with Infamy': Inscriptions of Poverty and Class in the United States." *Signs: Journal of Women in Culture and Society* 27 (2002): 451–473.

Adams, J. N. *The Latin Sexual Vocabulary.* Baltimore: Johns Hopkins University Press, 1982.

Alcoff, Linda Martín. *Visible Identities: Race, Gender, and the Self.* New York: Oxford University Press, 2006.

Allard, Paul. *Les Esclaves chrétiens depuis les premiers tempes de l'Eglise jusqu'à la fin de la domination romaine en Occident.* 1914. Reprint. Hildesheim: Georg Oms, 1974.

Ambrose. *On Abraham.* Trans. Theodosia Tomkinson. Etna, CA: Center for Traditionalist Orthodox Studies, 2000.

Andrews, Scott B. "Too Weak Not to Lead: The Form and Function of 2 Cor 11.23b–33." *New Testament Studies* 41 (1995): 263–276.

Aune, David E. "Odes of Solomon and Early Christian Prophecy." *New Testament Studies* 28 (1982): 435–460.

Barrett, C. K. *A Commentary on the Second Epistle to the Corinthians.* New York: Harper & Row, 1973.

Barton, Carlin A. *Roman Honor: The Fire in the Bones.* Berkeley and Los Angeles: University of California Press, 2001.

———. "Savage Miracles: The Redemption of Lost Honor in Roman Society and the Sacrament of the Gladiator and the Martyr." *Representations* 45 (1994): 41–71.

Basil of Caesarea. *Exegetic Homilies.* Trans. Agnes Clare Way. Fathers of the Church 46. Washington, DC: Catholic University of America Press, 1963.

Bataille, Georges. *Guilty.* Trans. Bruce Boone. Venice, CA: Lapis Press, 1988.

Bauckham, Richard. *The Fate of the Dead: Studies in Jewish and Christian Apocalypses.* Novum Testamentum Supplement Series 93. Leiden: Brill, 1998.

———. "Salome the Sister of Jesus, Salome the Disciple of Jesus, and the Secret Gospel of Mark." *Novum Testamentum* 33 (1991): 245–275.

Bauman, Richard A. *Crime and Punishment in Ancient Rome*. London: Routledge, 1996.

Benton, Cindy. "Split Vision: The Politics of the Gaze in Seneca's *Troades*." In *The Roman Gaze: Vision, Power, and the Body*, ed. David Fredrick, 31–56. Baltimore: Johns Hopkins University Press, 2002.

Best, Ernest. *Second Corinthians*. Interpretation Bible Commentary. Atlanta: John Knox Press, 1987.

Betz, Hans Dieter. "*De Laude Ipsius* (*Moralia* 539A–547B)." In *Plutarch's Ethical Writings and Early Christian Literature*, ed. Hans Dieter Betz, 367–393. Leiden: Brill, 1978.

———. "στίγμα." *Theological Dictionary of the New Testament* 7.657–664.

———. *Galatians: A Commentary on Paul's Letter to the Churches in Galatia*. Hermeneia. Philadelphia: Fortress Press, 1979.

Birgitta of Sweden: Life and Selected Revelations. Ed. Marguerite Tjader Harris. Trans. Albert Ryle Kezel. Classics of Western Spirituality. New York: Paulist Press, 1990.

Black, David Alan. *Paul, Apostle of Weakness: Astheneia and Its Cognates in the Pauline Literature*. New York: Peter Lang, 1984.

Black, Matthew. "Gnostic Elements in the 'Ascension of Isaiah.'" *New Testament Studies* 18 (1972): 221–226.

Bontemps, Alex. *The Punished Self: Surviving Slavery in the Colonial South*. Ithaca, NY: Cornell University Press, 2001.

Bourdieu, Pierre. *The Logic of Practice*. Trans. Richard Nice. Stanford: Stanford University Press, 1980.

———. "The Sentiment of Honour in Kayble Society." Trans. Philip Sherrard. In *Honour and Shame: The Values of Mediterranean Society*, ed. Jean G. Péristiany, 191–241. Chicago: University of Chicago Press, 1966.

Branham, Joan R. "Blood in Flux, Sanctity at Issue." *Res: Anthropology and Aesthetics* 31 (1997): 53–70.

———. "Bloody Women and Bloody Spaces." *Harvard Divinity Bulletin* 30.4 (2002), accessed February 16, 2009, at http://www.hds.harvard.edu/news/bulletin/articles/branham.html.

Branham, R. Bracht. *Unruly Eloquence: Lucian and the Comedy of Traditions*. Cambridge, MA: Harvard University Press, 1989.

Briggs, Sheila. "Can an Enslaved God Liberate? Hermeneutical Reflections on Philippians 2:6–11." *Semeia* 47 (1989): 137–153.

Brilliant, Richard. *Gesture and Rank in Roman Art: The Use of Gestures to Denote Status in Roman Sculpture and Coinage*. Memoirs of the Connecticut Academy of Arts & Sciences 14 (1963).

Brock, Sebastian. *The Luminous Eye: The Spiritual World Vision of Saint Ephrem*. Cistercian Studies Series 124. Kalamazoo, MI: Cistercian Publications, 1992.

Brown, William A. "A Lecture Delivered before the Female Anti-Slavery Society of Salem at Lyceum Hall, Nov. 14, 1947." In *Four Fugitive Slave Narratives*. Reading, MA: Addison-Wesley, 1969.

Brownson, James. "The Odes of Solomon and the Johannine Tradition." *Journal for the Study of the Pseudepigrapha* 2 (1988): 49–69.

Bruce, F. F. *The Epistle to the Galatians: A Commentary on the Greek Text*. New International Greek Testament Commentary. Grand Rapids, MI: Eerdmans, 1982.

Buchholz, Dennis D. *Your Eyes Will Be Opened: A Study of the Greek (Ethiopic) Apocalypse of Peter*. Society of Biblical Literature Dissertation Series 97. Atlanta: Scholars Press, 1988.

Buell, Denise Kimber. *Why This New Race? Ethnic Reasoning in Early Christianity*. New York: Columbia University Press, 2005.

Bultmann, Rudolf. *The Second Letter to the Corinthians*. Trans. Roy A. Harrisville. Minneapolis, MN: Augsburg, 1985.

Burghardt, Walter J. "Mary in Western Patristic Thought." In Carol, *Mariology*, 1.109–155.

———. "Mary in Eastern Patristic Thought." In Carol, *Mariology*, 2.88–153.

Burrus, Virginia. *Saving Shame: Martyrs, Saints, and Other Abject Subjects*. Divinations. Philadelphia: University of Pennsylvania Press, 2008.

Burton, Ernest Dewitt. *A Critical and Exegetical Commentary on the Epistle to the Galatians*. International Critical Commentary. Edinburgh: T. & T. Clark, 1921.

Bynum, Caroline Walker. "The Body of Christ in the Later Middle Ages: A Reply to Leo Steinberg." *Renaissance Quarterly* 39 (1986): 399–439.

Byron, Gay L. Byron. *Symbolic Blackness and Ethnic Difference in Early Christian Literature*. New York: Routledge, 2002.

Carol, Juniper B., ed. *Mariology*. 3 vols. Milwaukee: Bruce Publishing, 1954–1961.

Castelli, Elizabeth A. *Martyrdom and Memory: Early Christian Culture-Making*. Gender, Theory, and Religion. New York: Columbia University Press, 2004.

Catechism of the Catholic Church. 2nd ed. New York: Doubleday, 2003.

The Catechism of the Council of Trent for Parish Priests Issued by Order of Pope Pius V. Trans. John A. McHugh, O.P., and Charles J. Callan, O.P. New York: Joseph F. Wagner, 1945.

Charlesworth, James H. "The Odes of Solomon and the Jewish Wisdom Texts." In *The Wisdom Texts from Qumran and the Development of Sapiential Thought*, ed. C. Hempel, A. Lange, and H. Lichtenberger, 323–349. Bibliotheca Ephemeridum Theologicarum Lovaniensium 159. Leuven: University Press, 2002.

Clark, Elizabeth A. "Asceticism, Class, and Gender." *Late Ancient Christianity*, ed. Virginia Burrus, 27–45. A People's History of Christianity 2. Minneapolis: Fortress Press, 2005.

———. *The Origenist Controversy: The Cultural Construction of an Early Christian Debate*. Princeton: Princeton University Press, 1992.

Coetzee, J. M. *Waiting for the Barbarians*. London: Penguin, 1980.

Cohen, Shaye J. D. "Menstruants and the Sacred in Judaism and Christainity." *Women's History and Ancient History*, ed. Sarah B. Pomeroy, 273–299. Chapel Hill: University of North Carolina Press, 1991.

Cole, Susan Guettel. "*Gunaiki ou Themis:* Gender Difference in the Greek *Leges Sacrae*." *Helios* 19 (1992): 104–122.

Collins, Adela Yarbro. *Mark: A Commentary*. Hermeneia. Minneapolis: Fortress Press, 2007.

Constas, Nicholas. *Proclus of Constantinople and the Cult of the Virgin in Late Antiquity: Homilies 105, Texts and Translations*. Vigiliae Christianae Supplements 66. Leiden: Brill, 2003.

Corbeill, Anthony. *Nature Embodied: Gesture in Ancient Rome*. Princeton: Princeton University Press, 2004.

Cornell, Henrik. *The Iconography of the Nativity of Christ*. Uppsala: Uppsala Universitets Årsskrift, 1924.

Cosentino, Donald J. "Cosentino Replies." *African Arts* 43.1 (Spring 2001): 10.

Cousar, Charles B. *Galatians*. Interpretation Bible Commentary. Atlanta: John Knox Press, 1982.

Csordas, Thomas J. *Embodiment and Experience: The Existential Ground of Culture and Self*. Cambridge: Cambridge University Press, 1994.

D'Angelo, Mary Rose. "Gender and Power in the Gospel of Mark: The Daughter of Jairus and the Woman with the Flow of Blood." In *Miracles in Jewish and Christian Antiquity: Imagining Truth*, ed. John C. Cavadini, 83–110. Notre Dame, IN: Notre Dame University Press, 1999.

Danker, Frederick W. "Paul's Debt to the *De Corona* of Demosthenes: A Study of Rhetorical Techniques in Second Corinthians." In *Persuasive Artistry: Essays in New Testament Rhetoric in Honor of George A. Kennedy*, ed. Duane F. Watson, 262–280. Journal for the Study of the New Testament Supplement Series 50. Sheffield: Sheffield Academic Press, 1991.

———. *II Corinthians*. Augsburg Commentaries on the New Testament. Minneapolis: Augsburg Press, 1989.

Debby, Nirit Ben-Aryeh. "The Images of Saint Birgitta of Sweden in Santa Maria Novella in Florence." *Renaissance Studies* 18 (2004): 509–526.

Dewey, Arthur J. "A Matter of Honor: A Social-Historical Analysis of 2 Corinthians 10." *Harvard Theological Review* 78 (1985): 209–217.

Dewey, Joanna. "The Gospel of Mark." In Fiorenza et al., *Searching the Scriptures, Volume 2: A Feminist Commentary*, 470–509.

———. "Jesus' Healings of Women: Conformity and Non-conformity to Dominant Cultural Values as Clues for Historical Reconstruction." *Biblical Theology Bulletin* 24 (1994): 122–131.

The Digest of Justinian. Ed. Theodor Mommsen, Paul Krueger, and Alan Watson. 4 vols. Philadelphia: University of Pennsylvania Press, 1985.

Donahue, John R., and Daniel J. Harrington. *The Gospel of Mark*. Sacra Pagina 2. Collegeville, MN: Liturgical Press, 2002.

Douglass, Frederick. *My Bondage and My Freedom*. New York: Penguin, 2003.

Downing, F. Gerald. *Cynics, Paul and the Pauline Churches*. London: Routledge, 1998.

Drijvers, Hans J. W. "The 19th Ode of Solomon: Its Interpretation and Place in Syriac Christianity." *Journal of Theological Studies* 31 (1980): 337–365.

———. "Odes of Solomon and Psalms of Mani: Christians and Manichaeans in Third-Century Syria." In *Studies in Gnosticism and Hellenistic Religions: Presented to Gilles Quispel on the Occasion of his 65th Birthday*, ed. R. van den Broek and M. J. Vermaseren, 117–130. Leiden: Brill, 1981.

Dunhabin, Katherine M. *The Mosaics of Roman North Africa: Studies in Iconography and Patronage*. Oxford: Clarendon Press, 1978.

Dunkle, J. Roger. "The Greek Tyrant and Roman Political Invective of the Late Republic." *Transactions of the American Philological Association* 98 (1967): 151–171.

Dunn, Geoffrey D. "Mary's Virginity *In Partu* and Tertullian's Anti-docetism in *De Carne Christi* Reconsidered." *Journal of Theological Studies* 58 (2007): 467–484.

———. "Rhetoric and Tertullian's *De Virginibus Velandis*." *Vigiliae Christianae* 59 (2005): 1–30.

Dunn, James D. G. *The Epistle to the Galatians*. Black's New Testament Commentaries. Peabody, MA: Hendrickson, 1993.

Ebner, Martin. *Leidenslisten und Apostelbrief: Untersuchungen zu Form, Motivik und Funktion der Peristasenkataloge bei Paulus.* Forschung zur Bibel 66. Würzburg: Echter, 1991.

Edwards, Catharine. "The Suffering Body: Philosophy and Pain." In Porter, *Constructions of the Classical Body,* 252–268.

Egerton, Douglas R. *Gabriel's Rebellion: The Virginia Slave Conspiracies of 1800 and 1802.* Columbia: University of South Carolina Press, 1993.

———. *He Shall Go Out Free: The Lives of Denmark Vesey.* Rev. ed. Lanham, MD: Rowman & Littlefield, 2004.

Elliott, J. K. *The Apocryphal New Testament: A Collection of Apocryphal Christian Literature in an English Translation.* Oxford: Clarendon Press, 1993.

Elm, Susanna. *"Virgins of God": The Making of Asceticism in Late Antiquity.* Oxford: Clarendon Press, 1994.

Engels, Donald W. *Roman Corinth: An Alternative Model for the Classical City.* Chicago: University of Chicago Press, 1990.

Ensler, Eve. *The Vagina Monologues: The V-Day Edition.* New York: Villard, 2001.

Fagan, Garrett G. *Bathing in Public in the Roman World.* Ann Arbor: University of Michigan Press, 1999.

Fantham, Elaine. *Seneca's Troades: A Literary Introduction with Text, Translation, and Commentary.* Princeton: Princeton University Press, 1982.

Fiorenza, Elisabeth Schüssler, Shelly Matthews, and Ann Graham Brock, eds. *Searching the Scriptures, Volume 2: A Feminist Commentary.* New York, Crossroad: 1994.

Fisher, N. R. E. *"Hybris* and Dishonour: I." *Greece and Rome* 23 (1976): 177–193.

Fitzgerald, John T. *Cracks in an Earthen Vessel: An Examination of the Catalogues of Hardships in the Corinthian Correspondence.* Society of Biblical Literature Dissertation Series 99. Atlanta: Scholars Press, 1984.

———. "Paul, the Ancient Epistolary Theorists, and 2 Corinthians 10–13." In *Greeks, Romans, and Christians: Essays in Honor of Abraham J. Malherbe,* ed. David L. Balch, Everett Ferguson, and Wayne A. Meeks, 190–200. Minneapolis, MN: Fortress Press, 1990.

Fitzgerald, William. *Slavery and the Roman Literary Imagination.* Cambridge: Cambridge University Press, 2000.

Flemming, Rebecca. *Medicine and the Making of Roman Women: Gender, Nature, and Authority from Celsus to Galen.* Oxford: Oxford University Press, 2001.

———. *"Quae Corpore Quaestum Facit:* The Sexual Economy of Female Prostitution in the Roman Empire." *Journal of Roman Studies* 89 (1999): 38–61.

Fonrobert, Charlotte Elisheva. *Menstrual Purity: Rabbinic and Christian Reconstructions of Biblical Gender.* Stanford: Stanford University Press, 2000.

Forbes, Christopher. "Comparison, Self-Praise and Irony: Paul's Boasting and the Conventions of Hellenistic Rhetoric." *New Testament Studies* 32 (1986): 1–30.

Foskett, Mary F. *A Virgin Conceived: Mary and Classical Representations of Virginity.* Bloomington: Indiana University Press, 2002.

Frend, W. H. C. *The Donatist Church: A Movement of Protest in Roman North Africa.* 1952. Reprint. Oxford: Clarendon Press, 2000.

Fung, Ronald Y. K. *The Epistle to the Galatians.* New International Commentary on the New Testament. Grand Rapids, MI: Eerdmans, 1988.

Furnish, Victor Paul. *II Corinthians.* Anchor Bible 32A. Garden City, NY: Doubleday, 1984.

Gabler-Hover, Janet. *Dreaming Black/Writing White: The Hagar Myth in American Cultural History*. Lexington: University of Kentucky Press, 2000.

Gaddis, Michael. *There Is No Crime for Those Who Have Christ: Religious Violence in the Christian Roman Empire*. Berkeley: University of California Press, 2005.

Gambero, Luigi. *Mary and the Fathers of the Church: The Blessed Virgin Mary in Patristic Thought*. San Francisco: Ignatius Press, 1999.

Garland, David E. "Paul's Apostolic Authority: The Power of Christ's Sustaining Weakness (2 Corinthians 10–13)." *Review and Expositor* 86 (1989): 371–389.

Garnsey, Peter. *Ideas of Slavery from Aristotle to Augustine*. Cambridge: Cambridge University Press, 1996.

———. *Social Status and Legal Privilege in the Roman Empire*. Oxford: Clarendon Press, 1970.

Gaventa, Beverly Roberts. *First and Second Thessalonians*. Interpretation Bible Commentary. Louisville, KY: John Knox Press, 1998.

———. *Mary: Glimpses of the Mother of Jesus*. Minneapolis: Augsburg Fortress Press, 1999.

———. "The Maternity of Paul." In *Our Mother Saint Paul*, 29–40. Louisville, KY: Westminster John Knox Press, 2007.

Gaventa, Beverly Roberts, and Cynthia L. Rigby, eds. *Blessed One: Protestant Perspectives on Mary*. Louisville, KY: Westminster John Knox Press, 2002.

George, Michele. "Slave Disguise in Ancient Rome." In Wiedemann and Gardner, *Representing the Body of the Slave*, 41–54.

Glancy, Jennifer A. "The Mistress-Slave Dialectic: Paradoxes of Slavery in Three LXX Narratives." *Journal for the Study of the Old Testament* 21 (1996): 71–87.

———. *Slavery in Early Christianity*. New York: Oxford University Press, 2002.

———. "Torture: Flesh, Truth, and the Fourth Gospel." *Biblical Interpretation* 13 (2005): 107–136.

Gleason, Maud W. *Making Men: Sophists and Self-Presentation in Ancient Rome*. Princeton: Princeton University Press, 1995.

———. "Mutilated Messengers: Body Language in Josephus." In *Being Greek under Rome: Cultural Identity, the Second Sophistic and the Development of Empire*, ed. Simon Goldhill, 50–85. Cambridge: Cambridge University Press, 2001.

———. "Truth Contests and Talking Corpses." In Porter, *Constructions of the Classical Body*, 287–313.

Glucklich, Ariel. *Sacred Pain: Hurting the Body for the Sake of the Soul*. Oxford: Oxford University Press, 2001.

Grosz, Elizabeth. *Volatile Bodies: Toward a Corporeal Feminism*. Bloomington: Indiana University Press, 1994.

Gunderson, Erik. "Discovering the Body in Roman Oratory." In Wyke, *Parchments of Gender: Deciphering the Bodies of Antiquity*, 169–189.

———. *Staging Masculinity: The Rhetoric of Performance in the Roman World*. Ann Arbor: University of Michigan Press, 2000.

Guthrie, Donald. *Galatians*. New Century Bible Commentary. Grand Rapids, MI: Eerdmans, 1973.

Güttgemanns, Erhardt. *Der leidende apostel und sein Herr: Studien zu paulinischen Christologie*. Göttingen: Vandenhoeck & Ruprecht, 1966.

Hadot, Pierre. *Philosophy as a Way of Life: Spiritual Exercises from Socrates to Foucault.* Ed. Arnold Davidson. Oxford: Blackwell, 1995.

Hamerton-Kelly, Robert G. "A Girardian Interpretation of Paul: Rivalry, Mimesis and Victimage in the Corinthian Correspondence." *Semeia* 33 (1985): 65–81.

Hannah, Darrell D. "The Ascension of Isaiah and Docetic Christology." *Vigiliae Christianae* 53 (1999): 161–196.

———. "Isaiah's Vision in the Ascension of Isaiah and the Early Church." *Journal of Theological Studies* 50 (1999): 80–101.

Hanson, Ann Ellis. "The Logic of the Gynecological Prescriptions." *Tradatos Hipocráticos. Actas del VIIe Colloque International Hippocratique, Madrid 1990,* ed. J. A. López Férez, 235–250. Madrid: 1992.

———. "Talking Recipes in the Gynaecological Texts of the *Hippocratic Corpus*." In Wyke, *Parchments of Gender: Deciphering the Bodies of Antiquity,* 71–94.

Hanson, Ann Ellis, and Monica Helen Green. "Soranus of Ephesus: *Methodicorum princeps*." *Aufstieg und Niedergang der römischen Welt* 2.37.2 (1994): 968–1075.

Harrill, J. Albert. "The Domestic Enemy: A Moral Polarity of Household Slaves in Early Christian Apologies and Martyrdoms." In *Early Christian Families in Context: An Interdisciplinary Dialogue,* ed. David L. Balch and Carolyn Osiek, 249–253. Grand Rapids, MI: Eerdmans, 2003.

———. "Invective against Paul (2 Cor 10:10), the Physiognomics of the Ancient Slave Body, and the Greco-Roman Rhetoric of Manhood." In *Antiquity and Humanity: Essays on Ancient Religion and Philosophy,* ed. Adela Yarbro Collins and Margaret M. Mitchell, 189–213. Tübingen: Mohr Siebeck, 2001.

Hartman, Saidiya V. *Scenes of Subjection: Terror, Slavery, and Self-Making in Nineteenth-Century America.* New York: Oxford University Press, 1997.

Harvey, A. E. "Forty Strokes Save One: Social Aspects of Judaizing and Apostasy." In *Alternative Approaches to New Testament Study,* ed. A. E. Harvey, 79–96. London: SPCK, 1985.

———. *Renewal through Suffering: A Study of 2 Corinthians.* Edinburgh: T. & T. Clark, 1996.

Harvey, Susan Ashbrook. "Feminine Imagery for the Divine: The Holy Spirit, the Odes of Solomon, and Early Syriac Tradition." *St. Vladimir's Theological Quarterly* 37 (1993): 111–139.

———. "Odes of Solomon." In Fiorenza et al., *Searching the Scriptures Volume 2,* 86–98.

———. "On Mary's Voice: Gendered Words in Syriac Marian Tradition." In *The Cultural Turn in Late Ancient Studies: Gender, Historicism, and Historiography,* ed. Dale B. Martin and Patricia Cox Miller, 63–86. Durham, NC: Duke University Press, 2005.

Himmelfarb, Martha. "The Experience of the Visionary and Genre in the Ascension of Isaiah 6–11 and the Apocalypse of Paul." *Semeia* 36 (1986): 97–111.

———. *Tours of Hell: An Apocalyptic Form in Jewish and Christian Literature.* Philadelphia: University of Pennsylvania Press, 1983.

Hine, Darlene Clark. *Hine Sight: Black Women and the Re-construction of American History.* Bloomington: Indiana University Press, 1994.

Hock, Ronald F. *The Infancy Gospels of James and Thomas.* Santa Rosa: Polebridge, 1995.

———. *The Social Context of Paul's Ministry.* Philadelphia: Fortress, 1980.

Hodgson, Robert. "Paul the Apostle and First Century Tribulation Lists." *Zeitschrift für die Neutestamentliche Wissenschaft* 74 (1983): 59–80.

Holman, Susan R. "Molded as Wax: Formation and Feeding of the Ancient Newborn." *Helios* 24 (1997): 77–95.

———. "Rich City Burning: Social Welfare and Ecclesial Insecurity in Basil's Mission to Armenia." *Journal of Early Christian Studies* 12 (2004): 195–215.

Horn, Cornelia B. "The Virgin and the Perfect Virgin: Traces of Early Christian Mariology in the *Odes of Solomon*." In *Studia Patristica, vol. XL. Papers Presented at the Fourteenth International Conference on Patristic Studies Held in Oxford 2003. Liturgia et Cultus, Theologia et Philosophica, Critica et Philologica, Nachleben, First Two Centuries*, ed. F. Young, M. Edwards, and P. Parvis, 413–428. Leuven: Peeters, 2006.

Horner, Tim. "Jewish Aspects of the *Protevangelium of James*." *Journal of Early Christian Studies* 12 (2004): 313–335.

Hughes, Joseph J. "*Inter Tribunal et Scaenum:* Comedy and Rhetoric at Rome." In *Roman Eloquence: Rhetoric in Society and Literature*, ed. William J. Dominik, 182–197. London: Routledge, 1997.

Hughes, Philip Edgcumbe. *Paul's Second Epistle to the Corinthians*. Grand Rapids, MI: Eerdmans, 1962.

Hull, Vida J. "The Sex of the Savior in Renaissance Art: The *Revelations* of Saint Bridget and the Nude Christ Child in Renaissance Art." *Studies in Iconography* 15 (1993): 77–112.

Hynes, Nancy. "Africanizing Chris Ofili?" *African Arts* 43.1 (Spring 2001): 9–10.

Ignatius Loyola. *The Autobiography of St. Ignatius Loyola with Related Documents*. Ed. John C. Olin. Trans. Joseph F. O'Callaghan. New York: Fordham University Press, 1992.

Irenaeus. *Proof of the Apostolic Preaching*. Trans. J. P. Smith. Ancient Christian Writers 16. Westminster, MD: Newman Press, 1952.

Irigiray, Luce. *An Ethics of Sexual Difference*. Trans. Carolyn Burke and Gillian C. Gill. Ithaca, NY: Cornell University Press, 1993.

Irving, Toni. "Borders of the Body: Black Women, Sexual Assault, and Citizenship." *Women's Studies Quarterly* 35 (2007): 67–92.

Jacobs, Harriet. *Incidents in the Life of a Slave Girl*. New York: Oxford University Press, 1988.

Jay, Nancy. "Sacrifice as Remedy for Having Been Born of Woman." In *Immaculate and Powerful: The Female in Sacred Image and Social Reality*, eds. Clarissa W. Atkinson, Constance H. Buchanan, and Margaret R. Miles, 283–309. Boston: Beacon Press, 1985.

———. *Throughout Your Generations Forever: Sacrifice, Religion, and Paternity*. Chicago: University of Chicago Press, 1992.

Jenkins, Richard. *Pierre Bourdieu*. Rev. ed. London: Routledge, 2002.

Johnson, Elizabeth A. *Truly Our Sister: A Theology of Mary in the Communion of Saints*. New York: Continuum Press, 2003.

Johnson, Mark. *The Body in the Mind: The Bodily Basis of Meaning, Imagination, and Reason*. Chicago: University of Chicago Press, 1987.

Johnson, Walter. "On Agency." *Journal of Social History* 37 (2003): 113–124.

Jones, C. P. "Tattooing and Branding in Greco-Roman Antiquity." *Journal of Roman Studies* 77 (1987): 139–155.

Jordan, Kimberleigh. "The Body as Reader: African-Americans, Freedom, and the American Myth." In *The Bible and the American Myth: A Symposium on the Bible and Constructions of Meaning*, ed. Vincent L. Wimbush, 105–121. Studies in American Biblical Hermeneutics 16. Macon, GA: Mercer University Press, 1999.

Judge, E. A. *Social Distinctives of the Christians in the First Century: Pivotal Essays by E. A. Judge*. Ed. David M. Scholer. Peabody, MA: Hendrickson, 2008.

Kaster, R. A. "The Taxonomy of Patience, or When Is *Patentia* Not a Virtue." *Classical Philology* 97 (2002): 133–144.

Kennell, Nigel M. *The Gymnasium of Virtue: Education and Culture in Ancient Sparta*. Chapel Hill: University of North Carolina Press, 1995.

Keulen, Atze J. *L. Annaeus Seneca Troades. Introduction, Text, and Commentary*. Leiden: Brill, 2001.

King, Karen L. *The Secret Revelation of John*. Cambridge, MA: Harvard University Press, 2006.

———. *What Is Gnosticism?* Cambridge, MA: Belknap Press, 2003.

Klassen, Pamela E. *Blessed Events: Religion and Home Birth in America*. Princeton: Princeton University Press, 2001.

Klassen, William. "Galatians 6:17." *Expository Times* 81 (1970): 378.

Knight, Jonathan. *The Ascension of Isaiah*. Sheffield: Sheffield Academic Press, 1995.

———. "The Portrait of Mary in the Ascension of Isaiah." In *Which Mary? The Marys of Early Christian Tradition*, ed. F. Stanley Jones, 91–105. Society of Biblical Literature Symposium Series 19. Atlanta: Society of Biblical Literature, 2002.

Kristeva, Julia. *Powers of Horror: An Essay on Abjection*. Trans. Leon S. Roudiez. New York: Columbia University Press, 1982.

———. "Stabat Mater." In *The Kristeva Reader*, ed. Toril Moi, 160–186. New York: Columbia University Press, 1986.

Kruse, Colin G. *The Second Epistle of Paul to the Corinthians*. Tyndale New Testament Commentaries. Grand Rapids, MI: Eerdmans, 1987.

Kunitz, Daniel. "True 'Sensation.'" *Salon.com*. October 2, 1999. Accessed February 16, 2009 at http://www.salon.com/ent/feature/1999/10/02/dung/.

Lagrand, James. "How Was the Virgin Mary 'Like a Man'?" *Novum Testamentum* 22 (1980): 97–107.

Lambrecht, Jan. "Dangerous Boasting. Paul's Self-Commendation in 2 Cor 10–13." In *The Corinthian Correspondence*, ed. R. Bieringer, 325–346. Leuven: Leuven University Press, 1996.

———. *Second Corinthians*. Sacra Pagina 8. Collegeville, MN: Liturgical Press, 1999.

La Regina, Adriano, ed. *Sangue e Arena*. Rome: Electa, 2001.

Laskaris, Julie. "Error, Loss, and Change in the Generation of Therapies." In *Hippocrates in Context: Papers Read at the XIth International Hippocrates Colloquium, University of Newcastle upon Tyne*, ed. P. J. van der Eijk, 173–189. Studies in Ancient Medicine 31. Leiden: Brill, 2005.

Lateiner, David. "Nonverbal Behaviors in Ovid's Poetry, Primarily Metamorphoses 14." *Classical Journal* 93 (1996): 225–253.

Lattey, Cuthbert. "λαμβάνειν in 2 Cor xi.20." *Journal of Theological Studies* 44 (1943): 148.

Leigh, Matthew. *Lucan: Spectacle and Engagement*. Oxford: Clarendon Press, 1997.

————. "Wounding and Popular Rhetoric at Rome." *Bulletin of the Institute of Classical Studies* 40 (1995): 195–215.

Levine, Amy-Jill. "Discharging Responsibility: Matthean Jesus, Biblical Law, and Hemorrhaging Woman." In *A Feminist Companion to Matthew*, eds. Amy-Jill Levine and Marianne Blickenstaff, 70–88. Cleveland: Pilgrim Press, 2001.

Leyerle, Blake. "Blood Is Seed." *Journal of Religion* 81 (2001): 26–48.

Lührmann, Dieter. *Galatians: A Continental Commentary*. Trans. O. C. Dean Jr. Minneapolis: Fortress Press, 1992.

Malherbe, Abraham J. "Antisthenes and Odysseus, and Paul at War." *Harvard Theological Review* 76 (1983): 143–173.

Malina, Bruce J., and Jerome H. Neyrey. *Portraits of Paul: An Archaeology of Ancient Personality*. Louisville, KY: Westminster John Knox Press, 1996.

Marcus, Joel. *Mark 1–8: A New Translation with Introduction and Commentary*. Anchor Bible 27. New York: Doubleday, 2000.

Martin, Dale B. *Slavery as Salvation: The Metaphor of Slavery in Pauline Christianity*. New Haven: Yale University Press, 1990.

Martin, Joan M. *More Than Chains and Toil: A Christian Work Ethic of Enslaved Women*. Louisville, KY: Westminster John Knox Press, 2000.

Martyn, J. Louis. *Galatians*. Anchor Bible 33A. Garden City, NY: Doubleday, 1997.

Matera, Frank J. *Galatians*. Sacra Pagina 9. Collegeville, MN: Liturgical Press, 1992.

Mauss, Marcel. "Techniques of the Body." Trans. Ben Brewster. *Economy and Society* 2 (1973): 70–88.

McCarthy, Kathleen. *Slaves, Masters and the Art of Authority in Plautine Comedy*. Princeton: Princeton University Press, 2000.

McNeil, Brian. "The Odes of Solomon and the Scriptures." *Oriens Christianus* 67 (1983): 104–122.

————. "The Odes of Solomon and the Sufferings of Christ." *Symposium Syriacum*, 31–38. *Orientalia Christiana Analecta*. Rome: Pontificum Institutum Orientalium Studiorum, 1978.

————. "Suffering and Martyrdom in the Odes of Solomon." In *Suffering and Martyrdom in the New Testament*, eds. William Harbury and Brian McNeil, 136–142. Cambridge: Cambridge University Press, 1981.

McVey, Kathleen E. "Images of Joy in Ephrem's Hymns on Paradise: Returning to the Womb and the Breast." *Journal of the Canadian Society for Syriac Studies* 3 (2003): 139–161.

Meltzer, Françoise. *For Fear of the Fire: Joan of Arc and the Limits of Subjectivity*. Chicago: University of Chicago Press, 2001.

Merleau-Ponty, Maurice. *Maurice Merleau-Ponty: Basic Writings*. Ed. Thomas Baldwin. New York: Routledge, 2003.

————. *The Visible and the Invisible*. Trans. Alphonso Lingis. Evanston, IL: Northwestern University Press, 1968.

The Mishnah. Trans. Herbert Danby. Oxford: Oxford University Press, 1933.

Mitchell, Margaret M. "A Patristic Perspective on Pauline περιαυτολογία." *New Testament Studies* 47 (2001): 354–371.

Moore, Stephen D. *Empire and Apocalypse: Postcolonialism and the New Testament*. The Bible in the Modern World 12. Sheffield: Sheffield Phoenix Press, 2006.

————. *God's Gym: Divine Male Bodies of the Bible*. New York: Routledge, 1996.

Moore, Stephen D., and Janice Capel Anderson. "Taking It Like a Man: Masculinity in 4 Maccabees." *Journal of Biblical Literature* 117 (1998): 249–273.

Morrison, Toni. *A Mercy*. New York: Knopf, 2008.

———. *Playing in the Dark: Whiteness and the Literary Imagination*. New York: Vintage, 1993.

Moulton, James Hope. "The Marks of Jesus." *Expository Times* 21 (1910): 283–284.

Murphy-O'Connor, Jerome. *The Theology of the Second Letter to the Corinthians*. New Testament Theology. Cambridge: Cambridge University Press, 1991.

Newbold, R. F. "Non-verbal Communication in Suetonius and the Historia Augusta: Power, Postures and Proxemics." *Acta Classica* 43 (2000): 101–118.

"Obstetric Analgesia and Anesthesia." *American College of Obstetricians and Gynecologists Practice Bulletin* 36 (July 2002).

Olson, Kelly. *Dress and the Roman Woman: Self-Presentation and Society*. New York: Routledge, 2008.

Optatus: Against the Donatists. Trans. Mark Edwards. Translated Texts for Historians 27. Liverpool: Liverpool University Press, 1997.

Origen. *On First Principles*. Trans. G. W. Butterworth. London: SPCK, 1936.

Osborn, Eric. *Tertullian: First Theologian of the West*. Cambridge: Cambridge University Press, 1997.

Osiek, Carolyn. *Galatians*. New Testament Message 12. Wilmington, DE: Michael Glazier, 1980.

Otten, Willemien. "Christ's Birth of a Virgin Who Became a Wife: Flesh and Speech in Tertullian's *De Carne Christi*." *Vigiliae Christianae* 51 (1997): 247–260.

Park, Katherine. *Secrets of Women: Gender, Generation, and the Origins of Human Dissection*. New York: Zone Books, 2006.

Parker, Holt. "Crucially Funny, or Tranio on the Couch: The *Servus Callidus* and Jokes about Torture." *Transactions of the American Philological Association* 119 (1989): 233–246.

Penner, Todd, and Caroline Vander Stichele, eds. *Mapping Gender in Ancient Religious Discourses*. Leiden: Brill, 2007.

Perkins, Judith B. "The Rhetoric of the Maternal Body in the Passion of Perpetua." In Penner and Vander Stichele, *Mapping Gender in Ancient Religious Discourses*, 318–332.

———. "Social Geography in the Apocryphal Acts of the Apostles." In *Space in the Ancient Novel*, ed. Michael Paschalis and Stavros Fangouldis, 118–131. Groningen: Barkhuis, 2002.

———. *The Suffering Self: Pain and Narrative Representation in the Early Christian Era*. London: Routledge, 1995.

Playoust, Catherine Anne. *Lifted up from the Earth: The Ascension of Jesus and the Heavenly Ascents of Early Christians*. ThD diss., Harvard University, 2006.

Porter, James I., ed. *Constructions of the Classical Body*. Ann Arbor: University of Michigan Press, 1999.

Rahner, Karl. "The Body in the Order of Salvation." In *Theological Investigations XVII*, 71–89. Trans. Kevin Smyth. New York: Crossroad Press, 1981.

———. *"Virginitas in Partu."* In *Theological Investigations Volume IV: More Recent Writings*, 134–162. Trans. Kevin Smyth. Baltimore: Helicon Press, 1966.

Rejali, Darius. *Torture and Democracy*. Princeton: Princeton University Press, 2007.

Rhoads, David. "Jesus and the Syrophoenician Woman in Mark: A Narrative Study." *Journal of the American Academy of Religion* 62 (1994): 343–375.

Richard, Earl J. *First and Second Thessalonians*. Sacra Pagina 11. Collegeville, MN: Liturgical Press, 1995.

Richlin, Amy. "Sexuality in the Roman Empire." *A Companion to the Roman Empire*, ed. David S. Potter, 327–353. Oxford: Blackwell Press, 2006.

Ridderbos, Herman N. *The Epistle of Paul to the Churches of Galatia*. New International Commentary on the New Testament. Grand Rapids, MI: Eerdmans, 1956.

Rieff, David. *Swimming in a Sea of Death: A Son's Memoir*. New York: Simon & Schuster, 2008.

Ringe, Sharon H. "A Gentile Woman's Story Revisited: Rereading Mark 7:24–31." In *A Feminist Companion to Mark*, ed. Amy-Jill Levine and Marianne Blickenstaff, 79–100. Cleveland: Pilgrim Press, 2004.

Robinson, James M., ed. *The Nag Hammadi Library*. New York: Harper Collins, 1990.

Roller, Matthew. *Constructing Autocracy: Aristocrats and Emperors in Julio-Claudian Rome*. Princeton: Princeton University Press, 2001.

———. *Dining Posture in Ancient Rome: Bodies, Values, and Status*. Princeton: Princeton University Press, 2006.

Saller, Richard. "Corporal Punishment, Authority, and Obedience in the Roman Household." In *Marriage, Divorce, and Children in Ancient Rome*, ed. Beryl Rawson, 144–165. Oxford: Clarendon Press, 1991.

———. "*Pater Familias, Mater Familias*, and the Gendered Semantics of the Roman Household." *Classical Philology* 94 (1999): 182–197.

———. "Symbols of Gender and Status Hierarchies in the Roman Household." In *Women and Slaves in Greco-Roman Culture: Differential Equations*, ed. Sandra R. Joshel and Sheila Murnaghan, 85–91. London: Routledge, 1998.

Sanders, Jack T. "Nag Hammadi, Odes of Solomon, and New Testament Christological Hymns." In *Gnosticism and the Early Christian World: In Honor of James M. Robinson*, eds. J. E. Goehring, C. W. Hedrick, J. T. Sanders, and H. D. Betz, 51–66. Forum Fascicles 2. Sonoma, CA: Polebridge, 1990.

Satran, David. "Fingernails and Hair: Anatomy and Exegesis in Tertullian." *Journal of Theological Studies* 40 (1989): 116–120.

Savage, Timothy B. *Power through Weakness: Paul's Understanding of the Christian Ministry in 2 Corinthians*. Cambridge: Cambridge University Press, 1996.

Scarry, Elaine. *The Body in Pain: The Making and Unmaking of the World*. New York: Oxford University Press, 1987.

Schaberg, Jane. *The Illegitimacy of Jesus: A Feminist Theological Interpretation of the Infancy Narratives*. Exp. ed. Sheffield: Sheffield Phoenix Press, 2006.

Scheper-Hughes, Nancy, and Margaret M. Lock. "The Mindful Body: A Prolegomenon to Future Work in Medical Anthropology." *Medical Anthropology Quarterly*, n.s., 1.1 (March 1987): 6–41.

Schillebeeckx, Edward. *Mary: Mother of Redemption*. New York: Sheed and Ward, 1964.

Schiller, Gertrud. *Iconography of Christian Art*. Trans. Janet Seligman. 2 vols. London: Lund Humphries, 1971.

Schmitt, Jean-Claude. "The Ethics of Gesture." In *Fragments for a History of the Human Body Part Two*, ed. Michael Feher, 128–147. New York: Zone, 1989.

Schwartz, Saundra. "From Bedroom to Courtroom: The Adultery Type-Scene and the Acts of Andrew." In Penner and Vander Stichele, *Mapping Gender in Ancient Religious Discourses*, 267–311.

Segal, Erich. *Roman Laughter: The Comedy of Plautus*. 2nd ed. Cambridge, MA: Harvard University Press, 1987.

Setzer, Claudia. "Three Odd Couples: Women and Men in Mark and John." In *Mariam, the Magdalen, and the Mother*, ed. Deirdre Good, 75–92. Bloomington: Indiana University Press, 2005.

Shaw, Brent D. "Body/Power/Identity: Passions of the Martyrs." *Journal of Early Christian Studies* 4 (1996): 269–312.

———. "Who Were the Circumcellions?" *Vandals, Romans and Berbers: New Perspectives on Late Antique North Africa*, ed. A. H. Merrills, 227–258. Burlington, VT: Ashgate, 2004.

Silvas, Anna M. *The Asketikon of St Basil the Great*. Oxford: Oxford University Press, 2005.

Sissa, Giulia. *Greek Virginity*. Trans. Arthur Goldhammer. Cambridge: Cambridge University Press, 1990.

Smid, H. R. *Protevangelium Jacobi: A Commentary*. Assen: Van Gorcum, 1965.

Sontag, Susan. *Illness as Metaphor and AIDS and Its Metaphors*. New York: Anchor Books Doubleday, 1989.

Soranus. *Soranus' Gynecology*. Trans. Owsei Temkin. 1956. Reprint. Baltimore: Johns Hopkins University Press, 1991.

Spencer, F. Scott. *Dancing Girls, Loose Ladies, and Women of the Cloth: The Women in Jesus' Life*. New York: Continuum, 2004.

Spillers, Hortense J. "Mama's Baby, Papa's Maybe: An American Grammar Book." *Diacritics* 17.2 (Summer 1987): 64–81.

Steinberg, Leo. *The Sexuality of Christ in Renaissance Art and in Modern Oblivion*. New York: Pantheon/October, 1983.

Stowasser, Barbara Freyer. *Women in the Qur'an, Traditions, and Interpretation*. New York: Oxford University Press, 1996.

Stowe, Harriet Beecher. *Uncle Tom's Cabin*. New York: Airmont, 1967.

Stramara, Daniel F. "Gregory of Nyssa: An Ardent Abolitionist?" *St. Vladimir's Theological Quarterly* 41 (1997): 37–69.

Strathern, Andrew J. *Body Thoughts*. Ann Arbor: University of Michigan Press, 1996.

Tertullian. *De Anima Quinti Septimi Florentis Tertulliani*. Trans. and ed. Jan Hendrik Waszink. Amsterdam: J.M. Meulenhoff, 1947.

———. *Treatises on Marriage and Remarriage: To His Wife, an Exhortation to Chastity, Monogamy*. Trans. William P. Le Saint. Ancient Christian Writers 13. Westminster, MD: Newman, 1951.

Theissen, Gerd. *The Gospels in Context: Social and Political History in the Synoptic Tradition*. Trans. Linda M. Maloney. Edinburgh: T&T Clark, 1992.

Thomas, Christine M. "The Prehistory of the *Acts of Peter*." In *The Apocryphal Acts of the Apostles*, ed. François Bovon, Ann Graham Brock, and Christopher Matthews, 39–62. Harvard Divinity School Studies. Cambridge, MA: Harvard University Press, 1999.

Thomas, John Christopher. "'Stop Sinning Lest Something Worse Come upon You': The Man at the Pool in John 5." *Journal for the Study of the New Testament* 59 (1995): 3–20.

Thrall, Margaret E. *A Critical and Exegetical Commentary on the Second Epistle to the Cor-inthians.* 2 vols. International Critical Commentary. Edinburgh: T&T Clark, 1994–2000.

Tilley, Maureen. "The Ascetic Body and the (Un)Making of the World of the Martyr." *Journal of the American Academy of Religion* 59 (1991): 467–480.

Trout, Dennis. "Re-textualizing Lucretia: Cultural Subversion in the *City of God.*" *Journal of Early Christian Studies* 2 (1994): 53–70.

van der Horst, Pieter W. "Sex, Birth, Purity and Asceticism in the *Protevangelium Jacobi.*" *Neotestamentica* 28 (1994): 205–218.

von Campenhausen, Hans. *The Virgin Birth in the Theology of the Ancient Church.* Studies in Historical Theology 2. Naperville, IL: Allenson, 1964.

von Staden, Heinrich. "*Apud nos foediora uerba:* Celsus' Reluctant Construction of the Female Body." In *Le latin médical: La constitution d'un langage scientifique: Réalités et langage de la médicine dans le monde romain (Actes du IIIe Colloque international "Textes médicaux latins antiques"),* ed. G. Sabbah, 271–295. Saint-Étienne: L'Université de Saint-Étienne, 1991.

———. "Women and Dirt." *Helios* 19 (1992): 7–30.

Vorster, Willem S. "The Protevangelium of James and Intertextuality." In *Text and Testimony: Essays on New Testament and Apocryphal Literature in Honour of A. F. J. Klijn,* eds. T. Baarda, A. Hilhorst, G. P. Luttikuizen, and A. S. v. d. Woude, 262–275. Kampen: Kock, 1988.

Watson, Duane F. "Paul's Boasting in 2 Corinthians 10–13 as Defense of His Honor: A Socio-Rhetorical Analysis." In *Rhetorical Argumentation in Biblical Texts: Essays from the Lund 2000 Conference,* ed. Anders Erikssson, Thomas H. Olbricht, and Walter Über-lacker, 260–275. Harrisburg, PA: Trinity, 2002.

Wegner, Judith Romney. *Chattel or Person? The Status of Women in the Mishnah.* New York: Oxford University Press, 1988.

Weiler, Ingomar. "Inverted Kalokagathia." In Wiedemann and Gardner, *Representing the Body of the Slave,* 11–28.

Welborn, L. L. "The Runaway Paul." *Harvard Theological Review* 92 (1999): 115–163.

Whitmarsh, Tim. *Greek Literature and the Roman Empire: The Politics of Imitation.* Oxford: Oxford University Press, 2001.

Wiedemann, Thomas, and Jane Gardner, eds. *Representing the Body of the Slave.* London: Frank Cass, 2002.

Williams, Craig A. *Roman Homosexuality: Ideologies of Masculinity in Classical Antiquity.* New York: Oxford University Press, 1999.

Williams, Delores. *Sisters in the Wilderness: The Challenge of Womanist God-Talk.* Maryknoll, NY: Orbis, 1993.

Windisch, Hans. *Der zweite Korintherbrief.* Göttingen: Vandenhoeck & Ruprecht, 1924.

Winkler, John J. *The Constraints of Desire: The Anthropology of Sex and Gender in Ancient Greece.* New York: Routledge, 1990.

Wood, Marcus. *Slavery, Empathy, and Pornography.* Oxford: Oxford University Press, 2002.

Wyke, Maria, ed. *Parchments of Gender: Deciphering the Bodies of Antiquity.* Oxford: Clarendon Press, 1998.

Young, Iris Marion. *On Female Body Experience: "Throwing Like a Girl" and Other Essays.* Studies in Feminist Philosophy. New York: Oxford University Press, 2005.

Zervos, George T. "Seeking the Source of the Marian Myth: Have We Found the Missing Link?" In *Which Mary? The Marys of Early Christian Tradition*, ed. F. Stanley Jones, 107–120. Society of Biblical Literature Symposium Series 19. Atlanta: Society of Biblical Literature, 2002.

Zwelling, Elaine. "The History of Lamaze Continues: An Interview with Elisabeth Bing." *Journal of Perinatal Education* 9 (2000): 15–21. Accessed August 31, 2007, at http://www.pubmedcentral.nih.gov/articlerender.fcgi?artid=1595002.

Index of Ancient Sources

Greek and Roman

General Index

Acts of Andrew, 67–68
Adair, Vivyan, 51
Alcoff, Linda Martín
  on body as mind, 10, 52, 137
  on corporal selfhood, 9, 19, 21
  on disruptions of corporal knowledge,
    10, 55, 77, 80
  on race and gender, 10–12, 141n15
Allard, Paul, 71, 152n33
Ambrose of Milan, 66–67, 71–72
anesthesia, 87–90
Artemis Orthia and ritual flagellation,
    34–37
Ascension of Isaiah
  on bodies and selfhood, 19–20, 100–106,
    136
  dating, 92–93, 108
  nativity, 81, 100, 104–106, 108, 158n88
  on pain, 90, 100–102, 104
Augustine, 68, 72–74, 78–79

Barton, Carlin A., 43, 64
Basil of Caesarea, 70–71, 75–76, 77–78
Bataille, Georges, 147n73
battle scars
  Paul's *stigmata* and, 24, 47
  satirized, 34–35
  and valor, 25, 27–30, 33, 39, 40
Bauckham, Richard, 74, 159n95
Betz, Hans Dieter, 39
Birgitta of Sweden, 84, 105, 155n14
Blandina, 56, 59–61, 62
boasting
  corporal, 28–29

and Greco-Roman rhetoric, 27–28,
    38–40
Paul and, 24–25, 38, 41–47
in Roman comedy, 34–35
bodies, storytelling
  in childbirth, 82, 96, 107
  contemporary, 8, 82, 85–86, 139
  and cultural history, 8
  deceptive, 55–56
  and disability, 5, 9
  and humiliation, 49
  and sin, 5, 9, 96
  slavery and, 45, 55–56
  and the *Vagina Monologues,* 85–86
  violence and, 24–25, 45, 47
body and identity. *See* corporal
  selfhood
body language
  ancient, 14, 15–19, 25–26, 29
  contemporary, 10, 142n34
body as mind, 10, 12, 52, 137
Bourdieu, Pierre
  critiques of, 52, 75
  on habitus, 9, 26–27 (*see also* habitus)
  as scholarly influence, 13–14, 53,
    141n13
Branham, Joan R., 110–111
Brilliant, Richard, 12, 13, 14
Brock, Sebastian, 98, 157n62
Brooten, Bernadette, 71
Brown, Peter, 4, 21
Buchholz, Dennis D., 74
Buell, Denise Kimber, 143n51
Burghardt, Walter, 85, 95, 157n55

pudor and, 59, 64–65, 68–70, 72–73
and rejection of slaveholding, 50
resistance to, 56, 75–79, 80, 150n12,
    154n92
resurrection and, 70, 74
in Roman comedy, 32–33, 34–35
sexual ethics of, 54–55, 61–74, 153n68
and tattoos, 46
Smid, H. R., 85, 112
social location, as known in the body, 4,
    10–11, 13–14, 19, 48, 77, 137–139
Sontag, Susan, 6–7
Soranus
    on anatomy, 106
    on lactation, 113–114
    and Tertullian, 119, 121, 122, 133,
        161n140
Spencer, F. Scott, 16–17
Spillers, Hortense J., 79
Steinberg, Leo, 84
stigma, 24, 26, 27, 29–30, 37, 45–46
Stoicism and Stoics
    on abuse, 30, 40–41
    on pain, 101
    and paradox, 119–120
    on social status, 61–62
    and Tertullian, 119–120, 126
Stowe, Harriet Beecher, 61
Syrophoenician woman in Gospel of Mark,
    15–19

Tertullian
    on Artemis Orthia and ritual flagellation, 36
    and bad taste, 85
    on bodily fluids and moral degradation,
        112, 124–126
    on body as self, 20
    on childbirth as filthy, 81–82, 112,
        120–126, 129
    on childbirth as violent, 81–82, 116, 118,
        130–133
    influenced by competing discourses, 90,
        118–120, 125–126
    on lactation, 114, 131
    and Marcion, 94, 118, 120–126, 129,
        130, 133
    on Mary and Eve, 94–95
    on *pudor*, 69
    and Stoicism, 119–120, 126
    on womb as sewer, 121–124, 125, 127, 130

Theissen, Gerd, 143n50
Tilley, Maureen, 60
torture
    fetal life as, 124
    in martyrdom, 60–61, 101–102
    Seneca on, 41
    and truth, 137, 139–140
    See also Scarry, Elaine
Trent, Council of, 81, 86
Trout, Dennis, 72–73

urine, 42, 123, 125

Vagina Monologues, 85–86
van der Horst, Pieter, 113
violation
    childbirth as sexual, 133
    physical, 25, 27, 41, 46, 56–57
    slavery and sexual, 62, 64, 65, 68, 69,
        70–74
virginity
    and afterlife, 70
    in partu, 81, 86, 89, 100, 108, 116, 134
    as physical intactness, 81, 85, 108,
        109–110, 115–117, 131–132
    postpartum, 93, 105, 116
    threatened, 64–65, 71, 72, 73
virtue
    as embodied, 13, 42
    for men, 13, 25–26, 28, 36, 47, 101
    for women, 61–62, 64, 70–74, 116
von Campenhausen, 85
von Staden, Heinrich, 110, 123, 161n156

Waszink, J. H., 119
Welborn, Laurence L., 146n52
whippability
    at altar of Artemis Orthia, 36–37
    and dishonor, 30–33, 36–37, 40, 41, 47
    Paul and, 40, 41, 43, 46, 47
    in Roman comedy, 34–35
    as servile, 31, 32–35, 36–37, 56–57,
        145n28
Williams, Delores, 67
Wood, Marcus, 151n17
Woolf, Virginia, 3, 21, 136, 140

Young, Iris Marion, 151n14

Zervos, George, 93, 108